CAMBRIDGE STUDIES IN ECONOMIC HISTORY

PUBLISHED *with the aid of the Ellen McArthur Fund*

MANAGERS OF THE FUND
PROFESSOR C.H.WILSON, *Jesus College, Cambridge*
PROFESSOR D.C.COLEMAN, *Pembroke College, Cambridge*
DR C.H.FEINSTEIN, *Clare College, Cambridge*

PETERBOROUGH ABBEY 1086–1310

Peterborough Abbey
1086-1310

A STUDY IN THE LAND MARKET

EDMUND KING
LECTURER IN MEDIEVAL HISTORY
UNIVERSITY OF SHEFFIELD

CAMBRIDGE
AT THE UNIVERSITY PRESS 1973

Published by the Syndics of the Cambridge University Press
Bentley House, 200 Euston Road, London NW1 2DB
American Branch: 32 East 57th Street, New York, N.Y.10022

© Cambridge University Press 1973

Library of Congress Catalogue Card Number: 72–91959

ISBN: 0 521 20133 0

Printed in Great Britain by
William Clowes & Sons, Limited
London, Beccles and Colchester

FOR MY MOTHER AND IN MEMORY OF MY FATHER

Contents

TABLES

Abbreviations

Abbreviations

Canterbury	R. A. L. Smith, *Canterbury Cathedral Priory* (Cambridge, 1943).
Chr.P.	*Chronicon Petroburgense* (Camden Soc., XLVII, 1849), ed. T. Stapleton.
Davis	G. R. C. Davis, *Medieval Cartularies of Great Britain* (London, 1958).
D.B.	*Domesday Book* (2 vols, 1783).
E.C.E.E.	C. R. Hart, *The Early Charters of Eastern England* (Leicester, 1966).
E.H.R.	*English Historical Review.*
Early Northants Charters	*Facsimiles of Early Charters from Northamptonshire Collections* (Northants Rec. Soc., IV, 1930), ed. F. M. Stenton.
Econ.H.R.	*Economic History Review.*
Ely	E. Miller, *The Abbey and Bishopric of Ely* (Cambridge, 1951).
First Century	Sir Frank Stenton, *The First Century of English Feudalism* (2nd edn., Oxford, 1961).
Hugh Candidus	*The Chronicle of Hugh Candidus* (Oxford, 1949), ed. W. T. Mellows.
Lincs Domesday	*The Lincolnshire Domesday and the Lindsey Survey* (Lincs Rec. Soc., XIX, 1924), ed. C. W. Foster and T. Longley.
Monasticon	W. Dugdale, *Monasticon Anglicanum* (1846, edn. of J. Caley, H. Ellis and B. Bandinel).
P.N.Soc. Northants	J. E. B. Gover, A. Mawer and F. M. Stenton, *The Place-Names of Northamptonshire* (Cambridge, 1933).
Pytchley	*Henry of Pytchley's Book of Fees* (Northants Rec. Soc., II, 1927), ed. W. T. Mellows.
Ramsey	J. A. Raftis, *The Estates of Ramsey Abbey* (Toronto, 1957).
Regesta	*Regesta Regum Anglo-Normannorum. 1066–1154*, 3 vols. (1913–68).
Registrum Antiquissimum	*The Registrum Antiquissimum of the Cathedral Church of Lincoln*, ed. C. W. Foster and K. Major, 9 vols. (Lincs Rec. Soc., 1931–68).
Rural England	R. Lennard, *Rural England 1086–1135* (Oxford, 1959).

Abbreviations

Sparke J. Sparke (ed.), *Historiae Coenobii Burgensis Scriptores Varii* (London, 1723).

Tenure and J. A. Raftis, *Tenure and Mobility. Studies in the Social*
Mobility   *History of the Medieval English Village* (Toronto, 1964).

V.C.H.   *Victoria County History.*

William *The Book of William Morton* (Northants Rec. Soc., XVI,
Morton   1954), ed. W. T. Mellows, P. I. King and C. N. L.
           Brooke.

Preface

The various estate studies in print have a common form of title, but rather different emphases. Each community is different, each region is different, and the surviving records for each estate vary enormously. The distinctive feature of the Peterborough material is the wealth of cartularies and charter material of all kinds. The twelfth century cartulary contains a valuable set of records from the reign of Henry I. The mid-thirteenth-century cartulary, that of Robert of Swaffham, summarises a century of considerable activity. And for the early fourteenth century we have the *Carte Nativorum*, a unique record of land transactions among the peasantry. Over several drafts, this work has come to concentrate upon the land market, for which the Peterborough records are both full and wide-ranging.

My central preoccupation in this book is the character of the land market during the twelfth and thirteenth centuries: my central argument is that the land market must be studied as a whole if it is to be understood. A number of the chapters which follow deal with the endowment of the monastery itself, and with the way the monastic estate was managed, concentrating in particular on surveys of the early twelfth century and account rolls of the late thirteenth century. The endowment of the monastic departments is examined in detail, showing how the monastery used new land to compensate for a decline in the value of its fixed income. A chapter considers the origins of most of this new land, in the forest and fenland colonisation of Northamptonshire. A series of chapters deal with the monastery tenants. For both knightly and villein tenants the Peterborough material is exceptionally full. In both cases, conclusions of general application have been drawn from the material, and these conclusions are critically examined. Wherever possible in this study, the approach is via a family history, and looks at the family's acquisition of property and the use that was made of it. The history of the monastery is itself a family history.

This is an interesting area of scholarship, and there can be no doubt that it is a notably friendly one. I am most grateful to Professor M. M. Postan, who supervised my thesis, for his attention and for the constant stimulus of his ideas. Two other Cambridge scholars have read more recent drafts of this book, and have made invaluable suggestions for its improvement. To Mrs Marjorie Chibnall I am indebted for helpful criticism and for a lot of much appreciated encouragement. Dr Edward Miller fostered my interest in medieval studies ten years ago, and at Cambridge and more recently at Sheffield he has given me a very great deal of help. My more precise debts are no less important and no less gratefully acknowledged. I have been greatly assisted in being able to follow the work on Peterborough sources of Mr W. T. Mellows, and in being able to use his photographic collection, which is now in the Peterborough Dean and Chapter Library; for access to this library I am indebted to Canon J. L. Cartwright and Canon A. S. Gribble. For permission to print material in the appendices I am indebted to the Dean and Chapter of Peterborough Cathedral, and His Grace the Duke of Buccleuch. The calendar of a Crown-copyright record in the Public Record Office appears by permission of the Controller of H.M. Stationery Office. For permission to refer to their unpublished theses I am grateful to Dr J. Z. Titow and Dr Paul Hyams. The greater part of Chapter 2 of this book appeared in *Past and Present* in 1970, and I am grateful to the editor of that journal for permission to reprint it here. The publication of this article brought me a wealth of valuable comments; here I can acknowledge only the corrections, which I owe to Miss Katherine Naughton, and Drs Michael Clanchy, Paul Hyams and Clive Knowles. While at Sheffield I have been assisted by several grants from the University Research Fund. An earlier draft of the book was awarded an Ellen McArthur Prize in 1969; I am grateful to the Managers of the Fund for accepting the book in their series and for making a grant towards its publication. The staff of the Press have dealt with my manuscript with skill and with despatch, and I am most grateful to them. Finally, and most of all, I am indebted to my wife.

November 1972   EDMUND KING

The Abbot's Demesne Manors in 1300.

Walcot

Scotter

Fiskerton
LINCOLN

Collingham

BOSTON

Thurlby

KING'S LYNN

STAMFORD
Tinwell
G We
Wa E
C L PETERBOROUGH
Great Easton
Biggin
Cottingham
Warmington
Oundle Ashton

Kettering
Irthlingborough Stanwick

NORTHAMPTON

G — Glinton
We — Werrington
Wa — Walton
E — Eye
C — Castor
L — Longthorpe

10 8 6 4 2 0   10   20

Miles

Introduction

This study covers the period from the foundation of the monastery in the tenth century to the check in population expansion in the early fourteenth century. The range of the source material naturally determines the particular quality of the work, when compared with studies of other monastic estates, and it is the aim of the introduction to give a brief outline of the main sources used.[1]

The element of continuity in these sources is provided by the abbey chronicles. The best known of these, the Peterborough continuation of the *Anglo-Saxon Chronicle*,[2] is at the same time the least useful for the historian of the monastery. What it does vividly, most notably in the passage upon the atrocities of Stephen's reign, is to show concern over the harshness of Norman lordship. Its concern is the more interesting because all the other records for the period after the Conquest show the strength of the abbey's own lordship, which is never more impressive than in the early twelfth century. The monks elected an Anglo-Saxon abbot in 1098, but the extent to which the last entry in the *Chronicle*, symbolically recording the end of Norman lordship in 1154, reveals a house that was Anglo-Saxon in sympathy is an open question. In the twelfth century the number of Saxon sympathisers must have been small, and they are unlikely to have played a major part in the formation of policy or the exercise of lordship. Professor Knowles justly remarks that the house's Latin chroniclers show a similar and distinctive concern for the cloister monks, those who did not hold office in the abbey administration.[3]

Three chroniclers cover the period of this study. The first of them is Hugh Candidus, who takes the story from the foundation to around 1175;[4] his chronicle is largely independent of the *Anglo-*

---

[1] W. T. Mellows' full and very valuable description of the Peterborough sources in his introduction to *Pytchley* (pp. xxv–xxxvii, 156–7), and for the cartularies and registers G. R. C. Davis's more recent list (*Medieval Cartularies of Great Britain* (London, 1958), nos. 754–73), make an extended description of them unnecessary here.
[2] *The Peterborough Chronicle 1070–1154*, ed. C. Clark (2nd edn., Oxford, 1970).
[3] David Knowles, *The Monastic Order in England* (2nd edn., 1963), p. 507.
[4] *The Peterborough Chronicle of Hugh Candidus*, ed. W. T. Mellows (Oxford, 1949); for what is known of the life of Hugh see there, pp. xv–xvii.

Saxon Chronicle, but relies upon many of the same materials.[1] The second chronicler, Robert of Swaffham, takes the narrative from 1175 to 1246; the third, Walter of Whittlesey, continues until 1321.[2] Each of these chronicles is a composition at a single point of time. Each is distinctive in its subject matter, since for each of the periods covered there is a distinctive group of materials.

Hugh Candidus provides the most valuable chronicle of the three, for it is the only one to rely upon sources the greater number of which have not survived. Hugh's wrath is reserved for abbot Thorold,[3] but the extortions of the Norman kings, who preserved a peace under which Peterborough could build anew, are calmly chronicled. This is one of the most accurate sources for the early history of English feudalism,[4] and the materials for the period which it covers are, by the standards of other estates, almost abundant. *Domesday Book* provides the foundation of this as of every such study, and between them the Peterborough *Descriptio Militum*[5] and the *Northamptonshire Survey*[6] give an unusually good picture of 'the lost generation which followed the knights and barons of Domesday Book'.[7] The list of knights probably dates from the first ten years of the twelfth century; a survey of the Lincolnshire property is dated by Stenton at around 1100,[8] while surveys of the abbey's demesne manors, particulars of cash and food farms, and a list of the household, date from the vacancy of 1125 to 1128.[9] There are a few, very valuable, early twelfth-century charters.[10] This makes up a full range of material, from estate management to feudal and family history, which is particularly valuable for 'that time of rapid but obscure social development, the reign of Henry I'.[11]

---

[1] Clark, *Peterborough Chronicle*, p. xxvi–iii.

[2] The only edition of the later chronicles is that of J. Sparke, *Historiae Coenobii Burgensis Scriptores Varii* (London, 1723).

[3] It is suggested that Hugh may have been 'at least half Norman' (Clark, *Peterborough Chronicle*, p. xxviii), yet certainly he looks back to the late Anglo-Saxon period as a golden age. See below, pp. 12–13.

[4] Stenton refers to Hugh as 'an honest and unimaginative compiler of local history' (F. M. Stenton, *Preparatory to Anglo-Saxon England* (Oxford, 1970), p. 185 note 1), but for a later period he has the rare distinction of being praised in that graveyard of historical reputations, the Index to *Feudal England* (J. H. Round, *Feudal England* (1895), p. 582).

[5] See my article, 'The Peterborough "Descriptio Militum" (Henry I)', *E.H.R.*, LXXXIV (1969), 84–101.

[6] Round, *V.H.C. Northants*, I, 357–92.

[7] Stenton, *Preparatory to Anglo-Saxon England*, p. 333.

[8] *Chr.P.*, pp. 176–82; Stenton, *Types of Manorial Structure in the Northern Danelaw* (Oxford, 1910), pp. 6–7.

[9] *Chr.P.*, pp. 157–68.

[10] *P.B.C.*, fos. 24v–31v.

[11] Stenton, *First Century*, p. 155.

The next writer, Robert of Swaffham, provides a fuller chronicle, but one much more narrowly based. It is a record of property transactions in large part, and it adds next to nothing to the charters from which it was compiled. The period he covers has rightly been called 'the age of charters'.[1] The largest abbey cartulary bears Robert's name and dates from the 1250s; it is the major source for the century which preceded its composition.[2] The chronicle is the first item in it, followed by royal papal and episcopal charters. The chief value of this cartulary, however, lies in its having the fullest selection of private grants of property to the monastery, and a large number of glosses point out the riches for which no space can be found. Various grants from the abbots to the convent show the uses to which some of this land was put. Also contained in Swaffham, although the original is in an earlier cartulary, are early thirteenth-century surveys of the abbey's demesne manors in the Soke of Peterborough and in Lincolnshire.[3] There are no surveys for the abbey's manors in Northamptonshire. This is a serious limitation since, in the later thirteenth century, it is only for the Northamptonshire manors that a sufficient range of accounts survives to give any indication of changes in the exploitation of the demesne. Of the three main groups of sources for this estate study, (1) chronicles and charters, (2) surveys and (3) account and court rolls, it is the survey material which has the biggest gaps in it. Hence the chief respect in which this differs from other parallel studies; the study of lordship as it is reflected in peasant obligation is limited here both by the range of the sources and by the considerable geographical range of the estate.

While the mid-thirteenth century chronicle is written from the charters, that of the early fourteenth century is written from the accounts. Indeed, from 1299 to 1321 Walter of Whittlesey abandons narrative entirely, and lists year by year the major works, and purchases of vestments, jewellery and land.[4] Chronicle material of this

[1] F. R. H. Du Boulay, *The Lordship of Canterbury* (London, 1966), p. 9. The introductory chapter to this work provides an excellent survey of the source material available for an estate study.
[2] Peterborough Dean and Chapter MS. 1 (Davis, no. 757; *Pytchley*, p. xxviii). The series of abbatial charters to the convent is in the main hand up to the time of William Hotot, who died in 1249; the anniversary charter of John of Caux, dated 1256, is in a later hand (Swa. fo. 108v).
[3] See the note on these, *C.N.*, pp. lxi–lxiii. The Lincolnshire surveys date from 1231; were the two acres in *Beche* which Richard of Scotendon held in the Surveys (fo. 181v), the two acres there which he transferred to the almonry in Swa. fos. 213v–214r, then the surveys for the Soke could be dated to before 1233, and might reasonably be presumed to have been made in 1231 also.
[4] Sparke, pp. 153–74.

kind has considerable limitations for an economic historian.[1] The series of accounts is not a long one, but enough of them survive to illustrate the structure of the estate and the organisation of demesne production. The first fragment of account dates from 1280–1;[2] another larger fragment has accounts for rather over half the demesne manors, including all those in Northamptonshire and a couple in Lincolnshire.[3] Then, for 1300–1, 1307–8 and 1309–10 there are complete account rolls for all the demesne manors.[4] Thereafter there are again only fragments; the next full range of material is from the 1370s.[5] It is this gap in the account rolls which provides this study with its term.

While the accounts are limited in extent, they are nonetheless extremely full. In particular they contain details of entry fines, and other material usually found in this period not in accounts but in court rolls. No separate court rolls survive from before 1310; there are four from the next twenty years, and these are useful in enabling some peasant families to be traced over two or three generations.[6] From the same period there survives what is perhaps the estate's most remarkable document, the *Carte Nativorum*, preserved by Mr Mellows and recently splendidly edited.[7] This is 'a unique and important document of medieval rural social life'.[8] It contains villein transactions in free land, almost all of them from the villages surrounding the monastery in the Soke of Peterborough. From the account rolls, the court rolls and the peasant charters, a detailed picture can be built up of peasant society in this area in the generations around the year 1300.

This does not exhaust the charter material for the later middle ages. There is a substantial collection of charters in the archives of the Fitzwilliams of Milton Hall. These relate to the manors of

---

[1] See the strictures of R. H. Hilton, 'Rent and Capital Formation in Feudal Society', *Second International Conference of Economic History 1962* (Paris, 1965), p. 43.

[2] B. M. Add. Ch. 737.

[3] Sir Michael Culme-Seymour, Bart., Rockingham Castle, Northants; there is a microfilm of this in the Peterborough D and C Library.

[4] Fitzwilliam A/C Rolls, 2388, 233, 2389.

[5] The later accounts survive in two places. (1) In the Fitzwilliam collection, on which see the catalogue of I. H. Jeayes. (2) In the muniments of the Peterborough Dean and Chapter. Apart from two small fragments of 1308–9 and 1333–4, those at Peterborough all date from later than 1361.

[6] Peterborough D and C Muniments, Court Rolls, Box Ia (1320–1); Fitzwilliam Court Rolls, 139 (1336), 138 (1337–8) and 140 (?1340).

[7] *Carte Nativorum*, ed. C. N. L. Brooke and M. M. Postan (Northants Rec. Soc. xx, 1960).

[8] Hilton, in a review of the above, *E.H.R.* LXXVII (1962), 323.

Castor, Marholm, Woodcroft, Etton and Northborough, all of them to the west of Peterborough in the Soke, and bought by the first Sir William Fitzwilliam between 1502 and 1532.[1] The charters from Castor are particularly valuable, for the abbey had a demesne here also, so that for this village the *Carte Nativorum* and the Fitzwilliam charters may be compared. There is another collection of private charters at Boughton House, relating to property acquired after the dissolution by Sir Edward Montagu.[2] These, however, chiefly deal with land in Polebrook hundred, where Ramsey and Thorney abbeys had a greater interest than Peterborough, and it is more with the dealings of these houses that the charters are concerned.

The abundance of the charter material distinguishes the whole Peterborough archive, and in the following chapters this material has been given its head. The charters are abundant for every level of society, from the peasant land market to the crown's operations on that market at exactly the same time. Edward I's land dealings, we are told, 'might be described as studies in the fluidity of the land market. The king took a hand, as a landholder with capital to spare rather than as a king.'[3] That is Powicke's intuition perhaps, but it is sound, and superior to some more modern scholarship.[4] The range of sources available for this estate takes us from the family settlement of the Peterborough half-virgater to 'the seductive border region where politics grease the wheels of business and polite society smiles hopefully on both'.[5] While they cannot be presented together they must be kept together in the mind. The society is a single entity, and the land market, if it is to be understood, must be studied as a whole.

[1] See M. E. Finch, *The Wealth of Five Northamptonshire Families 1540–1640* (Northants Rec. Soc., XIX, 1956), Chapter V.
[2] *Complete Peerage*, IX (London, 1936), Appendix D.
[3] F. M. Powicke, *King Henry the Third and the Lord Edward* (Oxford, 1947), p. 704.
[4] K. B. McFarlane makes great play with this analogy in his article, 'Had Edward I a "policy" towards the Earls?', *History*, L (1965), 148–9. 'Is there no point', he asks, 'at which a difference in scale amounts to a difference of quality' (p. 148). McFarlane has a case against Powicke here, in that the king's activities in some of these transactions were somewhat dubiously founded on his own law, but Powicke's general analogy seems sound.
[5] R. H. Tawney, *Business and Politics under James I* (Cambridge, 1958), p. 83.

1   *The First Two Centuries, 966–1166*

The abbey of Peterborough was established by Bishop Ethelwold in 966, one of the earlier and more important foundations in the great spread of monasticism in the second half of the tenth century.[1] There was an earlier foundation on this site, at Medeshamstede, which 'must have been one of the greatest monasteries of the Mercian kingdom in the eighth century'.[2] The Danish invasions destroyed this; some records survived, but there was no visible continuity. It was the 'tireless pertinacity' of Ethelwold that built a community here,[3] on one of those islands in the fens that God had put there, according to Hugh Candidus, that they might be the dwelling places of his servants.[4]

In Ethelwold's lifetime, and for a period thereafter, Peterborough's fortunes were closely bound up with those of the other monasteries in his 'connexion' – Abingdon, Ely, Thorney, Crowland, the two Winchester houses and (probably) St Albans.[5] It is from charter material that the story must be pieced together.[6] It is the more complicated insofar as Ethelwold's fenland monasteries must be considered as a group.[7] Land bought by him might be allocated rather later;[8] adjacent estates might be granted to different houses,

---

[1] David Knowles, *The Monastic Order in England* (2nd edn., Cambridge, 1963), pp. 31–56.
[2] F. M. Stenton, 'Medeshamstede and its Colonies', in his collected papers, *Preparatory to Anglo-Saxon England* (Oxford, 1970), pp. 179–92, quotation from p. 191.
[3] *Ely*, p. 17.
[4] *Hugh Candidus*, pp. 4–5.
[5] E. John, 'The King and Monks in the Tenth-Century Reformation', reprinted in *Orbis Britanniae* (Leicester, 1966), p. 160.
[6] All of these charters have been several times printed, and frequently commented upon. A guide to all this work, and a comprehensive list of charters, is provided by P. H. Sawyer, *Anglo-Saxon Charters. An annotated list and bibliography* (London, 1968 – hereafter referred to as *A.S.C.*). C. R. Hart, *The Early Charters of Eastern England* (Leicester, 1966 – hereafter *E.C.E.E.*), lists the Peterborough charters, and contains useful critical discussion of them. Hart also lists (pp. 243–7; nos. 345–59) a series of grants which are recorded in narrative form in *Hugh Candidus* (pp. 67–71).
[7] This is the chief contribution of a further excellent article by John, 'Some Latin Charters of the Tenth-Century Reformation', reprinted in *Orbis Britanniae*, pp. 181–209. Hart's edition of the Thorney charters (*E.C.E.E.*, pp. 146–209), follows from this, and is extremely valuable.
[8] *E.C.E.E.*, p. 177.

and even single villages divided among them. Property granted out would frequently be exchanged.[1] The archives of these houses, in consequence, supplement one another, and they must be studied as a whole. Peterborough, for example, has the best text of an important Thorney charter of 973.[2] On the other hand, there is no mention in any Peterborough text of the anti-monastic reaction which followed the death of Edgar, for all that it affected the abbey drastically; the story here is found in the Ely chronicle, and in the Life of St Oswald of York.[3] These houses had a common origin, a common interest, and perhaps a common record. This last point is not certain, but there 'seems to have been some form of composite record' of Ethelwold's activities, which has since been lost.[4]

It was on this record that the two main charters relating to Peterborough's endowment seem to have been based. The first of them states that the abbey received the following land: Medeshamstede and its berewicks; Anlafestun and its berewicks; land at Yaxley and Farcet in Huntingdonshire, and half of Whittlesey Mere; Oundle and its berewicks, and Kettering.[5] Of this property Medeshamstede was the site of the monastery, Anlafestun was presumably in what is now the Soke of Peterborough, the Huntingdonshire manors were each less than five miles from the abbey, Oundle was twelve miles away in the Nene valley, and Kettering twenty-four miles away in the valley of one of the Nene's tributaries. Peterborough, Oundle and Kettering were seized by Leofsige in the reaction which followed the death of Edgar in 975, and lay uncultivated for two years.[6] 'His success would have meant the extinction of this monastery'; but they were regained, and the culprit killed.[7]

This endowment was then consolidated, seemingly in Ethelwold's lifetime, by purchases and gifts of land, within the Soke of Peterborough and along the upper Nene valley. The record of these transactions is provided by a long 'list of sureties', which is the

---

[1] Of two contiguous villages in the north of Huntingdonshire, Yaxley was given to Thorney, and Farcet to Peterborough (*Ibid.* p. 163). Farcet was subsequently acquired by Thorney in exchange for a grant to Peterborough of some property in the Soke (*Ibid.* pp. 163–4).
[2] *Ibid.* p. 173.
[3] *Liber Eliensis*, ed. E. O. Blake (Camden Soc., 3rd ser., xcii), pp. xii, 84–5.
[4] *E.C.E.E.*, p. 177.
[5] A. J. Robertson, *Anglo-Saxon Charters* (2nd edn., Cambridge, 1956), no. xxxix (pp. 73–5, notes pp. 325–30).
[6] *Liber Eliensis*, p. 85.
[7] D. Whitelock, foreword to *Liber Eliensis*, pp. xii–xiii.

second of the two main charters.[1] The section relating to Wittering provides a specimen of this record:[2]

In this document it is declared who are the sureties for the purchase of land which Bishop Ethelwold made from various men out at Wittering; first of all 24 acres from Gyreweard, and a good dwelling-house in addition, and it was given him for 12 mancuses of gold and 8 ores of pure white money, and his sureties were Frena and Sigeferth and Oggod. Then 60 acres were bought from Mannel and his wife for 3 pounds and one ore, and his sureties were Thurlac and Oggod. Then from Tuce and her son Clac 60 acres were bought for 10 pence each, and her sureties were Gunna and Hundulf and Saxa and Thurferth. And for the 20 acres which were bought from Ufi for 28 pence each, the sureties were Tunna his father, and Ulf and Osulf, and from his mother Aswig 60 acres were bought for 10 pence each, and the sureties were Wulfgar and Eadric and Osferth and Styrcyr and Ethlebrant.

Most of these transactions were purchases. They chiefly represent consolidation, and extended the abbey's range only very slightly. Of the manors named in this document, Ashton, Warmington and Lutton were in Northamptonshire between Oundle and the abbey; Benefield was adjacent to Kettering, and the other property was in the Soke. Three estates, Wittering, Oxney and Longthorpe, were obtained from Thorney in exchange for the manor of Farcet in Huntingdonshire.[3] At the same time an agreement with Thorney protected Peterborough's fishing rights in Whittlesey Mere.[4] In all of this there is evident 'an intensive land market',[5] in which not all of the factors were economic. Parts of the villages of Castor and Maxey were granted to Ethelwold because of the outlawry of their former owners.[6] Many must have accepted his ready cash the more readily for fear of the strong right arm of the king. Some, impoverished, would have accepted it anyway.[7] There may even have been a religious revival. Ethelwold's lifetime is the first, and a distinct, period in the abbey's endowment.

The next period which may be distinguished is that between 985 and 1025. In these two generations the abbey acquired Langton

---

[1] Robertson, *Anglo-Saxon Charters*, no. XL (pp. 75–83; notes pp. 330–2); *cf.* P. Vinogradoff, 'The Transfer of Land in the Old English Period', in *Collected Papers*, I (1928), pp. 149–67.

[2] Robertson, *Anglo-Saxon Charters*, p. 81.

[3] *E.C.E.E.*, pp. 163–4.

[4] *Ibid.* p. 183; *D.B.*, I, fo. 205a.

[5] *Ramsey*, p. 7.

[6] Robertson, *Anglo-Saxon Charters*, pp. 78–9, 80–1.

[7] D. J. V. Fisher, 'The Anti-Monastic Reaction in the Reign of Edward the Martyr', *Cambridge Historical Journal*, x (1952), 264.

in Leicestershire, and various estates in Northamptonshire near the Leicestershire border, together with property in southern Lincolnshire, and two estates nearby in Rutland.[1] From Thurkil Hoche it obtained rights in Stamford, a moneyer, and land on the southern bank of the Welland. This, around 1024, was also the first grant which geographically really extended the abbey's endowment, for he gave Collingham in Nottinghamshire as well, and this was forty-six miles from the abbey.[2] With this exception the property acquired in this period was within the same radius as before; Thurlby and Stamford were twelve miles from the abbey, Langton and Cottingham just under twenty-five miles away.

The third and last period of the endowment was the couple of generations before the Conquest, and the few months thereafter. Earl Ralph, nephew of Edward the Confessor, gave Great Easton in Leicestershire and Glaston in Rutland.[3] The widow Godgifu, who later married Earl Siward, gave land in Lincolnshire, Yorkshire, Northamptonshire and Rutland, very little of which the abbey retained.[4] Archbishop Cynesige of York, a see with which the abbey had strong links in Anglo-Saxon times,[5] gave Tinwell in Rutland.[6] The abbey obtained much its biggest single endowment from the family of Brand, the last Saxon abbot, 'in the doubtful time between the death of Harold and William's own coronation'.[7] This comprised Mushkam in Nottinghamshire, and nineteen estates in Lincolnshire, of which Fiskerton, Scotter, Scotton, Manton and Walcot-on-Humber were the chief. The total amount of land was fifty-two carucates.[8] These gifts were confirmed to Peterborough by the Conqueror in 1067, in one of the earliest of his writs to survive.[9]

---

[1] *E.C.E.E.*, nos 345–7, 349–50.   [2] *Ibid.* no. 351.
[3] *Ibid.* no. 352.   [4] *Ibid.* nos. 160, 353.
[5] D. Whitelock, 'The Dealings of the Kings of England with Northumbria in the Tenth and Eleventh Centuries', in *The Anglo-Saxons.* ed. P. Clemoes (London, 1959), pp. 75–6.
[6] *E.C.E.E.*, no. 355.
[7] On them see *Hugh Candidus, passim*; F. M. Stenton, int. to *Lincs Domesday*, pp. xl–xliv, and in *V.C.H. Notts*, I, 222–3.
[8] A full list of this property is given in *Hugh Candidus*, pp. 71–2, and other information about its acquisition pp. 40–2, 67. Various forged charters of Edward the Confessor in respect of this property probably have a genuine foundation (*A.S.C.*, nos. 1029, 1059–60 = *E.C.E.E.*, nos. 157–9, where see in particular the notes to no. 159).
[9] *Regesta*, I, 8; printed *Monasticon*, I, 383. It is accepted by Davis as correct in substance, although irregular in form, and it had also been accepted as genuine by Round (*The Commune of London* (1899), pp. 29–30). This would seem very likely; that the Anglo-Saxon witnesses occur before the Norman is in tune with the Conqueror's early policy of conciliation, but hardly an order which a later forger would invent.

They formed the largest estate owned in the *Lincolnshire Domesday* by any religious foundation, which is in itself an indication of the weakness of ecclesiastical lordship in this area.[1]

At the same time, more quietly, the abbey was building up a considerable estate within the area of its original influence, Nassaburgh and the upper Nene valley. The list of *Domesday* property proves this unmistakably. Some of the more distant manors were exchanged for others closer to hand. The Ramsey chronicle records that Ramsey gave Peterborough unspecified property in Marholm in return for nine virgates in Lutton, because of the advantage to each side.[2] Hugh Candidus records with disapproval that Abbot Earnwig in his simplicity exchanged the royal village (*regalem villam*)[3] of Olney in Buckinghamshire for Stoke Doyle in Northamptonshire, 'for no other reason than that it was easier for him to go for his farm to Stoke than to Olney'.[4] The problems of organisation, with which we are here confronted, were clearly considerable. In the early period the endowment was strictly localised, and carefully preserved. The only exception to this statement is King Edgar's gift of Barrow-on-Humber, which was lost around 1013.[5] But in the third period of endowment the scope broadened, and problems of control meant that much of the more scattered property was lost. One of Godgifu's manors, Binnington in the East Riding of Yorkshire, was over a hundred miles from Peterborough.[6] Olney was about forty-five miles away. Around 1016 some land in Walton and Peakirk, which were hamlets of Peterborough, was granted by Edmund Ironside to Winchester, New Minster.[7] Neither of these grants took effect. Of the abbey's Lincolnshire property only that

[1] F. M. Stenton, *Documents Illustrative of the Social and Economic History of the Danelaw* (London, 1920), introduction.

[2] *Ramsey Chronicle*, p. 165; *cf.* F. Harmer, *Anglo-Saxon Writs* (Manchester, 1952), no. 62, and pp. 252–6.

[3] It was presumably exchanged with Borret, 'an important Northamptonshire thegn', for Borret's land passed to the bishop of Coutances, who held Olney in Domesday (*D.B.*, 1, fo. 145b). On his rebellion early in Rufus's reign, the property passed to the crown. Olney remained in royal hands for the bulk of the twelfth century (*V.C.H. Bucks*, IV, 433), which explains why it is described as *regalem villam* here.

[4] *Hugh Candidus*, p. 65; *cf. Rural England*, p. 169 note 3. From the map, at any rate, it looks a sensible exchange: Stoke Doyle was in the extreme north of Borret's estate, and Olney was to the south of any other Peterborough manor. But Olney was worth more in 1086, £12 as against £8, and perhaps in Hugh's opinion the difference was greater still (*D.B.*, 1, fos. 145b, 221a–b).

[5] *Hugh Candidus*, p. 64; *Anglo-Saxon Chronicle* (E), s.a. 1013.

[6] *E.C.E.E.*, no. 353.

[7] *A.S.C.*, no. 947 = *E.C.E.E.*, no. 165, and pp. 200–3; but *cf.* Whitelock in *E.H.R.*, LXXXIV (1969), 113.

granted before and just after the Conquest survived, and this probably only because it was granted the Conqueror's firm peace almost as soon as it was obtained. This concession may well have been an act of policy, for Stenton suggests that 'it is highly probable that king William was moved to grant his peace to abbot Brand in 1066 not merely by the proffer of 40 marks of gold and the mediation of good men, but by a sense that it would be indiscreet at that moment to indulge his anger against an abbot with powerful kinsmen in the unquiet Danelaw'.[1] With this exception it must have been administrative convenience as well as the depredations of magnates that determined which property survived, and served to rationalise the rather undisciplined piety of the later Anglo-Saxons.

Three stages in the endowment can thus be distinguished. The first represents Ethelwold's initial gifts and his subsequent purchases. Of this first group of estates only Kettering lay more than twelve miles from the abbey. The base from which the abbey expanded was Nassaburgh, and the various properties to the south and west in the Nene valley. The next half-century is a distinct period, with the abbey expanding into Leicestershire, the western parts of Northamptonshire, Rutland, and the southern wapentakes of Elloe in Lincolnshire. Geographically, this second period represents the addition of property on the Lincolnshire Limestone to an estate in origin based on the heavy clays.[2] At the same time the expansion was fairly constricted, for none of this property lay more than twelve miles from the abbey. The last generation of the Anglo-Saxon period brought property from further afield; the manor of Collingham from the link with the diocese of York, and a considerable estate in Lincolnshire from the family of abbot Brand. The time of abbot Leofric (1052–66) was one of great prosperity for the abbey, and it was named 'the golden borough'. At the same time its strength lay more in its connexions than in its endowment, and so it had more to lose than many monasteries after the Conquest.[3]

An indication of this new world, and a reflexion of the old, is found in 'the first of the long series of Lincolnshire wills', that of Ulf and Madselin.[4] Ulf was another person of consequence who had

[1] Stenton, *Lincs Domesday*, p. xliv.
[2] This is 'the sheep and barley land par excellence': *Land Utilisation Survey*, ed. L. Dudley Stamp, part 53 (Rutland, 1938,) by M. E. Broughton, pp. 30–1; part 58 (Northamptonshire, 1943), by S. H. Beaver, p. 377.
[3] Compare Knowles, *Monastic Order*, pp. 73–4 and his table on pp. 702–3.
[4] Stenton, *Lincs Domesday*, p. xlii; D. Whitelock, *Anglo-Saxon Wills* (1930), no. XXXIX.

close links with the abbey, and shortly after the Conquest he decided to go on pilgrimage to Jerusalem. The will that he left behind granted away a considerable estate, most of it to religious foundations, of which Peterborough was the chief: the document, indeed, was described as an 'agreement' between himself and his wife on the one hand, and God and St Peter on the other.[1] It was not, however, an ideal time to leave property unguarded and go abroad. In 1086, most of the estates he had bequeathed were in the hands of Normans, 'and the predecessors of these are not Ulf's legatees'.[2] This episode is in complete contrast to the protection afforded the lands the abbey had held in 1066.

The first commentary on the Conquest and on the *Domesday* settlement comes from the mid-twelfth century, from the chronicle of Hugh Candidus. The perspective from there was quite clear: the Norman Conquest was a disaster, in no way relieved.[3] Now it is well known that the English monasteries clung tenaciously to their Anglo-Saxon past,[4] and at Peterborough the evidence for this is particularly strong. After thirty years of Norman rule the monks gave William Rufus 300 marks for their own election in 1098, and chose a brother of abbot Brand.[5] He, however, lived in a different world in more ways than one, for he was deposed for simony in 1102.[6] Then there is the much more powerful evidence of the *Anglo-Saxon Chronicle*. 'A patriotic and strangely melancholy spirit', writes Professor Knowles, 'pervades the entries in the last text of the old English chronicle.'[7]

Hugh Candidus was a young monk at this time, and he cannot have written long after the *Peterborough Chronicle* closed.[8] A first reaction might be to discount his chronicle as part and parcel of the same attitude, the product of a mind which lived in 'a kind of twilight between the world of reality and that of folklore'.[9] Hugh

---

[1] The twelfth-century Peterborough cartulary tidily preserved the record of their good intentions (Black Book, fo. 50v); in Swaffham's cartulary a century later the charter is omitted.

[2] Whitelock, *Anglo-Saxon Wills*, p. 208. The subsequent history of the individual estates can be traced in the notes to Professor Whitelock's text (*Ibid.* pp. 207–12).

[3] *Hugh Candidus*, pp. 80–6.

[4] See R. W. Southern, *St Anselm and his Biographer* (Cambridge, 1963), Chapter VII.

[5] *Hugh Candidus*, pp. 86–7.

[6] Clark, *Peterborough Chronicle*, p. 85; *Eadmer's History of Recent Events in England*, trans. G. Bosanquet (London, 1964), p. 150.

[7] *Monastic Order*, p. 127.

[8] Mellows, *Hugh Candidus*, pp. xv–xvii; Clark, *Peterborough Chronicle*, pp. xxvi–xxviii.

[9] Knowles, *Monastic Order*, p. 500.

Candidus, however, was not general but specific, and there are several sources against which his account may be tested. What he says about the settlement is therefore worth careful consideration.[1]

Then a monastery that had once been very rich was reduced to penury. From that day up to the present time nothing has been added or restored, and many things have been taken away. For the same abbot Thorold not only added nothing, but he badly broke up his compact estate, and gave lands to his kinsfolk and the knights who came with him, so that scarcely one third of the abbey estate remained in demesne. When he came the abbey was valued at one thousand and fifty pounds, which he so squandered that it was scarcely worth five hundred pounds.

There are a number of points here that must be examined. That Thorold enfeoffed his kinfolk is not open to doubt.[2] This was against the Rule, but it was a natural consequence of the settlement. The more general statements about the enfeoffment of knights, and about the size of the endowment, are more important and must be tested.

It should first be noted that what was staggering wealth in pre-Conquest terms ceased to be so in the tenurial revolution which followed the Conquest. On Corbett's calculations perhaps thirty lay baronies, ten monasteries and ten dioceses had lands worth £300 or more.[3] Around fifty estates in England, in terms of endowment, took rank with or before the abbey of Peterborough. Other and more specific factors must then be taken into account in considering the abbey's position in the Conqueror's day. This involves in particular a study of the *Domesday* picture with regard to subinfeudation, and this in turn involves considering the location of the abbey's property. The *Domesday* evidence as to enfeoffment is presented in outline in Table 1. Here the process was almost complete in 1086: the *Northamptonshire Domesday* has a separate section for 'St Peter's men', and subinfeudation was equally advanced in the other counties. The valuation of the enfeoffed property was nearly £147, out of a total of £317. Forty-six per cent of the abbey's property was in

---

[1] *Hugh Candidus*, pp. 84–5.
[2] The first tenant of the Southorpe fee is referred to as 'Geoffrey the abbot's nephew' (*Pytchley*, p. 68 note). He is also referred to as Geoffrey Infans, which makes it likely that the first tenant of the Torpel fee, Roger Infans, was a nephew of Thorold also (*Ibid.* p. 34 note). He is perhaps the 'Roger nephew of the abbot' who held of the abbey at Slipton in the Northants Survey (*V.C.H. Northants*, I, 365).
[3] W. J. Corbett, *Cambridge Medieval History*, v (Cambridge, 1926), 510–2.

the hands of its knights, not far from the chronicle's estimate. The figure is enormous, as will be seen when it is compared with that for three other ecclesiastical tenants-in-chief.

	Total Valuation	Enfeoffed Valuation	%
Canterbury[1]	£2234	£344	15
Winchester[2]	£1663	£338	20
Glastonbury[3]	£840	£250	30
Peterborough[4]	£317	£147	46

It might very properly be observed at this point that Peterborough is here being compared with estates of a different size and class. This is true, but each of these estates owed a *servitium debitum* of sixty fees. Peterborough, indeed, was the only non-cathedral monastery to sustain such an obligation, for the service due from the abbot of Glastonbury was reduced to forty early in Henry II's reign.[5]

The mention of military quotas takes this analysis beyond the

Table 1   *Valuation of Peterborough Property in 1086*

	Demesne	Knight-holdings
Northamptonshire	£92 18s 4d	£101 7s 0d
Leicestershire	£7	£5
Nottinghamshire	£11	—
Rutland	£7	—
Huntingdonshire	£12	£1
Lincolnshire	£36 5s 0d	£39 11s 0d
Bedfordshire	£1 10s 0d	—
Total	£167 13s 4d	£146 18s 0d

Total demesne	£167 13s 4d
Total enfeoffed	£146 18s 0d
Town property	£2 19s 8d
Total valuation	£317 11s 0d

[1] F. R. H. Du Boulay, *The Lordship of Canterbury* (London, 1966), pp. 57–8.
[2] *Rural England*, pp. 77–8.
[3] *D.B.*, I, fos. 43b, 59b, 66b, 77b, 90a–91a.
[4] *D.B.*, fos. 205a, 210b, 221a–222a, 231a, 284a, 345b–346a. See Table 1.
[5] J. H. Round, *Feudal England* (1895), pp. 251, 278.

Domesday Survey, but at Peterborough it takes it no more than a generation beyond. There survives from around 1105 a list of the abbey's tenants by military service, headed *Hec est Descriptio Militum de Abbatia de Burgo*, and referred to hereafter as the *Descriptio*.[1] This gives not only the name of the tenant but also the number of fees owed and, in most instances, a statement of the precise amount of land from which service was due. The list was slightly revised around 1130, when it was copied into an abbey register. This document is of crucial importance, for it is the abbey's first feudal record, and bridges almost exactly the gap between *Domesday* and the *Northamptonshire* and *Lindsey Surveys*. The earlier list records between sixty and sixty-two fees, and supplies clear evidence that the abbey was making up a contingent at the former figure. There would seem no cause to doubt the Peterborough tradition that the bulk of the enfeoffment was the work of abbot Thorold.[2] It is therefore not unreasonable to superimpose the figure of sixty fees on the *Domesday* valuations. This gives a figure of £2 10s the fee.[3] Now this figure is even more remarkable than that for the percentage of property enfeoffed. It is minute when set alongside Round's twenty librates, as he was the first to point out,[4] and it remains small even by the more sober standards of recent scholarship. At Canterbury, Winchester and Glastonbury the fees were worth on average between £5 and £6. To obtain a fee of this size the Peterborough knights would have needed to take over the whole estate.

The observation so far has tended to confirm the general picture of Hugh Candidus, though it shows his figures to be inflated. Clearly by the standards of other ecclesiastical estates, Peterborough carried on altogether exceptional burden of military tenure. This burden cannot be explained satisfactorily; the Conqueror's ignorance was probably as much responsible as Thorold's undoubtedly

---

[1] It was first printed by Thomas Stapleton, as an appendix to the late thirteenth-century material in the Black Book (*Chronicon Petroburgense*, ed. T. Stapleton (Camden Soc., XLVII, 1849), pp. 168–75). A revised text is established in my article, 'The Peterborough "Descriptio Militum" (Henry I)', *E.H.R.*, LXXXIV (1969), 84–101. This prints (pp. 97–101) a numbered version of the text, and it is to this that subsequent references will be made. (Thus *Descriptio*, no. 38 represents the tenancy of Roger of Lovetot, as there p. 100.)

[2] *Hugh Candidus*, pp. 84–5.

[3] All these figures are admittedly of limited usefulness; they are notional assessments, at a single point of time, and provide no indication of economic opportunity (Du Boulay, *Lordship of Canterbury*, pp. 93–4).

[4] *V.C.H. Northants*, I, 392.

unfortunate reputation.[1] It acquires some credibility if Peterborough is seen as a bulwark against Hereward and the Danes, the nearest the monastic order got to a marcher barony, mustered against a threat which never came.[2] But this is hypothesis, and if true it would provide only a limited explanation. Round's comment remains valid – the hand of the Conqueror 'lay heavy on the house'.[3]

At the same time this point should not be pushed too far. In the first place the comparison is with other ecclesiastical estates. These were in no way typical. Reference to Corbett's figures for the lay estates shows that 'quotas of forty or more knights were imposed on most of the baronies having revenues of over £200 a year'.[4] Peterborough had what would be a heavy, but not an excessive, burden for a lay estate of its size. And if the Conqueror's hand lay heavy on the house, it also lay selectively; the severity of the pressure was partly mitigated by the care with which the settlement was made, and the control which the abbey seems to have exercised over it.[5] When *Domesday Book* is examined closely, the principles underlying the abbey's attitude to enfeoffment can be discerned. Most of the manors retained in demesne were where the abbey owned the complete village. Only very rarely did the abbey keep a demesne in a village where another tenant-in-chief owned land. The exceptions here were Great Langton in Leicestershire, North Muskham in Nottinghamshire, and Elton in Northamptonshire, and in each of these cases the property was subsequently subinfeudated. The smaller demesne holdings were subinfeudated in the century after *Domesday*. Stanwick in Northamptonshire, rated at three hides and three virgates, was the smallest manor farmed by the abbot in

---

[1] For Thorold's career see *Hugh Candidus*, pp. 80–6, and the *Anglo-Saxon Chronicle* (E), s.a. 1070. Miss Chew sees the heavy quota as a punishment for 'the strong nationalist tendencies which the house had displayed during and after the Conquest' (H. M. Chew, *English Ecclesiastical Tenants-in-Chief and Knight Service* (Oxford, 1932), p. 8).

[2] Peterborough lay the farthest north of the religious houses owing military service: I. J. Sanders, *Feudal Military Service in England* (Oxford, 1956), p. 17.

[3] *V.C.H. Northants*, I, 283.

[4] *Cambridge Medieval History*, v, 512.

[5] Recent work on individual estates which concentrates on *Domesday* has tended to show far more design, and more control by the landlord, than earlier commentators had suggested. The model here is *Rural England*, Chapter IV; *cf.* also W. E. Wightman, *The Lacy Family in England and Normandy 1066–1194* (Oxford, 1966), Chapters I and IV. Against this must be set Du Boulay, *Lordship of Canterbury*, pp. 58–9, which suggests a picture of the knights of the house touring the countryside, and selecting the best property. At Peterborough, and perhaps elsewhere, the monks seem better judges of an estate's potential than a group of men trained for another purpose in another land.

the thirteenth century.[1] When the evidence for subinfeudation comes to be examined, this point must be borne in mind. The pressures to grant out land were strong, but in small part this may represent a rationalization of endowment which was in the abbey's interests.

While these were the general principles, the division of property within each area seems to have been governed by more specific factors.[2] The Soke of Peterborough, which the abbey owned almost in its entirety,[3] saw the creation of only two fees of any size, Torpel and St Medard. Each of these lay largely in the north and west of the Soke, the area of the poorest agricultural land.[4] The property nearest the abbey, with but a few exceptions, was retained. In Northamptonshire outside the Soke of Peterborough the abbey kept control of its ancient endowment, Oundle and Kettering, and of the larger manors along the Nene valley. The property subinfeudated was of various sorts. The majority of it was in villages of divided lordship. Where the abbey was the only lord, the granting out of a manor is sometimes to be explained by its size,[5] and sometimes by its distance from other Peterborough property.[6] Several of these manors lay firmly on the claylands towards the Huntingdonshire border.[7] Outside Northamptonshire and the Soke, where two-thirds of the abbey's property lay, the factors influencing subinfeudation seem to have been determined less by geography than by the size of the property. The largest estates, however distant, were retained in demesne. The others were granted to the knights.

[1] A number of the smaller manors that remained in demesne were later granted to individual departments. Of the manors of the abbot's part, Thurlby (Lincs.) was smaller than Stanwick, but this was retained less as an agricultural unit than as a staging post, for communication with the property to the north.

[2] The *Domesday* evidence is examined in more detail in my thesis, 'The Estates of Peterborough Abbey 1086–1310' (Univ. of Cambridge, Ph.D. thesis, 1968), pp. 33–40.

[3] In the Northamptonshire Survey there was 'in the demesne of the abbot of Peterborough 70 hides and 3½ virgates': other holdings amounted to 8½ hides, 1½ virgates (*V.C.H. Northants*, I, 367). The Survey does not give details of land ownership within the Soke; the first comprehensive picture of this comes from an abbey survey of around 1150 (Peterborough D and C MS. 5, fo. 24r–v; *cf. Pytchley*, p. xxxix, 8).

[4] J. Morton, *The Natural History of Northamptonshire* (1712), pp. 9–10; *Land Utilisation Survey*, part 59, by S. H. Beaver, pp. 408–9. The Soke was economically the least developed part of Northamptonshire at this time: *Ibid.*; *The Domesday Geography of Midland England*, ed. H. C. Darby and I. B. Terrett (2nd edn., Cambridge, 1971), p. 389.

[5] As perhaps with Cotterstock, which was rated at only three hides.

[6] As with Dallington, twelve miles west of the river Ise, which otherwise formed the boundary of the abbey's Northamptonshire holdings.

[7] *Land Utilisation Survey*, part 58, pp. 375–6, 380; part 75, pp. 442–3.

In consequence, the demesne manors to the north and the west of the abbey were widely scattered: one manor, Walcot, was on the south bank of the Humber, eighty miles from the abbey, and both Scotter and Collingham were over sixty miles away. The chronology of enfeoffment was the same in Lincolnshire as elsewhere on the estate. This point is possibly of interest in connexion with the 'under-enfeoffment which distinguishes many of the Lincolnshire honours', exposed to Danish attack, especially since it has been suggested that the heavy Peterborough quota may be in part a reflexion of this threat.[1]

The structure of the Norman settlement is basic to the whole of this study. It determined the organisation of the estate in the thirteenth century, no less than the workings of the honour in the twelfth, and it set the pattern of the abbey's relations with its tenants for as long as the bonds between them endured. The pressures on this settlement during the first century came neither from Danes nor from the native English, but from the Normans. They modified it only in small part. Put in the simplest terms there are two movements here. The first is the constant pressure on the abbey forcing it to devolve property; the second the necessary adjustment of feudal relationships in the twelfth century as feudal society changed. Each of these movements must be considered against a general background: the former against the political history of the Anglo-Norman period, the latter against the more debated history of 'the first century of English feudalism'. The latter is considered at greater length, for in this context the Peterborough records are substantial, and often very informative.

In *Domesday*, and far more clearly in the *Descriptio*, there is evidence of the continuous pressures on the lord to subinfeudate land. These pressures were many and various. They show within the honour some of the most important facets of the political history of the period: the largely unbridled opportunism of the first Norman sheriffs, the patronage of Henry I, and the enterprise of the baronial class during the subsequent anarchy.

The first example concerns the way an estate might be lost through royal pressure. At the end of the entry concerning Eudo Dapifer's manor of Easton in *Domesday Book* it is recorded laconically, 'this land belongs to Peterborough'.[2] The *Descriptio* provides

---

[1] *First Century*, p. 139 note. In any case the threat of Danish attack can hardly help to explain *twelfth-century* conditions.
[2] 'Hec terra est Sancti Petri de Burgo' (*D.B.*, I, fo. 227a).

the story behind this, in the entry relating to Ansketill of St Medard:[1]

From the fee of this knight king William the elder gave Eudo Dapifer one and a half hides in Easton; and from Normandy he sent his writs to the Bishop of Coutances and Robert d'Oilli in England ordering them to give the abbot in exchange an estate of equal value in whichever of the three neighbouring counties he chose. But the abbot refused.

Eudo is recorded elsewhere in the *Descriptio* as holding a small fee of three virgates at Little Casterton in Rutland and Wothorpe in Northamptonshire.[2] It is unlikely that the abbey ever obtained service from either tenancy; on Eudo's death in 1120 his property reverted to the Crown, and the abbey lost all claim on it.[3]

The chief pressure on the abbey estates, however, came from powerful local landowners. The extortions of men like Picot of Cambridge and Urse d'Abetot are well known. Other men built up considerable estates by these means, more quietly but no less effectively. Such a man was Robert d'Oilli, a royal constable, and an important member of the administrative baronage of the midlands. Robert seems to have held Cranford of the abbey in 1086.[4] His grandson certainly held a fee in the later text of the *Descriptio*, and in addition to this a further hide and a half 'for which he has not agreed any service'.[5] The family does not appear to have rendered any service until late in Henry I's time, and the original tenancy was used as a basis for subsequent and successful encroachments. Another such entrepreneur was Ivo Taillebois, sheriff of Lincolnshire. In 1086 he held the abbey manor of Walcot-on-Humber, but shortly thereafter abbot Thorold secured a recognition that this was for Ivo's lifetime only, and obtained royal confirmation of this.[6] When Ivo died around 1098 the manor returned to the monastery demesne, and it provided a farm of £4 10s in 1125.[7] These two episodes show the abbey struggling, with differing degrees of success, to maintain control over its more distant demesne holdings.

More characteristic of the early twelfth century is the picture of royal patronage provided by the early history of the manor of

[1] *Descriptio*, no. 1.
[2] *Ibid.* no. 39
[3] W. Farrer, *Honors and Knights' Fees*, III, 281–5; *Pytchley*, p. 134 note; *Rural England*, pp. 99–104.
[4] *D.B.*, I, fo. 222a. A knight held this of him.
[5] *Descriptio*, no. 40.
[6] *Lincs Domesday*, 8/28–30; *Regesta*, I, 409.
[7] *Chr.P.*, p. 166; but no *survey* survives for this period.

Pytchley. This in *Domesday* was rated at nine and a half hides, the bulk of which was held by Azo, who held two estates – one of five hides and a virgate, and the other of one and a half hides.[1] The two estates retained a separate identity. The smaller was part of the Engaine fee by the time of the *Northamptonshire Survey*, and represents a quiet and permanent loss of lordship.[2] The larger was the subject of intensive litigation in the Anglo-Norman period. The abbey claimed it as a demesne manor[3] and did indeed regain it. In 1102–3 abbot Matthew was able to grant the property to his brother, Geoffrey Ridel.[4] A further lease followed in 1117,[5] which Lennard suggested may have converted an oral agreement to a written lease.[6] On Geoffrey's death it was agreed that the property was to return to the abbey. He died in 1120, in the White Ship disaster. The property was recovered, and confirmed to the abbey in the following year.[7] What followed is described by Hugh Candidus.[8]

Abbot John recovered the village of Pytchley, giving the King sixty marks of silver for it, and it was confirmed to God and St Peter and the monks with the King's seal and authority. But then when the abbot died the King took a further sixty marks from Richard Basset and gave the village to him.

Now Basset was Geoffrey Ridel's son-in-law, but this does not explain his succession, for clearly the abbey held the property for at least five years, between 1120 and 1125, and afterwards during at least part of the vacancy.[9] Basset, a 'Midland creation' of Henry I,[10] was one of the vacancy commissioners.[11] This explains his acquisition of the manor, and royal patronage explains his successful tenure.[12] The abbey made various unsuccessful attempts to regain

---

[1] *D.B.*, I, fo. 222a.
[2] *V.C.H. Northants*, I, 383 note 6. This was a consolidation of the forest serjeanty which Engaine held in Pytchley and Laxton (*V.C.H. Northants*, I, 294; *Pytchley*, pp. 130–2).
[3] 'Hoc manerium fuit de firma monachorum, et ibi fuit dominicum aedificium': *D.B.*, I, fo. 222a.
[4] *Hugh Candidus*, pp. 88–9.
[5] Swa. fo. 113r.
[6] *Rural England*, p. 171 note 6.
[7] *Hugh Candidus*, pp. 88–9; *Regesta*, II, 1244.
[8] *Hugh Candidus*, p. 99.
[9] Pytchley was surveyed as part of the abbey demesne in 1125–8: *Chr.P.*, pp. 161–2. Round's analysis stopped at this point, and he therefore regarded the property as having been permanently regained: *V.C.H. Northants*, I, 284.
[10] R. W. Southern, 'King Henry I', in *Medieval Humanism and Other Studies* (Oxford, 1970), pp. 218–19.
[11] *Hugh Candidus*, p. 99.
[12] He accounted in 1130 for 25 marks 'pro Pisteslai de Abbatia de Burgo': *Pipe Roll 31 Henry I*, p. 82.

this manor,[1] and only finally abandoned its claims in 1218, when Ralph Basset was granted the manor in fee-farm for ten marks a year.[2]

While Henry I's reign saw a community of interest between king and church,[3] this remained elastic and could be overruled in the interests of the king's servants. The dispassionate tone of the chronicle perhaps confirms this. The monasteries gained from Henry I's heavy-handed justice, but no-one expected this justice to be completely even-handed. On the other hand not all royal servants were as successful. William Mauduit developed, initially by marriage, an interest in Leicestershire and Rutland, which came to impinge on the outlying manors of the abbey.[4] He was castellan of Rockingham castle, and it was probably from there that he took over the Peterborough manors of Cottingham and Great Easton during the civil war.[5] They were regained by the abbey, seemingly before the death of Martin of Bec in 1155.[6] On balance, in fact, the monastery seems not to have lost from the 'nineteen long winters' between 1135 and 1154. The Lincolnshire holdings are the only possible exception to this statement.

The dynamic of the tension between the monastery and its tenants in Lincolnshire was rather different from that so far considered. In 1086 lordship there was much less developed than elsewhere on the estate. The difficulty of the *Lincolnshire Domesday*, with its myriad of small tenancies and the complexities of its sokes, is a necessary reflexion of this. Subsequent records are also deficient, but behind them lordship slowly took some root. The history of the Bourne barony, which engrossed several Peterborough tenancies, is interesting in this context. It was created in the time of Henry I, 'from the lands of several small *Domesday* tenants-in-chief', and given to William de Rullos. His daughter married Bald-

---

[1] *Curia Regis Rolls*, II, 52, 261. In 1185–7 the abbey did, however, establish its claim to the church: Swa. fo. 93v; W. Holtzmann, *Papsturkunden in England* (Berlin, 1935–6), II, no. 248 (as against the date of 1200 to 1210 given in Swaffham's chronicle, Sparke, p. 106).

[2] Swa. fo. 207r.

[3] Southern, *Medieval Humanism*, pp. 232–3.

[4] *Regesta*, II, 1719, III, 581.

[5] The editors of the *Regesta* comment (p. xxxvii), 'it must be presumed that he stayed quietly on his English lands through most of the civil war'. It was presumably at Rockingham that he stayed, his national activities circumscribed by his being in an area in which the Empress had few friends (R. H. C. Davis, *King Stephen* (London, 1967), maps on pp. 74, 90), but with more than enough scope to be a considerable local nuisance.

[6] *Hugh Candidus*, pp. 123, 173.

win fitz Gilbert de Clare. Baldwin's daughter married Hugh Wake.[1] At some point in the twelfth century some Peterborough tenants, who held directly of the abbey in *Domesday*, came to hold of the Wake family, which in consequence held a mesne tenancy between themselves and the abbey.[2] It is very likely that this mesne lordship was created in the latter part of Stephen's reign, when the barony was held by Hugh Wake. Hugh was an important witness for Ranulf of Chester after around 1145,[3] and his chief lieutenant in Lincolnshire. This type of insinuation of an individual into the feudal hierarchy is a more subtle form of freebooting than some that went on during the anarchy, but freebooting it remained.[4]

The story of how the Wake family came to be tenants of Peterborough is of some interest in that it provides a clue to one of the darker passages in the history of Norman lordship, its spread in Lincolnshire in the century after the Conquest. The making of manors in Cambridgeshire is caught by the sudden flash-light of *Domesday*; the process was slower in the free communities of Lincolnshire, and can be traced from no single record. Yet this slow assertion of lordship, the engrossing of smaller men, was perhaps more widespread than has been recognised.[5] On the one estate, at the same time, there are local feudal societies at different stages of their evolution.

The pressures leading to subinfeudation were thus of several kinds. At Pytchley two estates were alienated in the century after the Conquest. In the one the Engaine family consolidated its forest serjeanty: in the other a disputed alienation was reclaimed by the abbey, then leased, then reclaimed and finally permanently lost as a result of royal patronage. The former is insidious pressure,

[1] On this see *Complete Peerage*, xii, ii, 295–7; Sanders, *English Baronies*, pp. 107–8; *Pytchley*, pp. 81–4.
[2] *Pytchley*, pp. 81–4 notes.
[3] R. H. C. Davis, 'An unknown Coventry charter', *E.H.R.*, LXXXVI (1971), 535. I hope to examine the twelfth-century history of the Wake family in a separate article, which would consider this episode in more detail.
[4] After the civil war, abbot William of Waterville 'pro confirmacione vero novem militum quos comes Simon tenuerat centum marcas dedit regi': *Hugh Candidus*, p. 128. This oblique entry might possibly refer to similar enterprise.
[5] Compare the expansion of Ralph Paynel's estate in Lindsey around the turn of the century (*Early Yorkshire Charters*, VI, 60–5), and the growth of manorialism at Stickney (D. M. Owen, 'Some Revesby Charters of the Soke of Bolingbroke', in *A Medieval Miscellany for D. M. Stenton* (Pipe Roll Soc., new ser., 36, 1962), pp. 221–34). See also Round's reference to 'the interesting though little-known process by which the holdings of English thegns were subordinated to the fief of a Norman baron' (*Rotuli de Dominabus* (Pipe Roll Soc., 35, 1913), p. xlvi).

the latter conspicuous. The former, for all this, was the more important, the more representative. This is what might be called 'creeping' subinfeudation, as seen with the Marmion tenancy, at Stoke Doyle, and in the history of the Wake fees.[1] Such instances are taken to demonstrate the growing strength of men of middling rank.[2] The movement was at its strongest in the two or three generations after *Domesday*; by 1166 it had all but ceased.

Later changes in landholding and in feudal services are necessarily less apparent. The Exchequer drew a line across a fluid society in 1166, and would not recognise further change. The abbey records can only reflect this unhistorical precision. Around 1105 the abbey had its quota of sixty fees, just about; around 1130 there were perhaps sixty-two;[3] in 1166 the abbey returned sixty-three and five-sixth fees,[4] and it is unlikely that it ever collected on more than sixty-five.[5] A list of 1235–6 makes a distinction between the 'new' fees and the 'old'.[6] The new fees there, assessed at a total of rather under five fees, represent those over and above the quota of sixty, referred to here and elsewhere as 'chamber fees'.[7] Now this is a late rationalisation of a highly complicated social development. The history and the invented history which lie behind this list are interesting in that they reflect many of the changes in the twelfth-century feudal society.

There is some invention already around 1105. Clearly to raise the abbey's quota of knights stretched its military resources to the limit. The last two entries in the *Descriptio* are quite explicit on this point. Vivian of Churchfield held a hide of land, and claimed a quarter hide, 'and he serves as a knight with assistance'.[8] The later text has more information both on his tenancy and on his service: 'he shall

---

[1] Table 2, nos. 6, 26, 12–14.
[2] See E. Miller, *Past and Present*, no. 23 (1962), pp. 79–80, citing S. Painter, *Studies in the History of the English Feudal Barony* (Baltimore, 1943), pp. 21–30. For a slightly different interpretation of subinfeudation in the 'first century' see *Ramsey*, pp. 24–33. Raftis sees the chief reason for the devolution of property as 'the rapacious administration of the royal servants' (p. 28). At Peterborough such cases, while they are the most conspicuous, are not the most representative.
[3] These two figures are based on the argument in my article, *E.H.R.*, LXXXIV, 90, 95.
[4] *Red Book of the Exchequer*, ed. H. Hall (Rolls Series, 99, 1896), I, 329.
[5] Mellows' list gives a total of 'about 69 fees' (*Pytchley*, p. xxi), but this conflates assessments at various points of time.
[6] Swa. fo. 286r.
[7] The term is explained in Chew, *English Ecclesiastical Tenants-in-Chief*, p. 138.
[8] *Descriptio*, no. 51.

Table 2   *Fees of the abbey in the early twelfth century*

Title of fee	Domesday tenant	Descriptio		Number of fees
		Tenant	Number	
1 St Medard	Anketil	Asketill of St Medard	1	6
2 Torpel	Roger	Roger Infans	3	6
3 De la Mare	—	Ralph de la Mare	9	3
4 Waterville of Marholm	Ascelin	Ascelin of Waterville	6	3
5 Dover-Marmyon	William	William son of Ralph	8	3
6 Marmyon of Fillongley	Abbey demesne	Roger Marmiun	42	2
7 Overton Waterville	Ansgered	—	—	1
8 Maufe	Roger	Roger Maufe	20	2
9 Gunthorpe	Geoffrey	Geoffrey nepos abbatis	5	3
10 Bassingbourne	Hugh	Richard son of Hugh	49	3
11 Milton	Roger	Turold of Milton	11	2
12 Wake	?Saxwalo	Hugh of Evremou	43	2
13 Wake	Ansford	Ansford	44	—
14 Wake	Robert	Robert of Gimiges	45	2
15 Fauvel	—	Gilbert Falvel	12	2
16 Burghley	Geoffrey	William of Burghley	7	2
17 Luvetot	Eustace the Sheriff	Roger of Luvetot	38	2
18 Neville of Walcote	Gilbert	Gilbert of Neville	13	1
19 Neville of Scotton	Ralph	Ralph of Neville	52	3
20 Tot	—	Geoffrey of Tot	18	1
21 Cranford-Daundelyn	Robert	Robert d'Oilli	40	1
22 Churchfield	—	Vivian	51, 54	1
23 Peverel	—	Walo of Paston	16	1
24 Engaine-Pytchley	William Engaine	Viel Engaine	4	1

Table 2 *Continued*

Title of fee	Domesday tenant	Descriptio		Number of fees
		Tenant	Number	
25 Bringhurst	—	Theobald of Bringhurst	15	1
26 Stoke Doyle	Abbey demesne	Wimund	50	1
27 Knight of Stoke	—	Hugh Olifard	53	1
28 Dallington	Richard	Robert son of Richard	48	2
29 Thorold of Castor	—	Turold of Castor	21	2
30 Sutton	—	Ansketill of Sutton	10	2
31 Avenel	—	Avenel	41	$\frac{1}{2}$
32 Dumar	—	Richard son of Herbert	22	$\frac{1}{2}$
33 Helpston	—	Pain of Helpston	17	$\frac{1}{3}$
34 —	Richard	Richard Engaine	2	1
35 —	Eudo Dapifer	Eudo Dapifer	39	1

be a knight in the army with two horses and his own arms, and the abbot will provide him with any other necessities'.[1] He had to turn up with two horses and a sword; the abbey would do the rest. Another tenant is recorded in the first list as holding three and a third virgates, 'and he serves as a knight'; the later text adds 'in the army and in guard-duty and in musters, with a corrody from the abbot'.[2] This corrody must represent a similar agreement. In both these cases a knight's service had been due from an estate of under a hide of land. They were fees of well below the estate average of two hides, which was anyway extremely small. The implication is that a tenancy this size could not support the obligations of knight-hood unaided. An indication of where the support came from appears in the sixteen entries in the original list which refer not to knights but to men who serve 'with the knights' (*cum militibus*). Six of these entries refer to groups of sokemen; the other ten refer to

[1] *Ibid.* no. 54.
[2] *Ibid.* no. 53.

serjeanty holders of various sorts. The entries in this category refer to just under 13 hides out of a total of 133½ hides – just under a tenth of the total land recorded. It would seem an obvious reading of the document that these men assisted the knights in their performance of military service.[1]

Even when the abbey was confronted with the need for precision, there was no point at which a division between knightly and non-knightly tenure could be clearly drawn. In the next century the Peterborough host, at best a precarious military entity, became a fiscal one entirely. This can be seen, for example, in the history of the honour's obligation to castle-guard, which was commuted at a rate of four shillings the fee in Henry I's time.[2] This represents a very early commutation, which shows the inadequacy of the abbey's knights, and in turn reflects the quite unrealistic burden of service due.

That there has been some adjustment to changing circumstances is apparent in the second text of the *Descriptio*, which was probably drawn up during the vacancy of 1125–8. Then the Churchfield and Knight of Stoke tenants served 'with assistance'; later still they owed the service of fractions of fees.[3] The same text also mentions for the first time three tenancies – Helpston, Dumar and Avenel – described as being held by the service of a fraction of a fee.[4] The appearance of these fractional knights is revealing, for it focuses attention on the holding rather than the knight. They show a society in which feudal terminology was becoming more explicit, and one in which external military pressure was beginning to disappear. When it disappeared there was no mention of the men who served 'with the knights'. It is in consequence almost impossible either to detail the obligations of these sub-military tenancies, or to trace the subsequent descent of their holdings. Perhaps they contributed equipment; perhaps they served as foot soldiers; more likely they paid money. It is clear that the contribution varied according to the size of the holding. But on this matter the evidence

---

[1] The points made in the previous two paragraphs are treated more fully in my article, as cited, pp. 89–92.

[2] Swa. fo. 46r; text printed in *Cal. Charter R. 1327–41*, p. 277. Compare S. Painter, 'Castle-Guard', in *Feudalism and Liberty* (Baltimore, 1961), p. 155, which is based on a misreading of the text.

[3] The service due from the Churchfield tenancy in the thirteenth century fluctuated between a quarter and a half fee (*Pytchley*, p. 121 note), while that from Knight of Stoke was a quarter fee throughout (*Ibid.* p. 147 note).

[4] *Descriptio*, nos. 17, 22, 41.

is late, and relates only to fiscal service; there is no indication of how it had been intended that the actual military service be raised.[1] The descendants of some of these freeholders held by the service of fractions of fees. Thus the John of Walton who held a quarter-fee of the abbey in 1236 was a descendant of the Swain who held three virgates and an acre in the *Descriptio*.[2] Geoffrey of Caxton, who then held one-thirteenth of a fee, had the holdings of the men who held at Winwick in the *Descriptio*, who presumably themselves represent the two serjeants who held in *Domesday*.[3] The Woodcroft fee in Paston was very likely constructed from a number of socage tenancies;[4] it was listed as a 'tenement' in 1146, but not as a fee.[5] Here again, it must have been an artificial line that was drawn, but it marks off the class for which feudal records survive.

It is easier to form a general picture of the Norman settlement, and of the factors which modified it as feudal society changed, than to grasp the honour, which we are told was 'a feudal state in miniature'.[6] The chief source here is a group of two dozen charters which describe the *acta* of the abbot's court in the first half of the twelfth century.[7] These are not charters as later formalised. They are narrative records of lawsuits and property transactions, which may have been cast initially in this form, or more likely written up from other records by a man with first hand knowledge of the events they describe. These charters give a fair amount of detail and, more important, they convey a certain amount of atmosphere.

The first document quoted is a good specimen of this material, and bears on a problem of considerable importance, that of the heritability of land.[8]

Be it known to all men both present and to come that in the year of our Lord 1147, the twelfth year of the reign of king Stephen, Robert of Torpel the son of Roger Infans of Torpel came a sick man into the chapel of

---

[1] For the argument of this paragraph see my article, as cited, pp. 91–3.
[2] *Descriptio*, no. 19; *Pytchley*, pp. 142–3.
[3] *Ibid.* p. 114 note; *Descriptio*, no. 33; *D.B.* I, fo. 221b.
[4] *Pytchley*, pp. 140–1.
[5] *Hugh Candidus*, p. 114. On the distinction between *tenementum* and *feodum* see C. W. Hollister, 'The Knights of Peterborough and the Anglo-Norman Fyrd', *E.H.R.*, LXXVII (1962), 418 note 5. Compare one of the items in the foundation charter of Revesby abbey in 1142, when two serjeanties were converted to form half a fee: Stenton, *Early Northants Charters*, pp. 2, 6.
[6] *First Century*, p. 51.
[7] P.B.C., fos. 24v–31v. The same documents have been copied from here and are found in a tidier version in Swa. fos. 112v–119v.
[8] P.B.C., fo. 27r–v.

St Leonard in the hospital of Peterborough. There in the presence of many who stood around, monks, clerks and laity, of his children also and of his men, he gave to God and St Peter and the church at Peterborough himself body and soul, together with all his land in Cotterstock and Glapthorne, to hold with every right, in wood and open country, in land and meadows, and in every other thing. This he granted as his just inheritance, of his own patrimony, to which he had succeeded on the death of his father, along with all the other lands and the honour of Torpel. This same property had in fact been given to his sister as a dowry on her marriage with Richard of Lambercourt,[1] and Robert had bought it back from Richard for forty marks. Previously when Robert was infirm and afflicted with leprosy his brother Roger had taken up the honour of Torpel, but the land here transferred – in the king's view and with the king's assent and that of many of the barons of the land – was to remain to Robert for him to hold and alienate as he please, without restriction. To confirm this gift to the church of Peterborough he sent his pledge twice a day by the hand of a monk of the house to the altar of palms, that is to say the green altar. And it was agreed that in his lifetime he should receive a monk's corrody, and four of his servants knights' corrodies, and on his death he should assume the monk's habit.

This document conveys the atmosphere of a feudal society. There is mention of royal assent to this transaction, but it must have been largely a formality. The strength of the landowner's position is clear. Here the son of a *Domesday* tenant grants land to the abbey, 'as his rightful inheritance which he had as part of his patrimony'. What is more there is the remarkable statement that this property had previously been granted away as a marriage portion, and then purchased back. There is a tenacity here which goes beyond feudal convention.

This evidence does not stand alone, or apply only to men of this rank. In charters concerning the smaller knights and freeholders the atmosphere is the same. A case from 1133 concerned rights in the church of Castor. It was contested by two brothers, the elder who was priest of the church, and the younger who held the fee – an interesting inversion of the standard pattern. The priest wished to become a monk and give his church to the monastery. The brother contested his right to do this: 'he said that the church was part of his fee, and he had the right to service from it as from the other parts of his fee'. Finally the younger brother abandoned his claim,

---

[1] It must be very likely that this is Richard of Reinbuedcurt, son of Guy, who occurs in the Northamptonshire Survey: Sanders, *English Baronies*, p. 33; *V.C.H. Northants*, I, 389.

on the advice of his friends, and his grant to the abbey was confirmed by his heirs in the abbot's court.[1]

The impression given by these charters is only confirmed by the
information concerning the descent of fees. Thus if we take the first
Descriptio list as a basis, and look at the descent of fees in the century after the Conquest, it becomes clear that the Peterborough
fees were heritable. Thirty-one entries in this list refer to knightly
tenures.[2] Two of these tenancies never subsequently owed the
abbey service.[3] Thirteen of the remaining twenty-nine tenancies
show clear evidence of continuity from *Domesday* to Henry II's day.[4]
Six were in some way discontinuous.[5] The evidence for the remaining eleven fees is equivocal; for four there is no information,[6]
and for the last seven the evidence is confused.[7] In the latter cases
the name of the tenant changes; this may represent a change of
family, but it may very easily not.[8] And where the evidence is
equivocal it is so with very little evidence of discontinuity.[9] This is
exactly what might be expected, taking into account the political history of the Anglo-Norman period. The turn-over at the top of each
honour is a necessary reflexion of the political instability of the
Anglo-Norman state. At a lower level, where political loyalty posed
fewer problems, continuity was massive.[10] Heritability was not an

---

[1] P.B.C., fos. 25v–26r; *Pytchley*, p. 153 note. In another of these charters,
Burmund the man of Ascelin of Tot came into the court with his daughter,
'quia non habuit alium heredem': P.B.C., fo. 26r, from around 1135.
[2] See Table 2, nos 1–6, 8–30, 34–5. No. 7 on this list, the fee of Orton
Waterville, must be a *Domesday* tenancy (*Pytchley*, pp. 54–5 notes;
Complete Peerage, XII, ii, 429), but it is not recorded in the *Descriptio*, and
so is not included here.
[3] Nos. 34, 35.   [4] Nos. 1, 2, 3, 4, 6, 8, 9, 11, 15, 18, 20, 29, 30.
[5] Nos. 10, 12, 13, 14, 17, 27.   [6] Nos. 19, 23, 25, 28.
[7] Nos. 5, 7, 16, 21, 22, 24, 26.
[8] A good example of the confusion of some of these early names is found
in the *Domesday* tenancy of Hugh of Waterville in Woodford, Addington
and Cotterstock. His son is referred to alternately as Richard son of
Hugh (*Descriptio*, no. 49; *V.C.H. Northants*, I, 388), Richard of Cotterstock (P.B.C., fo. 25v), and Richard of Addington (*Pipe Roll 31 Henry I*,
p. 81); and see also *Pytchley*, pp. 74–5.
[9] Three of these tenancies (nos. 12, 13, 14) came to owe service to Wake,
and have been considered above. Eustace the sheriff (no. 17) was succeeded by Richard of Lovetot: Farrer suggested that a daughter of Eustace married Richard of Lovetot (*Early Yorkshire Charters*, III, 3–5; cf.
Registrum Antiquissimum, VII, 211), but this faces the obstacle that it
was Roger, Richard's father, who held of the abbey in the *Descriptio*, no.
38. With Bassingbourne (no. 10) the son of the Domesday tenant seemingly left no heir (*Pytchley*, pp. 73–7). The tenancy of Knight of Stoke
(no. 28) was usurped by Gunthorpe in 1114 and regained by the abbey in
1120 (P.B.C., fo. 31r).
[10] cf. H. M. Colvin, 'A list of the archbishop of Canterbury's tenants
by knight-service in the reign of Henry II', in *Medieval Kentish Society*
(Kent Records, XVIII, 1964), p. 4.

issue here.[1] This is a problem which can be looked at from two
angles. The establishment of quotas, the necessary territorialisation
of the country's military resources, made heritability at least a
considerable convenience. And then there is the atavism of these
early charters. The family's attachment to property, the family
growing around its land almost, made heritability not just a convenience but also a way of life.[2]

The honour on an estate like this, on the other hand, was not a
way of life but a convenience. There was a feudal court.[3]

In this year also (1135) Pampelina the wife of Osbern, who held certain
lands in Peterborough, Werrington and Glinton, in which she had no
right, and to which she could show no title, came into the court of abbot
Martin. This was a full court on that day. There she returned into the
hands of the abbot, for God and St Peter, all the lands which she held, and
quit-claimed her rights to them and those of her heirs in perpetuity,
humbly asking that the abbot have mercy on her, for the love of God.
The abbot was moved by her clear piety and evident distress, as also by
the request of his barons, and returned to her the land of Wither of
Werrington, which she claimed her husband had bought. This land she
was to hold for sixpence a year for all service to the abbot. The abbot
remitted also a rent of ten shillings which she owed as the grand-daughter
of one John, and gave her a further ten shillings in addition. The whole
court witnessed this agreement.

The abbot's court was self-contained, it took none of its authority
from outside. The suitors at it were both 'judges and witnesses'.[4]
There is explicit reference to the barons of the honour advising
their lord. All these are facets of the honour, which Stenton has
made familiar, and which is his key to 'the first century of English
feudalism'.

The abbot of Peterborough had his court.[5] But when we look at
'the composition of that court, its procedure, and the kind of
business which came before it',[6] several of the particular features of

[1] As against the argument of R. H. C. Davis, 'What happened in Stephen's
Reign. 1135–1154', *History*, XLIX (1964), 1–12.
[2] Compare R. Genestal, 'Le Parage Normand', *Bibliotheque d'Historie du
Droit Normand*, 2nd ser.: études. Vol. 1, fasc. 2 (Caen. 1911), p. 38.
[3] P.B.C., fos. 25v–26r.
[4] *Ibid.* fo. 25r.
[5] 'Eodem siquidem anno idem abbas Martinus placita sua tenuit apud
Castram': *Ibid.* fo. 26r.
[6] *First Century*, p. 42.

ecclesiastical baronies become apparent.[1] Taking the question of procedure first of all. In a case already considered, from 1133, the elder son of the knightly family living in Castor wished to become a monk and bring his church and property to the abbey. He came first to the chapter house before the abbot and all the monks.[2]

The abbot on hearing his petition granted it, on condition that he appear in his court before his barons, and confirm in front of them what was done in the chapter house. Richard therefore came into the abbot's chamber, and before the abbot of Thorney and William d'Aubigny and Richard Basset, together with many of the barons of the honour, and many others who came with William and Richard, he granted his church of Castor to abbot Martin. . . . All these things were seen and heard by the following witnesses: Robert abbot of Thorney, Richard Basset, William d'Aubigny and all the court of Peterborough, which then was a full one, since this was the day that abbot Martin took the homages of his men.

The honorial court seems almost an *ad hoc* body here. It is meeting not at Castor but in the abbot's chamber. It accommodates royal officials like Richard Basset and William d'Aubigny seemingly with no stress at all. A court thus constituted cannot be strictly defined. And if several important transactions took place in this way in the abbot's chamber, it was in the abbey church that the full weight of spiritual sanction was imposed. Two brothers, granting property to the abbey, came 'before the high altar of the new church, on the feast of St Peter's Chair at Rome, just before the introit at the high mass of the day', and granted their inheritance to the abbey 'in the presence of abbot Martin, with the convent standing around, and in the presence of many sacred relics'.[3] Whatever the practice of lay transfer of land, that of an abbey like Peterborough used different sanctions and a rather different form.[4]

If the court's procedure was elastic, so also was its composition. It was compact, and it was open-ended. The abbey did not have, and we must presume it did not need, the extensive administrative framework which is found elsewhere. The litany of household officers found in a contemporary charter for Canterbury is absent

---

[1] Stenton excluded ecclesiastical baronies from his study: 'the feudalism which they represent has a certain artificiality which makes it unsafe to generalize from their history' (*Ibid*. p. viii).

[2] P.B.C., fos. 25v–26r.

[3] *Ibid*. fo. 27r.

[4] On this practice see D. C. Douglas, *Feudal Documents from the Abbey of Bury St Edmunds* (London, 1932), pp. xl–xliii.

here.[1] There can be no 'typical' list of witnesses to put in its place, but the following were the judges and witnesses when Leofwin the brother of Colgrim lost a case against the abbey in 1118: Ascelin of Waterville, Geoffrey of Gunthorpe, Roger of Torpel, Ralph Papilio, Vivian, William of Burghley, Martin of Papley, Geoffrey of Castor, William Dapifer, Walter son of Peter, Gilbert of Barnack, Godric of Thorpe.[2] Five of these men occur as knights in the *Descriptio*: Ascelin of Waterville and Roger of Torpel are men of substance within the honour; Geoffrey of Gunthorpe and Geoffrey of Castor are knights in the Soke; William of Burghley was the only military tenant of the abbey in Stamford.[3] Vivian held several serjeanties, and served as a knight 'with assistance'; Martin of Papley, Gilbert of Barnack and Godric of Thorpe are three of the ten or so men whose serjeanties became chamber fees. The others were probably freemen; one of them bears the interesting name *dapifer*, but there is no further information about his tenure.[4] There are one or two of the honorial baronage – often Torpel, often Waterville, often de la Mare. Then there are the smaller knights, whose property lies close to the abbey – men like Castor, Gunthorpe, Tot, Peverel, who may have been enfeoffed especially for this purpose. These then shade off into a larger group of serjeanty holders, among those duties that of suit of court bulked large.[5] Finally there are the household servants, bakers, door-keepers and cooks.[6]

Just as the honour was not a model honour by lay standards, so the two chief lay officers were not model officers. The Waterville family of Marholm were the hereditary stewards, and the de la Mares of Northborough the hereditary constables. In the early Norman period they had an important administrative part to play. It must have been as steward that Ascelin of Waterville occurs in royal writs of 1095–7 and 1107–14, and that his son Hugh appears in a writ for Bury St Edmunds later in Henry I's reign.[7] Both Hugh

---

[1] *First Century*, p. 71; Du Boulay, *Lordship of Canterbury*, pp. 251–3.
[2] P.B.C., fo. 25r.
[3] In the list of fees given in Table 2 these are nos. 4, 2, 9, 11 and 16 respectively.
[4] He was presumably a servant of the household, as was the steward Fulk Asketell at Ramsey (*Ramsey*, p. 51).
[5] *Ibid.* pp. 47–51, and the references there cited.
[6] On at least one occasion when reference is made to men *de curia nostra* it is these, not men of greater rank, who are implied: P.B.C., fo. 28r–v, a case from 1150.
[7] *Facsimiles of English Royal Writs to A.D. 1100*, ed. T. A. M. Bishop and P. Chaplais (Oxford, 1957), no. 21 (calendared *Regesta*, I, 409); *Regesta*, II, 924; *Regesta*, II, 1733 (printed Douglas, *Feudal Documents*, p. 76).

of Waterville and Ralph de la Mare accounted 'for the revenues of the abbey of Peterborough' in the Pipe Roll of 1130, which suggests that they had had some responsibility as feudal officers during the preceding vacancy.[1] But while both families performed their duties, getting the service due from them was quite another matter. The abbot of Peterborough could not offer a Hugh of Waterville the rewards laymen could offer men of comparable status – which Ranulf of Chester, for example, could offer Hugh Wake. Not surprisingly, he did not get the same loyalty.

The Waterville family, in addition to holding three fees of the abbey, controlled three of the more distant demesne manors in Northamptonshire – Irthlingborough, Stanwick and Aldwincle.[2] Each of these is recorded as being in demesne in the surveys of 1125, but they appear as the last three entries in the document, and the information on them is much less full than that for the other property.[3] The abbey chronicle mentions Hugh of Waterville as one of the powerful men from whom abbot Martin recovered property, and the agreement with him has survived.[4] The abbey regained control over the greater part of Irthlingborough and Stanwick, but lost Aldwincle, which Hugh retained for a fee-farm of 60s a year. In all this, and for the next half-century, there is no mention of the stewardship. Then between 1194 and 1199, Geoffrey of Barnack married a daughter of another Hugh of Waterville, and took over the stewardship from him.[5] Hugh was given twelve marks not to claim the office during the current abbot's lifetime.[6] A 'new man' becomes steward. Yet he married a daughter of the old steward, and he had to be made a knight, for while his substance suggested the dignity his tenure was not a military one.[7] There are elements in this both of the new administration and of the old.

There is less information on the constableship, but the pattern

---

[1] *Pipe Roll 31 Henry I*, p. 83.
[2] *V.C.H. Northants*, I, 365, 377, 388; cf. *Pytchley*, pp. 41–5.
[3] At this date the manors supplied no farm, although it was presumably for them that Ascelin of Waterville was paying £20 a year: *Chr.P.*, p. 167. If the other Peterborough demesne manors were farmed, as received opinion suggests most manors would be at this date, it would be interesting to know why only Ascelin was recorded in this way.
[4] *Hugh Candidus*, p. 123 (cf. *Anglo-Saxon Chronicle* (E), s.a. 1137); Swa. fos. 204v–205r (printed *Monasticon*, I, 393).
[5] *Pytchley*, p. 45 note.
[6] *Abbreviatio Placitorum* (1811), p. 3. He reserved the right to claim thereafter, but seems not to have done so.
[7] *C.N.* 505. Previously Geoffrey had paid a rent of 8s a year; now he was to serve as a quarter of a knight. Geoffrey's father, however, had been recorded as a knight in a list of witnesses of 1150: P.B.C., fo. 28v.

was the same. Late in the thirteenth century a charter of between 1115 and 1125 was produced which had granted Ralph de la Mare the hereditary constableship of Peterborough.[1] It would seem to have been based on a genuine confirmation, although it is unlikely that the office was created at so late a date. By the end of Stephen's reign the links with the honour were fairly tenuous, and abbot William had to give Henry II a hundred marks to recover 'the fee and the service of the constable Geoffrey de la Mare'.[2] Charters of the late twelfth century will sometimes refer to the de la Mares as constables.[3] But for the thirteenth century there is no mention of the constableship until 1296, when another Geoffrey was paid sixty marks and the office extinguished.[4] By then it was merely another form of privileged tenure. Its anachronism, indeed, is amusingly highlighted by a case concerning the de la Mares held under the Dictum of Kenilworth. Geoffrey de la Mare had been one of those defending Northampton against the king, and had for-feited his lands in consequence. He explained his conduct as follows. He held, he said, of the abbot of Peterborough, who ordered him to go to Northampton, and, when he refused, distrained him to do so. He went, therefore, with his lord, but he remained loyal to the king, shunning the company of those who held the town, and generally keeping out of the way.[5] There is no record that the justices were in any way impressed by this unlikely story, but for our purposes the picture of the hereditary constable of Peterborough, cowering in a corner of a besieged town, unarmed, is an interesting example of a 'decayed serjeanty'. It provides a late, but perhaps not entirely unsuitable, conclusion to a chapter which has largely been con-cerned with the military importance of the Norman settlement.

[1] *Chr.P.*, pp. 130–1. If the document is exactly reproduced, and it pre-sumably passed muster at the abbey, then its emphasis on hereditary tenure is interesting. On the Peterborough constableship see Round, *V.C.H. Northants*, I, 391, and Chew, *English Ecclesiastical Tenants-in-Chief*, pp. 84–6.

[2] *Hugh Candidus*, p. 128.

[3] Black Book, fo. 173r; *C.N.* 504; P.B.C., fos. 29v, 30r.

[4] Vesp. E. 22, fo. 1ff.

[5] *Rotuli Selecti*, ed. J. Hunter (1834), pp. 120–1.

Knighthood was an elastic category, and early on a comprehensive one. It was not only the knights of the honour who held by military service in the early years of the twelfth century. In the *status domus* of 1125, the eight heads of department among the abbey servants had a knight's corrody, without presumably anyone feeling the social order was prejudiced thereby.[1] When Robert of Torpel entered the monastery in 1147 he received a monk's corrody, while four of his servants were to have knights' corrodies.[2] In 1309, however, Robert of Thorpe, one of the abbey's major tenants, was allocated 'half a width of the better kind of clerical cloth, with a fur lining suitable for a clerk', on his appointment as steward.[3] His son was granted a knight's corrody on appointment to the same office in 1330; and yet he was not a knight.[4] When in the next generation Robert's grandson was appointed chief justice of the common bench, he was ordered to take knighthood, and given £40 annually from the exchequer to sustain him in this estate.[5]

In the terms of the thirteenth century we cannot regard as knights more than a fraction of the motley crew raised by abbot Thorold towards the feudal host. In this period witness lists to charters, the best evidence of a man's status within the local community, and the feudal records may give two quite distinct impressions. Thus in 1100 Turold of Castor had two hides and a virgate, for which he owed the service of two knights. Service of half a knight was remitted when his son gave the advowson and some land to the abbey. His successors, whose holding seems not to have changed greatly, owed the service of one and a half knights throughout the thirteenth century.[6] But this ceases to be a knightly family. In 1242 'the lord William son of Thorold' was chief witness to a charter; in the 1280s his son was described as 'Henry who is called the lord of Castor'.[7]

[1] *Chr.P.*, pp. 167–8.
[2] See above, pp. 27–8.
[3] Vesp. E.22, fo. 116r.
[4] Vesp. E.21, fos. 70v–71r.
[5] *Cal. Patent R. 1354–8*, p. 465.
[6] *Descriptio*, no. 21; P.B.C., fos. 25v–26r; *Pytchley*, p. 153.
[7] 'Dominus Willelmus filius Thoraldi', Fitzwilliam Ch. 4; 'Henricus dictus le lord de Castre', *Pytchley*, p. 64.

This is a nickname, not a title of rank. Others may have been more fortunate in their friends, for instance the Peverel family. They were descended from Walo of Paston, who in 1100 had a hide and a virgate in Paston and Warmington and owed the service of one knight. The Peverels sold the Warmington portion to the abbey in the last quarter of the twelfth century, and in the thirteenth owed the service of two-thirds of a knight. Yet it is as freeholders that a succession of Robert Peverels appear in the chronicle and in charters.[1] Only the feudal records regard this as a knightly family, and their definition is no more than Bracton's definition of military tenure: anyone who pays even a halfpenny in scutage holds thus.[2]

Along with this process of redefinition from outside, as it were, there were changes in the economic position of each family from one generation to the next. Yet the records which we have for the knightly tenants of Peterborough as a group fail to show either dynamic. The *cartae* of 1166 are the first of a whole series of central and local records which present the honour as a social group.[3] This raises problems even for the 'first century', and by 1200 the honour was patently decayed. The honorial court was indeed summoned in 1218, for a final settlement of the century-old dispute with the Basset family; but here it is no practical thing, rather an instrument of revenge.[4] It had been a local not a feudal unit, 'the knights and freeholders of Nassaburgh', that three years earlier had purchased the disafforestation of the area.[5] This by-passes the whole concept of 'the knights of Peterborough barony'; it is not a meaningful group either socially or geographically. And yet the government records, in 1212 and again in 1242, have still to record men in these units. The Peterborough list of 1212 starts 'Roger of Torpel six knights', as though the previous six generations had never been.[6] It was left to individual lords, in their feodaries, to look behind this, and 'Henry of Pytchley's Book of Fees' is a model of its kind. Yet it also will not say anything of the occupancy of these six fees in 1212,

---

[1] *Descriptio*, no. 16; *Pytchley*, pp. 69, 123; Sparke, p. 112; *C.N.*, p. lxii.

[2] Bracton. *On the Laws and Customs of England*, ed. G. E. Woodbine, trans. etc. S. E. Thorne (Cambridge, Mass., 1968), II, 117.

[3] *Red Book of the Exchequer*, I, 329, II, 618–19; and *Pytchley*, pp. xxxvii–xlvi.

[4] The fine begins, 'hec est finalis concordia facta in curia de Castre coram militibus baronie Burgi': Swa. fo. 207r–v, and also B. M. Sloane Roll 31/4. The Ely honorial court was last assembled in 1229: Miller, *Ely*, pp. 193–4.

[5] At one point six knights sealed a charter as the representatives of this group; its activities are considered on pp. 74–5, and some texts presented in Appendix A.

[6] *Red Book of the Exchequer*, II, 618.

and evidence of this must therefore come from elsewhere. Here we must chiefly rely on charters, and the Peterborough cartularies also are models of their kind. These massive monastic records cause fresh problems of interpretation, however, for they show only landlord enterprise, and tracing knights through them is necessarily a somewhat morbid exercise.

A way to avoid at least some of these difficulties is to look at the land market from a different viewpoint. 'The proper unit of study is the individual family; it must be seen from the inside; and the most fruitful path in this field is the detailed study of particular cases, based upon the family documents, where these are available.'[1] The main part of this chapter is therefore devoted to a consideration of just seven families.[2] They have been chosen because they can be studied in some detail, and they are a sample in this respect only. There is no family here which remained relatively stable during the thirteenth century, for stable families leave few records. Each family history is presented in a similar way. It starts with the knightly estate around 1100, the size of the properties of which it was composed and the pattern of their distribution. It then notes any changes in this pattern during the twelfth century, in particular grants away from the fee either to members of the family or to the church. Then in the thirteenth century the first five of these families decline, and the latter two prosper. The stages in either process will be worked out as fully as possible.

The devolution of property at the knightly level was for a long time controlled. From one point of view this is surprising, for there was pressure on the knights to devolve land no less than upon their lords. The claims of relatives, and the claims of piety, had each to be met according to the fashion of the group; this stress existed even if the family's economic position was assured.[3] There was some natural pressure towards fragmentation, for the knight's holding was often no more an economic unit than was the great estate.[4] In this it probably differed from a normal freehold. Thus, of the Peterborough fees, that at Milton included six bovates in Cleatham, a good sixty

---

[1] H. J. Habakkuk, int. to M. E. Finch, *The Wealth of Five Northamptonshire Families, 1540–1640* (Northants Rec. Soc., XIX, 1956), p. xix.

[2] I have considered this material in a slightly broader context in my article, 'Large and Small Landowners in Thirteenth-Century England', *Past and Present*, no. 47 (1970), pp. 26–50.

[3] The best general discussion of these matters is in S. Painter, 'The Family and the Feudal System in Twelfth-Century England', *Feudalism and Liberty* (Baltimore, 1961), pp. 195–219.

[4] Stenton, *First Century*, pp. 158–9, 169.

miles away in Lincolnshire. The small Tot fee in Paston was partly made up of land in Prestgrave, Leicestershire, nearly twenty-five miles away. The baronial fees within the honour show the same distribution. St Medard, with six fees, had land in six villages in three counties; Torpel, with the same, had land in fourteen villages in Northamptonshire; Gunthorpe, with three fees, had land in thirteen.[1] Already in 1086 there are on most knightly estates properties clearly marked out for subinfeudation. When did this happen? At this point, with this question, each of the family histories starts.

Torpel was one of two families to owe the service of six knights, the other being St Medard. The property of each of them was assessed at four fees within the Soke of Peterborough, and two outside. In each case the latter became separate tenancies in the midtwelfth century. The Torpel manors in this category were Cotterstock and Glapthorne, twelve miles from the abbey and the same distance from the manor of Torpel. Around 1100 their occupation was disputed. Perhaps still in dispute, for such was an ideal portion, they were given to Roger of Torpel's daughter on her marriage to Richard of Reinbuedcurt. They were purchased back by Roger's heir, Robert, and sometime before 1135 given to Robert as a separate tenancy when infirmity forced him to hand on the honour to his younger brother.[2] This land was given him, we are told, 'with the assent of King Henry and many of the barons of the land, to hold and alienate as he please'.[3] He then gave the two manors to the hospital of St Leonard outside Peterborough when he entered it in Stephen's reign, and in this way details of a very interesting family settlement have been preserved. The family regained control in the next reign, and these were demesne manors of the Torpel fee in the thirteenth century. The Torpels were the chief of the honorial barons; it was a powerful family which could regain property from an abbey like Peterborough.

The next event materially affecting the family's position was the marriage of the second Roger of Torpel with Asceline of Waterville. This was an alliance with another Peterborough family of similar rank. Around 1100 Ascelin of Waterville had held fourteen hides in Northamptonshire, as three fees.[4] This comprised two large manors

---

[1] The Peterborough knights' holdings are usefully tabulated in *Pytchley*, pp. xviii–xxi, from where these figures are taken.
[2] *Descriptio*, no. 3; P.B.C., fo. 27r–v; *Pytchley*, pp. 28–34.
[3] P.B.C., fo. 27r–v; entry translated above, pp. 27–8.
[4] *Descriptio*, no. 6; *Pytchley*, pp. 41–5.

in the Soke, Marholm and Upton, and an interest in several manors in the Nene valley. A charter of between 1133 and 1155 shows the family settlement of the next generation. The manors in the Soke, each rated at two hides and a virgate, went to Ascelin's two sons, Hugh and Geoffrey. His two daughters each had a virgate, one in Stanwick and one in Irthlingborough – his two most distant manors, and those where his lordship was least secure.[1] The younger son Geoffrey was a knight of Robert earl of Gloucester early in the civil war, and married Asceline, the youngest of the four sisters of Pain Peverel, who were his heirs to the barony of Bourn. He was lucky in his generation and lucky in his marriage; in such circumstances a younger brother might thrive. Their son died without heirs, and their two daughters, Asceline and Maud, inherited. It was the elder of these who married Roger of Torpel.[2]

The manors of Torpel and Upton, together thereafter and much transferred, are the tenurial product of this union. At the end of the century grants were made from them, by Asceline and Maud de Dive her sister, chiefly to the nuns of Stamford. Asceline's great-grandson, William of Torpel, died in 1242 and was succeeded by his sister, who naturally found a husband within the year.[3] This man, Ralph de Camoys, held Torpel and Upton, as did his son. But by this stage the family was heavily in debt both to Jew and Gentile.[4] When in 1280 Ralph's grandson, John de Camoys, first leased and then sold the manors of Torpel and Upton to the Crown,[5] this was but one of a whole string of family alienations, which culminated in the transfer of his wife and her property to William Paynel.[6] Early in 1281 Edward granted Torpel and Upton to Queen Eleanor, who seems to have been everywhere in the property dealings of the day. She leased them in turn to Geoffrey of Southorpe, another Peterborough tenant whose family is the next considered, and to Gilbert Pecche as a life tenancy, after she had been granted the whole of his

---

[1] Swa. fos. 204v–205r; printed *Monasticon*, I, 393.

[2] *Regesta*, III, 58, 68, 115–6; *Sir Christopher Hatton's Book of Seals*, ed. L. C. Loyd and D. M. Stenton (Oxford, 1950), no. 212; Sanders, *English Baronies*, pp. 19–20.

[3] Francis Peck, *Academia Tertia Anglicana; or, the Antiquarian Annals of Stanford* (1727), VI, 16–21; Sanders, *English Baronies*, p. 19; P.R.O., CP. 25(1) 173/32/469.

[4] *Cal. Close R. 1268–72*, p. 392; *Ibid. 1272–9*, p. 259.

[5] *Ibid. 1279–88*, p. 46; *Cal. Patent R. 1272–81*, pp. 366–7; *Cal. Close R. 1279–88*, pp. 66, 81.

[6] In 1267 Ralph de Camoys had granted two Hampshire manors to one of his creditors, Robert Waleround (*V.C.H. Hants*, IV, 82, 547); for the transfer of his wife see *Complete Peerage*, II, 506.

estate. When she died in 1290 the manors were granted to the abbey to farm for £100 a year.[1] The wheel had come full circle, but the lordship remained with the Crown. The properties were granted successively to Piers Gaveston and Edmund of Woodstock. Their history merges with that of Edward II's patronage, yet to understand that history we must start with the family history of a couple of Peterborough tenants in the mid twelfth century.

What were then transferred were the two manors which Torpel and then Camoys retained in demesne. Now this was not the whole property which had earlier owed the service of four knights. Lordship and land occupancy were two quite different things. The fragmentation of the original Torpel fee cannot be examined in detail, but several fractions of fees can be identified early in the thirteenth century. One of them, half a fee, was held by Geoffrey of Northborough.[2] There were many like him, and about most of them we know little. But this half-fee was purchased by Peterborough in the next quarter-century, and the central and local records give an unusually full picture of it. If looked at carefully they may show more than a simple history of decline.

Geoffrey occurs as a juror in the early part of the century. Between 1214 and 1222 he sold twenty acres of meadow to the abbey, and was given forty marks, to acquit him of a debt to the Jews.[3] He died in 1225 and his wife brought claims for dower; then one gets behind the feudal facade. There had been numerous alienations in Geoffrey's lifetime. His younger son, the priest of the church, had been given a third of the estate, which he had then sold.[4] His three daughters had their portions, subsequently bought by the abbey for £20, £4 and £2, which may roughly indicate the scale of their respective endowments. There had been other alienations. And at the time of his death the whole of his tenancy was leased to his lord, Roger of Torpel.[5]

What was left of this estate when the claims of family and creditors had been met was purchased by Peterborough abbey. The younger brother gave it the tithes from the estate, while he gave the advowson to Fineshade priory. Other entries in the Peterborough

---

[1] Peterborough D and C MS. 6, fo. 151r; *Cal. Patent R. 1281–92*, pp. 114, 421.
[2] *Pytchley*, p. 34 note.
[3] Swa. fo. 224v.
[4] Geoffrey's younger brother Richard had been the priest of the church before this: Swa. fo. 224r.
[5] *Curia Regis Rolls*, XII, nos. 230, 916, 967, 998, 2336; Swa. fos. 181v–182r.

cartulary clearly represent an attempt at consolidation. The daughters' portions have already been mentioned; rather earlier a tenancy was purchased from William Blevet for seven marks; finally, in 1258, the abbey bought the advowson and the land which had been given to Fineshade.[1] As well as the abbey there were several parties with an interest in this property in 1225 – Roger of Torpel, Robert of Braybrooke,[2] and Fineshade priory. The abbey saw its competitors off the field, and in the second quarter of the century largely rebuilt the estate which Geoffrey of Northborough had dissipated in the first.

From Northborough we now go up the scale, as it were, to the family of Southorpe. In 1100 Geoffrey 'the abbot's nephew' had eight hides in Northamptonshire, for the service of three knights.[3] As with Torpel and St Medard the proportion was two fees in the Soke to one outside. The chief manors in the Soke were Gunthorpe and Southorpe, while Stoke Doyle and Hemington were in the Nene valley ten miles away. As above, it is the family settlement that is first considered; after this their thirteenth-century history is traced from the abbey records, for this was the most substantial of the families forced by indebtedness to sell to the abbey.

Geoffrey had four sons. The eldest, Ives, had the whole of the estate for a good forty years, from around 1135 to at least 1178. The second son, Richard, had a part of the third fee, in Hemington, by 1176. Of the third son nothing is known. The fourth occurs around 1150 holding a virgate in Helpston, 'of the fee of Ives his brother'.[4] Ives, the tenant of the main fee, was in debt to the abbey by the middle of Henry II's reign. To redeem this, shortly after 1170, he mortgaged the smaller part of the third fee, Stoke Doyle, and the services (not the land) of his tenants in Etton, Gunthorpe and

[1] Swa. fos. 219r–220r, 224r–v; Fineshade Cartulary (Lambeth Palace, Records of the Court of Arches, MS. Ff. 291), fo. 27r; Swa. fos. 231r, 246r, 290r.

[2] On Robert see H. G. Richardson, *The English Jewry under Angevin Kings* (London, 1960), pp. 100–2, 270–80; and for his dealings in Northborough see his cartulary, B.M. MS. Sloane 986, fo. 17r–v. His chief interest in Northborough was in the de la Mare fee. Robert de la Mare sold Robert of Braybrooke half his tenancy (*Ibid.*), and in 1219 sold three virgates to Brian de la Mare (P.R.O., CP. 25(1) 172/16/63). Robert would seem to be the younger brother of Brian, tenant of the main de la Mare fee (*Pytchley*, p. 40 note). A younger brother's portion of the turn of the century was largely bought out, partly by the elder brother and partly by this ubiquitous royal servant.

[3] *Descriptio*, no. 5.

[4] *Pytchley*, pp. 68–9; Stenton, *Early Northants Charters*, p. 66; P.B.C., fo. 24v.

Paston.[1] What is noteworthy here is the tight hold which was kept right through the twelfth century on the two main fees; it was the property ten miles away that was used to meet the various economic and dynastic pressures on the family in the second half of the twelfth century.

GENEALOGY OF THE FAMILY OF SOUTHORPE

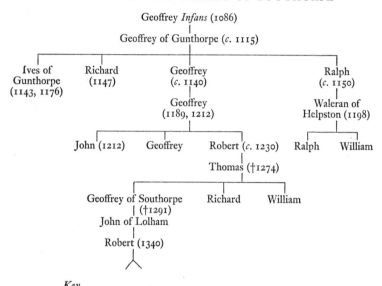

Geoffrey *Infans* (1086)

Geoffrey of Gunthorpe (*c.* 1115)

Ives of Gunthorpe (1143, 1176)

Richard (1147)

Geoffrey (*c.* 1140)

Geoffrey (1189, 1212)

Ralph (*c.* 1150)

Waleran of Helpston (1198)

John (1212)   Geoffrey   Robert (*c.* 1230)   Ralph   William

Thomas (†1274)

Geoffrey of Southorpe (†1291)   Richard   William

John of Lolham

Robert (1340)

Key
†   Date of death. Other dates are of references to the persons concerned;
c.   Indicates that such a date is approximate.

There were a number of alienations to the abbey in the period 1175–1225, a good deal of woodland, and ten solidates of rent for the almonry.[2] Such transactions seem common to all the tenants of this rank in the Soke. Clearly these things did not improve the family's economic position, but these were major tenants and the alienations are not remarkable. Between 1275 and 1290, however, the patrimony, the two carefully guarded fees in the Soke, was bought by the abbey of Peterborough, and as a knightly family that of Southorpe disappeared. The story of its demise is told in great detail in the various Peterborough sources,[3] and in its barest outline it is as follows.

[1] *Hugh Candidus*, p. 129.
[2] Swa. fos. 205r–206r.
[3] In particular, *Pytchley*, pp. 61–72.

Geoffrey of Southorpe sold Gunthorpe to the abbey *c.* 1276, for 550 marks.[1] Late in 1278 he got 300 marks from the sale of his holding in Hemingford and Yelling.[2] This did not succeed in getting the family out of debt, however, and by 1280 the last demesne manor, Southorpe, was in the hands of a London merchant, Stephen of Cornhill. Stephen was foreclosing on his own debts, and perhaps providing capital for Geoffrey to settle his debts with other merchants.[3] Geoffrey retired to the small manor of Lolham in the north of the Soke, which was his wife's marriage portion, and there prepared to build anew. As already seen, he leased Torpel and Upton *from* Queen Eleanor in 1281, and he seems also to have borrowed money from her. Yet the profits which were thus to revive the family fortunes proved illusory and brought only more debt. In 1285 a case came up concerning some of this property, and seemingly the whole area vouched him to warranty – that is to say he had alienated most of it in small portions for ready cash.[4] This was unwise. A year later the Queen's administration took the manors back and took Geoffrey to the debtor's prison. While he was thus occupied the abbey purchased Southorpe from Stephen of Cornhill.[5]

Geoffrey secured his release in 1289 by creating a perpetual rent-charge of £10 a year on Lolham, which was all that was left to him.[6] Then, *Pytchley* says:[7]

He returned and was at Lolham on the vigil of St. Nicholas the bishop, and forthwith broke out into malicious repudiation, saying that all the deeds which he had executed had been executed in prison under duress, and were therefore of no effect. But William of Woodford, then sacristan, having respect to his poverty and in order to avoid a scandal, gave him ten marks in ready money, and two horses to the value of ten marks.

And thus, with the last vestiges of gentility, he leaves the Peterborough record. Shortly afterwards Richard of Southorpe witnessed a charter as 'Richard, brother of the lord Geoffrey who was

---

[1] Swa. fo. 36v; *Ch.P.*, p. 25.

[2] P.R.O., CP. 25(1) 93/14/12.

[3] *Cal. Close R. 1272–9*, pp. 233, 248; *Ibid. 1279–88*, p. 53. Stephen was 'one of the rulers of the City of London, a draper and an important exporter of wool': M. M. Postan, 'Credit in Medieval Trade', in *Essays in Economic History*, I, 74; see also, G. A. Williams, *Medieval London* (London, 1963), espec. p. 128.

[4] *C.Inq.P.M.*, III, no. 38; Peterborough D and C MS. 6, fo. 151r–v; P.R.O., CP. 25(1) 175/56/252, 174/54/184.

[5] *Pytchley*, pp. 62–4.

[6] P.R.O., CP. 25(1) 175/56/252.

[7] *Pytchley*, p. 70.

once lord of Southorpe'.[1] What seems to have been the end of the story is related by Francis Peck.[2]

At this time divers most excellent soldiers of the equestrian rank, stroke with admiration at the holy lives of several White Friars then living, became Carmelites, of which number Sir Geoffrey Southorpe, who entered himself into their monastery at Stanford, was one.

Southorpe, Torpel and Waterville were substantial tenants of the abbey, and each of them had scope to alienate parts of their holding in the twelfth century. Torpel, the largest, did so by the second quarter of the century, then Waterville in the mid century, and finally Southorpe in the third quarter. Alienation was possible because 'there was a good deal of play in the joints of the average fee'.[3] In some fees, however, those of men at the bottom of the feudal ladder, there was no play at all. These will be called 'basic fees'; all of the families which follow had holdings of this sort.

In 1100 Geoffrey of Tot had a hide in Paston, a hamlet of Peterborough, and a virgate at Prestgrave in Leicestershire.[4] This tenancy descended as a single unit throughout the twelfth century. It was held as one fee until 1199, when the service was reduced by a half. In 1191, Elias of Tot owed nearly £15 among the debts of Aaron the Jew.[5] This of itself was in no way remarkable; he was in good company. Yet there is at least the suggestion here of a discrepancy between the family's economic position and its feudal position. And this was precisely the area of the abbey's most dynamic lordship in the next half-century. The family went under during this period, and an archive of twenty charters enables the story to be traced step by step.

Between 1200 and 1210, Robert of Tot was given six marks for a grant of woodland and arable, 'to acquit him of his debts to the Jews'. Other transactions in the same period brought a further twenty acres to the abbey. In the next generation his son, another Robert, made three further alienations, the largest of them a grant

---

[1] 'Richardi fratris domini Galfridi quondam militis de Sutthorp', *Chr.P.*, p. 147.
[2] *Antiquarian Annals of Stanford*, XI, 45. Geoffrey's son and grandson appear as freeholders, 'of Lolham', in the next century: Buccleuch Charters, BI. nos. 314, 327.
[3] S. E. Thorne, 'English Feudalism and Estates in Land', *Cambridge Law Journal* (1959), p. 205.
[4] *Descriptio*, no. 18.
[5] *Pytchley*, pp. 107–10; *Feet of Fines 10 Richard I* (Pipe Roll Soc. XXIV, 1900), no. 245; *Pipe Roll 3 and 4 Richard I*, p. 159.

of woodland for which he was given five marks.[1] Finally, in 1222, he mortgaged the bulk of his estate to the abbey for twenty years. He was given sixteen marks for this, to acquit him 'against the Jews of Stamford and against others', and the abbey undertook to pay £10 'for the debts of Aaron the Jew'.[2] This treble pressure – from the Exchequer, from the Jews, and from other creditors – seems finally to have extinguished this fee. In charters between 1220 and 1240 Geoffrey of Tot appears in witness lists among freeholders of only modest size, and on his death his wife was granted a corrody sufficiently substantial to suggest that it was conclusive.[3] Geoffrey's daughter was similarly pensioned off; while in 1284 his granddaughter brought a claim for some woodland clearly sold half a century before. It must have been more a plea for alms than a serious suit; the abbot, we are told, 'out of the kindness of his heart', gave her a mark.[4] A century later the last vestige of the family lay in the name *Totisgore*, and when the Paston demesne was surveyed it was noted that this referred to a certain Robert of Tot, 'who was once one of the lords of Paston'.[5]

The Milton family was slightly more substantial than that of Tot, and lasted slightly longer. Turold of Milton had in 1100 two hides in Milton, a hamlet of Castor, and six bovates in Cleatham in Lincolnshire, for a service of two knights.[6] The property descended in the male line throughout the twelfth century. Then, around the turn of the century, it was subdivided to provide for a younger son. His portion was bought by the abbey around 1230.[7] The main fee broke up in the next generation, the final but hardly the decisive blow being that Geoffrey of Milton backed the wrong side in the civil war of Henry III's reign. In 1267 Geoffrey was in debt to various Jews for about £180. In December 1267 these Jews sold their rights to William Charles, a knight of the household, who had been granted the Milton lands after the battle of Evesham.[8] It remained only to make a decent settlement, and in 1268 Geoffrey made over the Milton estate to William Charles in return for a corrody of 24

---

[1] Swa. fos. 218v–221r.
[2] Franceys, pp. 40–1.
[3] She promised to keep 'as quiet as she could' about this transaction: 'ego vero Emma ad predictam dotem meam adquirendam omnem quam potero apponam siligenciam' (*Ibid.* p. 43).
[4] *Ibid.* pp. 45–7, 59–60, 95–6; *Ch.P.*, p. 71.
[5] Franceys, p. 427.
[6] *Descriptio*, no. 11.
[7] *Pytchley*, pp. 78–80; Swa. fos. 216r, 243r–v.
[8] P.R.O., C. 55/3, m. 2 (I owe this reference to the kindness of Dr C. H. Knowles); *Cal. Plea Rolls of the Exchequer of the Jews*, I, 195.

marks a year.[1] The Lincolnshire estate was apparently alienated around the same time. Shortly afterwards, in an exchange of land, he described himself as 'Geoffrey son of Robert the knight, formerly lord of Milton'.[2]

Each of the above, the four main families, and the two considered along with Torpel, have one thing in common: their main property was in the Soke of Peterborough. They are chiefly studied from sources compiled at the abbey, and it is not surprising that in them the abbey appears as the dominant agent. Yet the detail of the sources is valuable, for it illustrates the chronology of knightly indebtedness, and the various steps taken to meet it. The range of the sources is now extended and a new element introduced into the discussion by the history of two families which held of the honour of Peterborough and can be studied from their own records. These families are Hotot of Clapton and Thorpe of Longthorpe near Peterborough.

The Phillips collection recently disclosed a small family cartulary, Richard of Hotot's 'estate book', apparently one of the earliest lay cartularies to survive.[3] It is called an estate book, perhaps, after that of another Northamptonshire man of similar substance, Henry de Bray.[4] But this is from the first half of the thirteenth century; shorter, a lot less polished, and at least as interesting. There is no tradition behind this document. It is difficult to convey its atmosphere in print, but when handled it gives a vivid impression of the small landowner at the very beginning of literacy. It starts with a family chronicle; not Richard's family, but that into which his father had married. The size of the script here matches any monastic cartulary, though the spelling does not. The chronicle turns into a list of Richard's purchases of land; then there are details of the services he owed, and that were owed to him. In the middle of the document there is a quire comprising Magna Carta 1215, the Charter of the Forest, and a couple of ecclesiastical records from the reign of John. Some smaller pieces of parchment are attached at the end, and contain memoranda of Richard's son.[5] He had his own

---

[1] *Cal. Close R. 1264–8*, pp. 531–2.

[2] *Pytchley*, p. 79; 'Galfridi filii Roberti militis quondam domini de Melletona', Fitzwilliam charter, no. 1360.

[3] B.M. Add. MS. 54228 (= Davis, *Medieval Cartularies*, no. 1256).

[4] *The Estate Book of Henry de Bray*, ed. D. Willis (Camden Soc., 3rd ser., XXVII, 1916).

[5] For a summary list of the contents of this volume see the Sotheby catalogue, 28 November 1967, pp. 33–4. I hope to edit this volume, alongside the thirteenth-century Basset records, for the Northamptonshire Record Society.

estate book, which although now lost was seen in the eighteenth century by John Bridges, who transcribed parts of a much fuller family history from it.[1]

The short history of the family in the earlier book begins as follows.

Turold abbot of Peterborough gave Roger of Lovetot baron of Southoe a fee of two knights in Clapton, Polebrook and Catworth, to hold of the said abbot and his successors. The same Roger of Lovetot gave the same Alfred de Grauntcourt his knight the whole fee which he had by gift of the said abbot in Clapton, namely four hides as one knight's fee. And the same Roger gave the same Alfred in the same vill of Clapton one hide and one virgate for a quarter fee, and this was of Roger of Southoe's own barony, not pertaining to Peterborough in any way, save only that it was in the liberty of the said abbot.

That is the description of the Clapton holding. It goes on to say that he had land in Polebrook, which was also held partly by Peterborough and partly of Roger of Lovetot, and a hide and a virgate in Thurning.[2] This is the liberty of Peterborough seen from the outside, and a family history which was quite independent of the abbey.

This estate differs in several respects from those previously considered. Territorially it was more compact, for these three villages were almost contiguous. Its obligations, further, were calculated at four or five hides the fee, not the Peterborough average of two hides. And in *Domesday* we find that this Alfred had previously held of Eustace the sheriff, the tenant-in-chief before Roger of Lovetot.[3] Thus, as on many other estates around the turn of the century, there was continuity of occupancy through a change of lordship. The estate descended in its entirety to William son of Walter. This William de Grauntcourt, so the tradition went in the thirteenth century, became known as William of Clapton, 'from the difficulty the lower people found in pronouncing his Norman name'.[4]

Between 1175 and 1190, what had previously been maintained as a single tenancy was divided into numerous parcels. In this it resembles every family of 'basic' knightly rank so far considered. Here the alienation was particularly extensive, and from the family's own records, combined with the feudal records, can be traced in considerable detail. William, we are told, had four brothers and

---

[1] Bridges, II, 367–72.
[2] B.M. Add. MS. 54228, fo. 1r–v.
[3] *Domesday Book*, I, fo. 228a.
[4] Bridges, II, 367.

three sisters.[1] Robert, the eldest of the brothers, was given the Polebrook estate.[2] The next brother, Walter, had unspecified land in Kingsthorpe;[3] the next had two virgates in Clapton; the youngest was priest of the church. There is no obvious logic in the descent of the rest of William's holding. Some land went to the church; the bulk of it was divided between a nephew and a niece's husband. The nephew was Thomas of Hotot, the father of the man who compiled the estate book, who was given sixty acres of demesne and two virgates. The niece's husband was William Dacus, who was given a larger estate – 120 acres of demesne, the service of the freemen, seven virgates of villeinage, and the quarter fee in Thurning. William of Clapton's gifts to the church are similar in scale to those of the other men of his rank considered. He gave two virgates of land to the nuns of Stamford, with his daughter, and twenty-four acres of demesne to the nuns of Chicksand in Bedfordshire. To Peterborough he gave at least three virgates, professed himself a monk, and there died.[4] It should be noted that the Peterborough cartulary tells only a very small portion of the story.

The dynamic of this story is now in the line of Thomas Hotot and Richard his son. Briefly, it sees Richard's partial reconstitution and extension of the estate his great-uncle had dissipated. Richard succeeded his father around 1213 and died around 1250. He spent in all 413 marks in acquiring the portions of Isabella and Maud his cousins. Isabella's first husband came from Somerset, and 'was found in a wood barbarously murdered with his head cut off'. She moved north, married a man who held three fees of the bishop of Lincoln, and they sold the Clapton estate to Richard around 1240. About this time he also purchased the other sister's portion. The estate book records at least forty smaller purchases in Clapton, and several elsewhere, the largest of these being at Turvey in Bedfordshire, eighteen miles away, where he spent 182 marks.[5] In all Richard spent at least a thousand marks on these purchases, roughly the same amount as Peterborough abbey spent in acquiring Gunthorpe and Southorpe, and this half a century earlier. This man is not in the *Book of Fees*, and not in any Peterborough cartulary –

---

[1] The information in this paragraph is taken from the estate book, unless otherwise stated.
[2] *Curia Regis Rolls*, I, 117, 119–20.
[3] *The Earliest Northamptonshire Assize Rolls, A.D. 1202 and 1203*, ed. D. M. Stenton (Northants Rec. Soc., V, 1930), pp. 46–7.
[4] Swa. fos. 249v–250r; Bridges, II, 368; *Curia Regis Rolls*, I, 117.
[5] B.M. Add. MS. 54228, fos. 2v, 3v–4r, 13v; Bridges, II, 368.

GENEALOGY OF THE FAMILY OF HOTOT OF CLAPTON

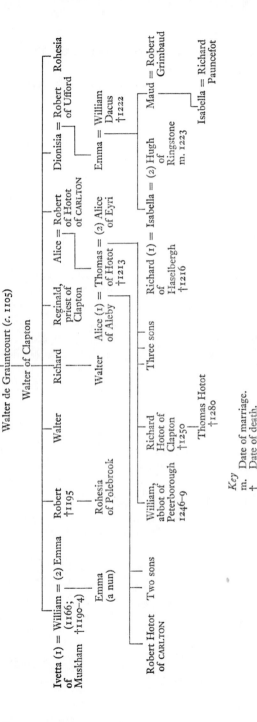

Alured (1086)

Walter de Grauntcourt (c. 1105)

Walter of Clapton

Ivetta (1) = William = (2) Emma   Robert   Walter   Richard   Reginald,   Alice = Robert   Dionisia = Robert   Rohesia
of   (1166;   †1195   priest of   of Hotot   of Ufford
Muskham   †1190–4)   Clapton   of CARLTON

Rohesia
of Polebrook

Emma = William
Dacus
†1222

Emma
(a nun)

Walter   Alice (1) = Thomas = (2) Alice
of Aleby   of Hotot   of Eyri
†1213

Richard (1) = Isabella = (2) Hugh
of   of
Haselbergh   Ringstone
†1216   m. 1223

Maud = Robert
Grimbaud

Isabella = Richard
Pauncefot

Three sons

William,
abbot of
Peterborough
1246–9

Richard
Hotot of
Clapton
†1250

Thomas Hotot
†1280

Robert Hotot   Two sons
of CARLTON

Key
m.   Date of marriage.
†   Date of death.
      Other dates are of references to the persons concerned.
c.   Indicates that such a date is approximate.

'in no way pertaining to Peterborough, save only that he was in the said abbot's liberty'.

Whether this capital was generated entirely by good management it is impossible to say. There is a less creditable explanation. Though there is no hint of the relationship in the estate book, it is very likely that Richard's elder brother was the William Hotot who was abbot of Peterborough from 1246 to 1249. Now William was apparently a bad lot; he was deposed, says Matthew Paris, accused of 'dilapidation and gifts to his kinsmen, of whom there were an inordinate number hanging around'.[1] But most of Richard Hotot's major purchases were made before this abbacy. Clearly it did a family no harm when one of its members was the most powerful churchman in the area, but whether peculation contributed substantially to the Hotot fortune is open to doubt.

Richard Hotot must have died within a year of his brother's deposition. His son Thomas inherited a viable estate. He acquired little, save significantly a large tenancy which he bought from Robert Hotot of Carlton, and which must have been the holding of the elder branch of the family.[2] He conserved, and we know that he compiled a family chronicle a good deal more circumstantial than that of his father. The long and colourful generation of the late twelfth century is shifted back to Stephen's reign, and becomes longer and more colourful still.[3]

Of Dionisia the second daughter of Walter de Grauntcourt it is recorded that when a maiden, clad in a tunic, with a hat upon her head and armed only with a hollow shield, about the seventeenth year of King Stephen she attacked a certain knight, with one blow of her spear bringing him to the ground, and carried off his horse.

This may not be true, but in a sense it needed to be. There is in all this evidence of a landed family, secure in its position in the world, a position acquired by its industry and defended by 'the charters'.

For the last knightly family considered there are no twelfth-century records, for then they were freemen.[4] It is only at the time of the thirteenth-century surveys, around 1230, that we can gain an

---

[1] *Matthaei Parisiensis Chronica Majora*, ed. H. R. Luard, v (Rolls ser., 57, 1880), p. 84.
[2] B.M. Add. MS. 54228, fos. 22r, 23r.
[3] Bridges, II, 368.
[4] In my earlier article on this material, following Mellows (*Pytchley*, p. 55 note), I stated that this family held in villeinage in the twelfth century: 'Large and Small Landowners', p. 44. I am indebted to Dr Paul Hyams for querying this, and thus forcing me to look again at the material.

indication of their substance. According to them William son of Thurstan of Thorpe held two of the four major freeholds in Longthorpe, for one of which he owed riding service. He probably also held land on the other side of the river Nene, for in the Hundred Rolls it was stated that he was the former tenant of two virgates at Orton Waterville in Huntingdonshire.[1] Yet from these records we get only half the picture. Around 1270 William of Thorpe got permission from the abbey to rebuild the chapel in Longthorpe, which was described as being so far from the village that 'the old and infirm often die without the sacraments, and the cure of souls is neglected to a considerable extent'.[2] The work was to be done at William's own expense. At the same time, alongside, William built a new manor house. William was not a knight;[3] but there can have been little doubt who was lord of Longthorpe. Around 1300 his son Robert added a tower three storeys high to the manor house, and it was he who was appointed steward in 1309. It is a remarkable building, reminiscent of the peel towers of the border counties, not of a manor house in the midlands. In the next generation Robert's son in turn commissioned in the great chamber a magnificent series of wall paintings, among the earliest and most impressive of those which survive.[4]

The context of lordship within which the family operated changed over the period. In the twelfth century the Thorpes were sub-tenants of the Watervilles of Orton. Early in the thirteenth century the abbey was granted the service direct, and the Waterville mesne lordship was extinguished.[5] In the mid century William of Thorpe seems to have been bound by ties of neighbourhood to the Watervilles of the adjacent manor of Marholm, one of the dominant knightly families of the Soke. When William of Thorpe was captured at Northampton in 1264, he claimed he had been in the *familia* of Reginald de Waterville, and shared the pardon granted to him.[6] Reginald died in 1287, and the property was divided between three

---

[1] Surveys, fos. 183v, 184v; *Rotuli Hundredorum*, II, 638a.

[2] *Peterborough Local Administration*, ed. W. T. Mellows, I (Northants Rec. Soc., IX, 1939), pp. 205–6.

[3] William does not appear among the knights in charters of the 1280s: Fitzwilliam Charters, nos. 83, 1362, 1364.

[4] M. Wood, *The English Medieval House* (London, 1965), pp. 166–7, 399–401; E. C. Rouse and A. Baker, 'The Wall Paintings at Longthorpe Tower, near Peterborough, Northants', *Archaeologia*, XCVI (1955), 1–57.

[5] Black Book, fo. 180v; Society of Antiquaries MS. 38, fo. 234v.

[6] P.R.O. Just. Itin. 1/618, m. 6d; reference from Dr C. H. Knowles, whose edition of this document will shortly be published by the Northamptonshire Record Society.

daughters.[1] It may be a small factor in the rise of the Thorpes that after 1287 they were no longer overshadowed by a resident lord at Marholm; and when the family started to expand in the early fourteenth century Marholm was the first manor it acquired.

There would appear to be at least some common pattern in these family histories. Perhaps what we are considering in the twelfth century represents the 'third stage' of Norman feudalism, the knightly families of the Norman settlement, and their attitude to their property. A distinction has been made between the greater knights of the honour, those with three to six fees, and the 'basic knights' with two or one. The greater knights can each be shown to have alienated parts of their holding by the mid century; the more substantial the family, the earlier the devolution. Until the last quarter of the century there is a devolution down to, but not beyond, this basic fee. The integrity of the fee was maintained. This is the more remarkable for a number of reasons. First, because continuity of occupancy was maintained through changes of lordship. Secondly, because these were feudal units, not economic ones; parcels of even the smallest fees were widely scattered. Thirdly, because a number of these fees were so small that there must have been a considerable tension between economic position and feudal position and obligation long before the end of the twelfth century.

During the last quarter of the twelfth century this basic fee was dissolved. The knights for the first time made visible independent provision for their daughters and younger sons. For the first time also, and at each level of society these two things seem to go together, they provided for their souls: two or three virgates of land found their way to various foundations, laden with four or five generations of guilt. All the Peterborough families have a phase of this sort; those considered show it clearly; and with Hotot we can form a picture as complete as the sources for this period are ever likely to allow. From it we get a good impression of the resources of a family of this rank, and this puts in perspective the grants by similar families in the various Peterborough cartularies.

In the thirteenth century, with the disappearance of the feudal units we see the construction – at times the reconstruction – of economic units. Hotot of Clapton is the model here again; in the next village but one a succession of Richards of Hemington seem to

---

[1] *Pytchley*, p. 45 note.

be doing the same thing;[1] two miles from the monastery there was
Thorpe of Longthorpe also.[2] The accidents of feudal geography
may well have created a number of areas particularly suited to enterprise of this sort. Within the Peterborough area of influence there
was perhaps the greatest turn-over in the Nene valley, for here lay
the most dispensable units of several fees which had their core near
the abbey. Here once again, the Norman settlement provides the
key to later changes.

Finally it is necessary to consider this part of the land market
from the point of view of the abbey, and to look at the chronology
of the abbey's investment in land. The part which this land played
in the monastic economy is examined elsewhere.[3] If it is accepted
that the basic fee only broke up around 1175, it might follow that
only from then can we speak of a land market at the knightly level.[4]
From 1175 to around 1300 the movement of property to the abbey
was a continuous one. The nearest that there was to a lull came in
the third quarter of the thirteenth century. The gap may not be a
real one, for Swaffham's cartulary is the work of the mid century.
Yet there are several indications of a slackening of interest, which
may be connected with the dual problems of incompetent management and the crushing burden of the civil war. The abbey bought a
part of the Milton fee around 1230, but when the main part came
under the hammer after the civil war it was bought by others.[5]

While the abbey's interest was a continuous one, however, the
dynamic behind the continuity changed a great deal. The acquisitions after the mid century are the first set of transfers of land to the
abbey as a group clearly inspired by economic necessity. The point,
indeed, might be better put the other way round. Between the
Conquest and the Reformation, the only general phase of pious
benefaction to this monastery was that of its own knightly tenants
in the late twelfth and early thirteenth centuries. The baronage of
the Norman settlement had their spiritual homes in Normandy.[6]
The newer houses met the resources and the needs of the 'new

[1] Buccleuch Charters, BI. nos. 136–251, *passim*.
[2] For the records of an interesting and perhaps comparable estate in
Ewell (Surrey) see, *Fitznells Cartulary*, ed. C. A. F. Meekings and P.
Shearman (Surrey Rec. Soc., XXVI, 1968).
[3] See below, Chapter 5.
[4] Following the argument of P. R. Hyams, 'The Origins of a Peasant Land
Market in England', *Econ.H.R.*, 2nd ser., XXIII (1970), 18–31.
[5] See above, pp. 45–6.
[6] D. J. A. Matthew, *The Norman Monasteries and their English Possessions*
(Oxford, 1962).

men' of the twelfth century.[1] After the mid-thirteenth century lay piety passed most institutions by: they represented too catholic a concern. A baron of Peterborough, Nicholas of St Medard, founded his own chantry at Thornhaugh in 1323. The abbot of Peterborough is concerned in this transaction only as a landlord, taking his cut, which amounted to six marks.[2] Like the other major landlords of the period, the abbots were concerned only with preserving the profits of a changing feudalism, a feudalism, indeed, which was largely kept alive for its profitability.

[1] R. W. Southern, *Western Society and the Church in the Middle Ages* (Harmondsworth, 1970), pp. 240–72.
[2] *Pytchley*, pp. 24–5; *cf.* K. L. Wood-Legh, *Perpetual Chantries in Britain* (Cambridge, 1965), pp. 47–8.

3   *The Development of Freehold*

When we come to consider freehold and the market in freehold we come up against the same problems as with knightly tenures, in a good deal less tractable form. There is no Conquest to provide a starting point, and only with serjeanty is there a social function to add to the stability of tenures over a period of time. Many strands went into the making of freehold; it is possible to identify these, and to outline the main features of their development.[1] More difficulty arises in trying to identify a market in freehold. There are of course a multiplicity of transactions; the problems are in defining an agreed group of freeholders, and in identifying an acceptable sample among them. Consideration of these problems is a necessary prelude to any discussion of the part played by the abbey in the market for freehold land. These matters will be dealt with in turn.

THE ORIGINS OF FREEHOLD

The discussion will be confined to the Soke of Peterborough, and two main groups of freeholders will be identified. The earliest chronologically and arguably the most important overall were the pre-Conquest freeholders, amongst whom were a large group of sokemen. Then there are the monastery servants, an important group from the beginning of the monastery, but whose landed endowment was largely the work of the twelfth century. Each of these groups had new holdings, representing the colonisation of the post-Conquest period, and it is this that provides the most conspicuous element in the thirteenth-century market for freehold.

A large number – possibly the majority – of thirteenth-century freeholders must be the descendants of the sokemen of *Domesday* and of those recorded as free in the surveys of the twelfth century. Here we are concerned with a group firmly established before the abbey was founded, and who remained largely independent of it.

In the cases of some of the more substantial tenures, their descent from the sokeland of *Domesday* can be traced fairly easily. At

---

[1] For such an approach to freehold see Miller, *Ely*, pp. 114–36.

Longthorpe in 1086 there were three sokemen with two ploughs.[1] Part of this land would seem to be referred to in the following entries from 1125.[2]

Et unus sochemannus facit servicium cum equo. Et Willelmus filius Anseredi tenet quartam partem de 3 virgis per servicium militare. Et Willelmus filius Odardi Coci tenet quartam de 3 virgis per servicium coquine abbatis . . . Et Godricus tenet quartam de 3 virgis, et inde ille et equus suus debent facere servicium abbatis cum victu suo.

Three of these four tenancies were held for the same services in the thirteenth-century surveys.[3] That of William son of Ansered, which had been held by military service in the twelfth century, had been purchased from the Waterville family by Robert of Lindsey between 1214 and 1222, and was now held directly of the abbey for 6s 8d a year.[4] There was also a virgate which had been enfranchised, and assart land totalling just over twenty-five acres. With these exceptions, the pattern of freehold revealed by the surveys was as it had been a century earlier. It is open to question how accurately this picture reflects a century of rapid social change.

At Ailsworth there were eight sokemen in 1086.[5] In the 1125 surveys this was included as a hamlet of Castor, and four sokemen were recorded.[6]

Et est ibi Hugo sochemannus qui tenet dimidiam parvam virgam, et prestat carrucam suam semel ad hivernage, et semel ad tremeis, et metit dimidiam acram de consuetudine. Et 3 alii sochemanni tenent 1 hidam. Duo eorum, scilicet Leofricus et Willelmus nepos suus, metunt 3 acras, et tertius scilicet Robertus dimidiam acram de consuetudine.

A century later there are six tenancies which must represent the same holdings, for they performed fractions of this ancient reaping service.[7] Robert Brito and Ascelin Tot held virgates for 10s and 5s respectively, for which they owed various ploughing services, and had to reap half an acre each *pro vigilia*. Geoffrey Illing had a virgate and a half in Castor for which he reaped one acre, and a virgate in Ailsworth whose services (including half an acre's reaping) had been

---

[1] *D.B.*, I, fo. 221a.
[2] *Chr.P.*, p. 159.
[3] Surveys, fo. 183r.
[4] William was a younger son of Ansered, *Domesday* tenant of the fee of Orton Waterville: *Pytchley*, pp. 54–5 notes.
[5] *D.B.*, I, fo. 221a.
[6] *Chr.P.*, p. 163.
[7] Surveys, fo. 186r–v.

remitted by charter for a rent of 6s 8d.[1] Three other tenancies each reaped half an acre: Ralph son of Robert for a virgate and a half, William son of William for a virgate, and Robert of Paston for a virgate in Ailsworth. 'There was nothing derogatory in such works,' commented Stenton on similar obligations, 'they may reasonably be understood as a survival of pre-manorial conditions'.[2]

More often than not, however, it is difficult to tie down holders in socage even to this extent. 'The terminology of twelfth-century texts is in itself too vague to permit the identification of members of this class; the common formulas which assert the fact of a peasant's tenure tell nothing as to its condition. It follows from the nature of the extant material that the freeholder of small estate is most clearly revealed to us through his power of disposing of his land by charter.'[3] For most sokemen the only evidence is from charters, and it is only the charter material that supplies evidence of social change.

One set of evidence is from personal names, and since in this matter the tenacity of the native peasantry had waned by the end of the century, it is on the earliest charters that we chiefly depend.[4] The abbey seems to have subinfeudated most of the manors which had large concentrations of sokemen, and so the abbey surveys do not supply an adequate estimate of the importance of this group of tenants. The witness lists to knightly charters, however, reveal several communities of unmistakable native descent. A dispute in 1120 concerning a holding of the Gunthorpe fee in Werrington, was settled on the oath of the following.[5]

Swein et Lefsi de Waltona. Levenoth de Estona. Elfric Wicing. Lefuuinus Stircele. Godricus Burri. Sumerde filii Brunwine. Sumerde de Ciceboie de Wirintona. Turoldus et Wither et Ordach de Pastona. De hominibus ipsius Galfridi (de Gunethorpe), Segge eius prepositus et Lefuuine Folescanche.

Very few of the men named here can subsequently be traced. The Folesank family is one, and one of Leofwin's descendants in the

---

[1] Swa. fo. 223r; the matching charter of the abbot is in Society of Antiquaries MS. 38, fo. 184v.

[2] F. M. Stenton, *Documents Illustrative of the Social and Economic History of the Danelaw* (London, 1920), pp. cix–cx.

[3] *Ibid.* pp. lxxxviii–lxxxix.

[4] On the evidence of Scandinavian names there is a masterly account, *Ibid.* pp. xcviii–cxviii; *cf.* also W. G. Hoskins, *The Midland Peasant* (London, 1957), pp. 34–5.

[5] P.B.C., fo. 31r.

early thirteenth century bore the equally revealing name of Ingenolf.[1] The Goci who held of the Gunthorp fee a generation later was of native origin also, as was the family of Anglicus.[2] The Soke of Peterborough had many of the characteristics of the Danelaw; one of them was this large body of free peasants, which can be glimpsed only imperfectly in the abbey's records.[3]

This is the first of the component elements of freehold in the Soke. A second is provided by the monastery servants. The list of 1125 gives the number of these as forty.[4] The majority at this time were probably landless men, who received their board and their keep; if some of them held land in addition, most likely they are to be sought among the fifty-five men who owed only rent and suit of court.[5] The apparent exceptions here are a solitary reference to a serjeanty of the kitchen in Longthorpe,[6] and the record under Peterborough of 'ten servants who hold their land by serjeanty, and if they are not servants they pay a customary rent of one mark'.[7] Six servants had houses in the town; probably these were major servants of the convent, eight of whom received a knight's livery in 1125.[8] It was men described as serjeants, along with the smaller knights and freeholders, who were the regular witnesses in the abbot's court in the early twelfth century.[9]

When charters became abundant in the late twelfth century, it becomes clear that the descendants of these servants had received some form of landed endowment. How, and when, had this come about? The point may be introduced by quoting a highly interesting

---

[1] *Curia Regis Rolls*, VI, 368. This is an important family, on which see *C.N.* 247 note. A Richard Folesank occurs in Stoke Doyle between 1227 and 1240 (P.R.O., CP. 25(1) 172/18/125, 172/24/262, 173/30/407), and may be a member of the same family, for the Gunthorpe fee had a holding in Stoke Doyle: *Pytchley*, p. xix.

[2] On Goci, P.B.C. fo. 24r, and *Early Northants Charters*, p. 112; on Anglicus, P.B.C. fo. 27r, *Hugh Candidus*, p. 172, Swa. fos. 206v–207r.

[3] Round, *V.C.H. Northants*, I, 268–9, 278–9. Thirty-six per cent of the recorded population of the hundred of Nassaburgh were sokemen in 1086, by far the highest proportion in the county: *Domesday Geography of Midland England* (2nd edn.), p. 400.

[4] *Chr.P.*, pp. 167–8; *cf.* Knowles, *Monastic Order*, p. 440.

[5] *Chr.P.*, p. 161.

[6] *Ibid.* p. 159.

[7] *Ibid.* p. 161.

[8] *Ibid.* pp. 161, 167–8. This full livery was received by two bakers, a winnower, a brewer, two cooks, a refectorer, and a mason.

[9] An idea of the range of service is given by the following list of names from charters of the twelfth century: Benecok, Cambellanus, Carpentarius, Coci, Dapifer, Faber, Forestarius, Peliparius, Pincerna, Piscator, Pistores, Portarius, Prefectus, Pudding, Secretarius, Squilarius, Speciarius, Vanour, Vigilator, Whitecok, Wortecok.

passage from Mellows' work on the early history of Peterborough. He remarked that the unfree tenants in the town originated from the lower grade of servants, and then continued. 'To provide each of them with a customary holding apart from his toft in Bondgate, the abbot asserted part of the wood of Eastwood, and granted holdings each containing four or five acres of this reclaimed land to these *nativi* of the inner vill.'[1] Mellows provided no evidence for this statement, nor has a search of the records revealed it. As formulated here, his point is open to certain objections. He drew a distinction between the *nativi* of the town and those who held in serjeanty, which would now be seen as begging the question for the twelfth century,[2] and which certainly did not apply in the thirteenth. We know that in a charter of between 1215 and 1222 abbot Robert freed the men of Peterborough from tallage, merchet and agricultural services, in return for a substantial increase in their rents.[3] Again, there seems no evidence that the lesser servants all lived in Bondgate. The holdings seem more broadly scattered; there are several in Hithegate, in Priestgate and in Cowgate, and there is no obvious pattern in their distribution.[4] The suggestion that the monastery servants had uniform tenancies of asserted land is nonetheless worth considering, for several thirteenth-century charters would be very tolerant indeed of such an explanation.

An analysis of three charters may perhaps serve to make this point. The earliest of them is a grant to Thomas son of William of the almonry of his father's holding in Peterborough. The date of the charter is between 1214 and 1222, and since this is the father's holding, the tenancy can reasonably be taken back to the last quarter of the twelfth century. It then comprised.[5]

> *A* a messuage in Priestgate
> a messuage towards the Bondgate
> 5 acres in Eastfield
> 3 acres on the other side of the road
> 2 acres at the park gate.

[1] *The Local Government of Peterborough* (Peterborough, n.d.), p. 195.
[2] The most recent examination of the implications of villeinage in the twelfth century is in R. H. Hilton, 'Freedom and Villeinage in England', *Past and Present*, no. 31 (1965), pp. 3–19.
[3] Swa. fos. 228r–229v. There is a similar charter for Oundle, Swa. fos. 227r–228r. These two charters are printed in my note, 'Two Charters of Liberty', *Northamptonshire Past and Present*, v, pt. 1 (1972–3).
[4] The main series of charters relating to property in the town is in Franceys, pp. 1–38; see also *C.N.* 496–548, *passim*.
[5] *C.N.* 499.

This is a strikingly regular holding. With it may be compared two later charters. Around 1250, Roger son of Benedict of Peterborough gave his daughter a marriage portion of twenty acres of land, in parcels as follows.[1]

> B a messuage in Hithegate
>   2 acres in Newark
>   5 acres in Stibbings
>   1½ acres in Benecroft
>   2 acres on Eastfield gate
>   2 acres extra le Beche
>   ½ acre citra Beche
>   1 acre citra Westwood
>   1 acre citra molendinum
>   1 acre in Bethwaite
>   4 acres super Bechedike

In 1333, Alam le Almoner sold the *Dangerousmister* serjeanty in the town, which had appurtenant to it the following.[2]

> C a messuage
>   4½ acres in Bethwaite
>   1 acre near Wareynes bridge
>   4 acres in le Stibbings
>   2 acres que vocantur le Buttys

It is unfortunate that the land in the first of these charters (*A*) is not more precisely described. It is very probable, however, that the five acres in Eastfield of *A* correspond to the five acres in Stibbings of *B*, and the four acres in Stibbings of *C*. Further it is possible that the two acres at the park gate of *A* correspond to the two acres at Eastfield gate of *B*, which might correspond to le Buttys. The enclosure of *A* might possibly be the Bethwaite of *C*; many of those with messuages in Peterborough had holdings in Bethwaite.[3] It could be argued from a comparison of these charters that *A* is a tenancy newly created, that *B* is a serjeanty enlarged by purchase two generations later, and that *C* is such a holding, after more than a century, far less transformed.[4] In 1294 William le Swon remitted

---

[1] *Pytchley*, p. 118. This is described as being the serjeanty of the butler of the refectory (*Ibid.* p. 117).

[2] *Ibid.* p. 12. In 1308 this comprised ten acres of land: Vesp. E.22, fos. 90v–91r.

[3] The first reference to an assart in Bethwaite is from around 1140, in a charter printed below, p. 78.

[4] The four or five acres that Mellows noted are the parcels of land in *Stibbings*, and not the complete holdings, which seem rather to have been of ten or twelve acres.

his rights to all corrodies and payments 'by right of the swineherd's fee of this abbey', which he claimed to hold in virtue of the following land:[1]

> a messuage and a croft in Westgate
> 1 acre ultra le Beche

One reading of this charter would be that the fee was claimed *because* he held land in these places. If this were accepted, our argument concerning the origin of these tenures would be strengthened by what is an interesting and clearly a dishonest piece of antiquarianism.

What is not open to doubt is that this land was recently assarted. *Stibbing* and the several compounds of *thwaite* are transparent.[2] Other of the named property can be shown to have been in the same area; thus land in le Beche is once described as lying towards Eastwood, and on another occasion as abutting on *Stibbings*.[3] Charters of around 1200 will frequently associate messuages in Peterborough with a holding in *Stibbings*.[4] The townsmen of Peterborough profited from, if they were not actively engaged in, the colonisation of the surrounding countryside. They were the last group of abbey tenants to acquire a landed base. The endowment first of the knights, then of the military serjeants, and then of the servants of lower rank, show the same force at work – the pressure on the lord to devolve land.

THE MARKET FOR FREEHOLD

When we come to consider the market for freehold in the thirteenth century, we find an abundance of charter material. A striking feature of many of these charters is that the land transferred is 'new land', gained from the forest in the twelfth and the first half of the thirteenth centuries. In the Soke of Peterborough the total amount of land cleared can scarcely be less than one thousand acres. There can be no doubt that the freeholding class was in the van of this movement, with the abbey administration acting on a smaller scale, clearing land itself and engrossing the clearances of others.[5] The large number of grants of holdings which appear in the abbey

---

[1] *C.N.* 484.
[2] *P.N. Soc. Northants*, p. 270.
[3] *C.N.* 24, 84.
[4] A good example of such charters will be found in Swa. fo. 184r–v.
[5] This paragraph summarises some of the conclusions of Chapter 4.

cartularies reflects this movement. It mirrors also the part played by 'conquest', in this case from the forest, in the family settlements of this period. When we are looking at the assart holdings of the free-holders we are looking at the most volatile element in the land market considered in this book. It is a land market of a peculiar intensity, and on an estimate of its direction and extent depends any assessment of the fortunes of the freeholding class in this area in the thirteenth century.

The difficulty comes in finding material which makes possible a considered judgement on these matters. The nearest that we can get to examining the freeholding community of a single village is at Castor. In addition to the surveys and the abbey cartularies, there is a large group of charters from the Fitzwilliam archives. This material demonstrates clearly, what in any case would have been suspected, that the abbey had lordship over only a small percentage of the free men of the village. And because the land was gathered in only much later, it shows the build up as well as the dissipation of small freeholds.

The first Fitzwilliam archive is that of Geoffrey Illing. In the thirteenth-century surveys he held two and a half virgates, and in the cartularies there were several grants in connexion with the foundation of the grange at Belsize.[1] The first charter in the archive dates from the first quarter of the thirteenth century, when he gave a virgate in Sutton to an aunt.[2] While he had a substantial holding, he seems to have been under some pressure in the mid-century. There are two leases of property to the chaplain of Castor, from 1242 and 1256;[3] the former was a six-year lease of two acres of land and four solidates of rent, for which he was paid 36s. These trans-actions may be the result of unpaid loans. The largest grant made by Geoffrey was four acres of land, which he sold 'in his great necessity' to Robert Butler. Other transactions make up a total of just over six acres of land sold, the leases specified, and six and a half acres granted to his brother to hold of him for a shilling a year.[4] The grants were all to members of other freeholding families – Paris, Mason, Butler, Herlewin and Silvester of Castor.

Richard of Lilford held a half virgate in the abbey surveys. In the charters, he and his daughter appear in several small transactions,

---

[1] Surveys, fo. 186r; Swa. fo. 223r.
[2] Fitzwilliam Charter, no. 1540.
[3] *Ibid.* nos. 4, 12. The village priest may often have been a moneylender: Postan, *Cambridge Economic History*, I, 627.
[4] His archive is Fitzwilliam Charters, nos. 4–13.

all of them alienations, involving just over three and a half acres of land.[1] By contrast, the family of Robert Butler, who held a small tenancy of the abbey, occur frequently and seem to have expanded their holding in the thirteenth century. Robert bought his park of Bovetownhay from Andrew Russell; he had the lease and then the grant of unspecified land in Castor, while there were two separate grants to him of four acres of land.[2] In the next generation there is an interesting charter by which Peter Asselin undertook to pay 3s 6d an acre for every acre owned by John Butler in the fields of Castor. This is difficult to interpret, but it would seem to indicate some fairly substantial loan. A second document mentions a tenancy of forty acres, and most of this seems to have come to him also.[3] All this seems to be the early history of the establishment of a substantial holding; this was known as Butler's manor up to the early sixteenth century, when it was bought by the Fitzwilliam family.[4]

The freeholders who did not hold of the abbey presumably held of the knightly tenants of the village. And they would seem to have been the larger group – the Cordels, the Silvesters, the Masons, the Paris and Ashton families. Of the early archives here the most conspicuous is that of Ralph the son of William Mason. He bought an estate of just under twelve acres of land, acquired in fourteen charters from seven different families.[5] For it he paid sums totalling £10 6s 4d, the price of the land working out at just under a pound an acre. Sometime in the 1270s he gave half of this to his wife for her lifetime, when it was described as being 'of my acquisition and free purchase'.[6] A man's acquisitions would be used to satisfy any extra demands made on him, leaving the patrimonial inheritance intact wherever possible.

The Castor charters enable us to trace the transfer of land within the freeholding class. Some families such as Mason and Butler can be seen to have grown in the thirteenth century, while others such as Illing and Lilford possibly declined. Geoffrey Illing, however, had at least seventy-five acres of land, and so we cannot deduce very much from two leases and twelve acres granted away. However we interpret the 'great necessity' clauses in these charters, they need not refer to endemic debt. Without any picture at a single

[1] Surveys, fo. 186v; Fitzwilliam Charters nos. 50–1, 54, 59, 68–71.
[2] Surveys, fo. 186v; Fitzwilliam Charters, nos. 24, 60, 74, 80, 83.
[3] *Ibid.* nos. 79, 78.
[4] *Pytchley*, p. 49 note.
[5] Fitzwilliam Charters, nos. 6–8, 18, 20, 22–3, 26–8, 38, 43, 52, 58, 63.
[6] *Ibid.* no. 43.

point of time, such as is provided by a good survey, it is difficult to feel any confidence in the use of such material. It certainly cannot be used to prove any thesis of a free peasantry's rise or decline.[1]

The sources show more clearly the land which did not remain within the freeholding sector, but which moved out of it. It moved in two directions. Some was granted to the abbey, and some was purchased by unfree men and appended to their customary holdings. In either case the abbey administration had an interest in it, for not only did it record its own purchases, it also claimed to control the property dealings of its villeins. The fruits of the latter policy are found in the *Carte Nativorum*, a register of the 1340s, which shows that in the late thirteenth and early fourteenth centuries a large amount of free land in the Soke of Peterborough passed into the hands of unfree men.[2] Freemen were the chief sellers of land in this cartulary, and so it also must be taken into account when considering the thirteenth-century market for freehold. The sales to villeins will be considered first, and then those to the abbey.

In the thirteenth-century surveys the Puttock and Blakeman families appear as the most substantial freeholding families in Walton, and theirs are the two main archives in the Walton section of the *Carte Nativorum*.[3] In the early part of the century Henry Puttock had a serjeanty of summoning the court of Castor, and in addition he had half a virgate at farm of the hospital of St Leonard outside Peterborough. He made his contribution to the abbey's assarting phase, making over woodland and some of the land that he had already cleared for thirteen marks. At the same time he sold the sacristy a small amount of rent for 20s. He was granted twelve acres of assart land in Paston in 1227, but the fact that only 8s was paid suggests that he was settling a claim made on his property on no very strong foundation.[4] The next evidence comes from the end of the century. By then the tenant was another Henry, the grandson of

---

[1] This point is made since it was on the basis of a similar collection of deeds from the Buckinghamshire manor of Wooton Underwood that Powicke drew his roseate picture of the English freeholder in the thirteenth century: F. M. Powicke, 'Observations on the English Freeholder in the Thirteenth Century', *Wirtschaft und Kultur. Festschrift . . . Alfons Dopsch* (Leipzig, 1938), pp. 382–93.

[2] The *Carte Nativorum* is considered very fully in Chapter 6, where evidence for the statements in this paragraph will be found. At Ramsey also, 'it would appear that villeins were gaining control of considerable local freeholds' (*Tenure and Mobility*, p. 82).

[3] *C.N.*, p. xiv.

[4] Surveys, fo. 188r–v; Swa. fo. 35r; P.R.O., CP. 25(1) 172/19/128.

the one above. He granted rents both to the sacrist and to the abbot.[1]
He sold his serjeanty, including its capital messuage, to William
of Amewell, and lands and rents to Roger Thorold at the same
period.[2] Other charters in the collection refer to his selling land in
Walton, Paston and Werrington.[3] It is impossible to say how large
a part of the family's holding this represented, but the sale of the
capital messuage suggests weakness. It is very likely that this family
lost ground in the thirteenth century, at the expense of the abbey on
the one hand and of its villeins on the other.

The same would seem to be true of the family of Blakeman.
William Blakeman held a virgate at farm of the abbey in the surveys. The first record of his dealings is again in connexion with the
movement of colonisation; between 1233 and 1245 he relinquished
his rights of common in 'the abbey's assarts in Walton'. One and a
half acres in Paston were granted to the abbey in 1261.[4] Then there
is a fair-sized archive in the *Carte Nativorum*. Of the twelve transactions involving this family, all were sales, seven of them to holders
of the small fee in Walton.[5] Like Henry Puttock, Gilbert Blakeman
both sold land to William of Amewell and sold rent to the abbot.[6]
In the early fourteenth century his son sold some land in Warmington to Ralph of Thorney, one of the abbey's bailiffs.[7] The last entry
serves as a reminder that he might have owned land in several
villages in the Soke.

With any freeholder there is at least the possibility that he held
land on more than one manor.[8] A variety of sources show that
Ralph of Berkhamstead held a messuage in Peterborough, by grant
of John le Almoner; a messuage in Ailsworth; two acres of land in
Longthorpe; and a virgate at farm in Castor.[9] The sacrist's register
under Pilsgate mentions Robert Peverel, John of Helpston and
William Avenel, all of them major freeholders who held small fees

---

[1] Franceys, pp. 90–1; Fitzwilliam A/C Roll 2388, m. 6r.
[2] *C.N.* 130, 138, 147, 158–60, 163.
[3] *Ibid.* 126, 142, 188–90, 192–3, 196–7, 214.
[4] Surveys, fo. 188r; Swa. fo. 239r; P.B.C., fos. 112v–113r; P.R.O., CP. 25(1) 174/50/90.
[5] *C.N.* 125, 129, 132–4, 136, 140; on the Walton fee see *C.N.*, p. xiii, 131 note, and *Pytchley*, pp. 142–3.
[6] *C.N.* 166; Fitzwilliam A/C Roll 2388, m. 6r.
[7] *C.N.* 483.
[8] For a good example of a freeholder with land in several different villages see P. D. A. Harvey, *A Medieval Oxfordshire Village. Cuxham 1240 to 1400* (Oxford, 1965), pp. 115–16.
[9] *C.N.* 53, 360; Fitzwilliam A/C Roll 2388, m. 4d. The Longthorpe hold-ing was sold to Robert of Thorpe in 1305: CP. 25(1) 175/60/473.

of the abbey.[1] Two of the chief tenants in Longthorpe also held property in Orton, on the opposite bank of the Nene. William of Thorpe and William de Menyl each held two virgates of the fee of the bishop of Lincoln, and the latter also held four virgates of the Waterville fee.[2] A fine of 1309 shows William de Menyl either purchasing or defending a hundred acres of land in Longthorpe.[3] Yet in the Peterborough sources there is only a grant in the *Carte Nativorum* of three acres in Glinton, coupled with an indication that a good deal of his property later came to Richard of Crowland.[4] Without the central records here, there would be no indication of this man's real substance.

The interests of Adam le Almoner, a tenant in the town of Peterborough, extended even further afield. He was a member of a family which held originally by serjeanty, and in the late thirteenth and early fourteenth centuries he appears in a variety of transactions. He purchased and then resold two shops at Yaxley in Huntingdonshire, which came eventually to Thorney abbey.[5] He had a messuage in Peterborough, by grant of Robert Gere, which came to Ralph of Berkhamstead in 1282, and thence to Peterborough abbey.[6] A serjeanty of the kitchen was acquired rather later from Robert of Oxney, and granted to a couple of clerks, who seem to have been the abbey's agents.[7] He seems to have acted as a property developer in a small way also, since the 1308 account records a halfpenny of rent due to him as middleman, 'for the new cottages at the end of town'.[8] Here both Adam and the abbey itself seem to be speculating in urban property.

THE ABBEY'S PART IN THE LAND MARKET

The abbey played an important part in this market, at every level, and over a long period. Some part of this concern has already been seen, for there is no division to be made between knightly land and freehold, and many of the knightly estates purchased were consolidated by the purchase of their free holdings. Manors acquired

[1] B.M. Cotton MS. Faustina B.3, fo. 11r–v.
[2] *Rotuli Hundredorum*, II, 637b–638a.
[3] CP. 25(1) 175/62/47.
[4] *C.N.* 325, held of him for an annual rent of 1 lb. of cumin and a pair of white gloves: Vesp. E.21, fo. 79v.
[5] Red Book of Thorney, fo. 55v.
[6] *C.N.* 53; *Pytchley*, pp. 12–13.
[7] Vesp. E.21, fo. 91r; *Pytchley*, p. 12, and *cf. C.N.* 62, 113.
[8] Fitzwilliam A/C Roll 233, m. 2r.

were granted, as extra endowment, to the various monastic departments, and these built up areas of lordship. Most of the manors in
the Soke of Peterborough, and several outside, were subject to an
interest of this sort from at least one of the departments. The work
of the obedientiaries in building up holdings is parallel to, and
follows the same pattern as, that of several of the knightly families
already examined.[1] It shows that the availability of capital, when
combined with a continuous vigilance, could bring a steady flow of
property to the abbey. At times, however, vigilance became aggres-
sion. For two periods, from 1215 to 1225 and from 1265 to 1280,
the evidence is so full and localised that it can only indicate sus-
tained campaigns.

The first real campaign of property acquisition seems to have
come with the endowment of the cellarer's grange at Belsize. The
core of this grange was to be the fee of Thorold of Castor, and it was
here that the campaign was at its strongest.[2] At the time of the
disafforestation fifty acres of woodland were recorded here,[3] all of
which the abbey seems to have bought for assarting in the next ten
years. The woodland of the freeholders was engrossed along with
that of the fee; Thorold's charter of sale confirmed a grant from one
of his tenants, and all of them, Ralph son of Silvester, Christiana
Paris and Reginald of Aston, sold their woodland around the same
time.[4] Portions of other fees were purchased also, from Geoffrey
Illing, a sub-tenant of the Milton fee, and from Ralph Munioie.[5]
The tenancy was then further consolidated by a large number of
exchanges and purchases which established a new mill at Cuswick.[6]

A similar example, although later and larger in extent, is provided
by the manor which the sacristy slowly built up out of freeholdings
in Paston. In this case the basic holding seems to have been the Tot
fee.[7] The evidence is extremely full because of the survival of the
sacristy registers, whose charters are given a pattern by a fourteenth-
century survey, describing the land parcel by parcel and also giving
names of former tenants.[8] The survey reads as a roll-call of the dead,

---

[1] This point is developed below, Chapter 5.
[2] *Pytchley*, pp. 152–3.
[3] Appendix A. no. 1.
[4] Swa. fos. 208r, 222v, 223v.
[5] Swa. fos. 223r, 247v; *Pytchley*, p. 79.
[6] Swa. fos. 208r, 222v, 223r, 231r, 232r, 233r, 242r.
[7] *Pytchley*, pp. 107–10, and see above pp. 44–5.
[8] This survey is set out as Appendix D, and is there analysed further. The
leases which relate to this property show a considerable decrease in its
value between 1291 and 1400. In 1291 the manor was leased for £6 10s a
year, and this figure excluded rents and services (Franceys, pp. 99–100),

and to anyone who has studied the thirteenth-century sources these are very familiar names indeed. First there was Robert of Tot, 'who was once one of the lords of Paston', then Gernun and Neville, Underwood and Dene, Reginald the chaplain and Richard of Scotendon – each of these men has a large archive in the various Peterborough registers. Much of this is clearly land recently reclaimed. Around 1260, Alice of Scotter, widow of a former steward, granted the sacristy nine and a half acres of assart land in le Nab.[1] Eight acres given by Margery of Gernun were described as lying between *Chirchestibbing* and *Tythestibbing iuxta le Theweytes*.[2]

To found Belsize grange, the abbey in part bought cleared land, in part woodland for clearance. Three generations later the work of clearance has ceased, and the abbey is engaged in buying up the assart land of its freeholders. Some of the holdings are substantial, and show consolidation by the freeholders before their grant to the abbey. To take an entry of average size. 'Item quarantena que vocatur Nevilswong continens 10 acras.' The tenant here had been William Neville. Two of his grants, dating from the 1260s or 1270s, are printed in the *Carte Nativorum*.[3] The sacrist's register contains a further nine of his charters.[4] Five of them conveyed land to the abbey. The greater part of his land, however, came to it at one remove. The two main transactions were grants to Richard of Dene; one of five acres, for which he was given £5, the other eight acres, for twenty marks. This went towards the large holding, thirty acres of land, which came to the sacristy from the Dene family. The tenancy bears all the marks of having been formed for this purpose; along with it came a grant of forty marks, and the total gift served as endowment for a chaplain saying mass for their souls.[5] This is a new form of piety, which could only just be maintained within a monastic framework.

while around 1400 the value of the manor was £2 (*Ibid*. pp. 100–3). The extent of 1400 refers to much of this land as either *incultus* or *non aratus*, and some of the land in the latter lay 'beneath Eastwood'. It could be that these Paston assarts were marginal land.

[1] *C.N.* 524; this and related transactions are discussed in Appendix D note 1. An earlier charter transferring this land refers to 'septem acras terre in assarto in Nabbe': *Pytchley*, p. 109.

[2] Swa. fo. 166v.

[3] *C.N.* 107, 157. Both the recipients were men of substance; Thurstan son of Robert of Thorpe was presumably a member of the chief landowning family in Longthorpe (*Pytchley*, p. 55 note), and William of Amewell was bailiff of the western group of manors in 1281 (B.M. Add. Ch. 737; *C.N.* 143 note and p. xiv).

[4] Franceys, pp. 48–55.

[5] *Ibid*. p. 26.

It is clear that the part of the abbey in the market for freehold, when isolated, amounted to rather less than appears at first sight of the charters. There are two sides to the movement of property to the abbey, and it is important that they be distinguished. There is the consolidation of various obedientary holdings; this adds to the abbey's rent roll, but it does not take land out of the market. The land remained with the freeholding class, although of course not necessarily with the family that had granted it out. Quite different is the formation of demesnes from freehold, with the cellarer's manor of Belsize and with the sacrist's manor of Paston. The one is the abbey's assart consolidated, the other the consolidation of free-holders' assart holdings. Here there was pressure on freeholders; although it must be noted that freeholders were the main assarters, and this was an area of particularly active growth.

When we are looking at consolidation we are looking at a move-ment within freehold, not a destruction of it. If however the campaigns were more general that would be another matter, for whatever qualifications are made freeholders were clearly under pressure in such areas. We know that there were similar campaigns on part of the Ramsey estate also.[1] Both at Peterborough and at Ramsey they did not apply over the whole of the estate, but only at the centre where the power of lordship was most strong. Lordship was becoming more concentrated.

[1] For the relevant comparisons with Ramsey see Raftis, *Ramsey*, p. 112 note 60, and *Tenure and Mobility*, p. 82.

4   *The Colonisation of Northamptonshire*

Burch is founded in the country of the Gyrvii; for there beginneth the Fen, on the east side thereof, which reacheth LX miles, or more, in length: which Fen is of no small benefit to the bordering people; for there they have wood and other fuel for the fire, and hay for fodder; as also reed for thatching of their houses; with many other necessaries. There are likewise divers rivers, waters, and great meers, for fishing, the country abounding in such things: in the best part whereof Burch is seated; having on the one side of it the Fen and river; and on the other upland ground, with woods, meadows, and many pastures; which do render it most beautiful on every part, having a meet access to it by land, except towards the east; on which side, without boats, there is no coming to it.

This, in Dugdale's translation, is how Hugh Candidus described the location of Peterborough.[1] In the *Anglo-Saxon Chronicle* there is a picture of the monks coming to restore Medeshamstede, and finding there 'only old walls and wild woods', although fortunately the walls were found to contain copies of the original foundation charters.[2] Other, genuine, charters confirm the picture of the chronicles. In the list of sureties for the estates acquired by Ethelwold the standard description of land was that it consisted of so many acres 'of woodland and open country'.[3] It was in that order, perhaps, that the countryside presented itself to the eye. Very likely it was the forest that predominated, for *Domesday Book* notes an agreement between the abbeys of Thorney and Peterborough which suggests that Thorney had fen to spare and Peterborough woodland.[4]

We must imagine Peterborough as for centuries a small island of habitation between the forest and the fen. The clearance of woodland, and reclamation from the fen, must from the beginning have

---

[1] *Hugh Candidus*, p. 5, in the translation of W. Dugdale, *The History of Imbanking and Draining of Divers Fens and Marshes* (2nd edn., 1772), p. 367.
[2] *Anglo-Saxon Chronicle* (E), s.a. 963 (Everyman edn., pp. 115–7).
[3] Robertson, *Anglo-Saxon Charters*, pp. 77, 79.
[4] A quarter of Whittlesey Mere was held, 'of the abbot of Thorney by the abbot of Peterborough, and in return for these he provides sufficient pasture for 120 pigs, and if pasture fails, he feeds and fattens 60 pigs with corn. Moreover he finds timber for one house of 60 ft, and poles for the enclosure around the house. He also repairs the house and enclosure when they are decayed' (*D.B.*, I, fo. 205a; *cf.* Hart, *E.C.E.E.*, p. 183).

been a continuous occupation. Yet none of this evidence shows the work of clearance in progress, and for the pre-Conquest period the movement of colonisation must be left to the imagination. A slightly more precise indication of the abbey's commitment is found in *Domesday*, and in particular in the maps which have been constructed from it. The abbey's lands lay in the most densely wooded area of Northamptonshire. At Oundle there was the biggest stretch of woodland in the county, three leagues by two, and several of the abbey manors approached this figure.[1] The figures for plough-teams, and for density of population, whatever their quantitative value, give the same relative impression.[2] The poorest areas of Northamptonshire were in the north and south-east. 'In the former area, the Rockingham Forest district and the Soke of Peterborough had plough-team densities of about 2 or under and population densities of about 5 per square mile.'[3] This was definitely under-developed land. Yet *Domesday* does not show the extent to which much development, in the form of much undocumented colonisation in the centuries before 1086, had already taken place.

What must represent the bulk of the colonisation of Northamptonshire can therefore only be a prologue to this chapter. The chapter proper starts, where the records allow it to start, in the early twelfth century. These records are essentially of two kinds. The first, chronologically, are those of the central government: charters granting license to assart, fines for forest offences, and surveys of the regarders – the fruits of the tight control which the Angevins kept, right through this period, over their forest land. The limitation of this material is that, at least for the twelfth century, it is unsystematic, and shows the colonisation of Northamptonshire only incidentally. The second group of material comprises the charters in the Peterborough cartularies. They also are unsystematic, in that it is the abbey's entrepreneurship which they show at first hand, not the history of the colonisation. The precise part played by the abbey in the movement of colonisation is one of the chief problems raised by the material. With these limitations, common to all the sources for

---

[1] *D.B.*, I, fo. 221a. The figure for Werrington, which included the hamlet of Paston, was two leagues by one (*Ibid.*). The Oundle measurement represented 'perhaps 4½ miles by 3 miles': Lennard, *Rural England*, p. 11; cf. Round, *V.C.H. Northants*, I, 279–81. A picture of the Domesday woodland of Northants is given by the map in *The Domesday Geography of Midland England*, ed. H. C. Darby and I. B. Terrett (2nd edn., Cambridge, 1971), p. 405.

[2] *Ibid.* pp. 396, 398.

[3] *Ibid.* p. 404.

the early history of colonisation, the Peterborough archive is a full
one, and in several ways interesting.

The central records will be considered first. The earliest of these
are two charters of Stephen. The more specific of the two confirmed
to the abbey '200 acres of assart' in the Soke of Peterborough – 115
acres in Longthorpe, 55 acres in Walton and 70 acres in Castor and
Ailsworth, amounting in fact to 240 acres.[1] The second charter
granted the abbey all its assarts up to the date of the charter, June
1143, 'free and quit of all secular impositions and from every forest
regard'.[2] The mention of the regard is early, as Cronne points out;
indeed it is probably too early, for the word 'regard' is likely
either interpolated or a later translation of some more general
phrase. It is possible that the precise date is interpolated too.[3] This
document, in fact, takes us into the reign of Henry II. According to
the Huntingdonshire jurors in 1218, it was Henry II who put all
their county in the regard, when he came to the throne. 'By whose
advice he did it they knew not', but who his agent was they remembered only too well. It was Alan de Neville, who established
innumerable 'bad customs', and imposed the system of verderers,
wardens and regarders of the forest for the first time.[4] Whether or
not this was so, there is no doubt of the activity of the intervening
years, and the central and local material combine to provide a neat
example of the mounting pressure of Angevin administration.

The eyres of Alan de Neville, which still lived in popular memory
fifty years later, were those of 1162–3 and 1166–7.[5] In the first of
them the abbey paid fines for assarting in Werrington, Cottingham,
Oundle and Great Easton. A large number of its knights and free
tenants, especially in the Soke of Peterborough, paid fines also.[6]
Four years later most of the same entries appear, while the whole
village paid a fine of half a mark in the Peterborough hamlet of
Paston.[7] It is in the next reign, however, that the pressure starts to
mount, and with it the amount of the material. Swaffham's cartulary

[1] *Regesta*, III, 657.
[2] *Regesta*, III, 655.
[3] H. A. Cronne, *The Reign of Stephen* (London, 1970), p. 282. No other
charter of Stephen's reign uses the word 'regard'.
[4] P.R.O. E. 32/38 m. 1; for the date see M. Bazeley, 'The Extent of the
English Forest in the Thirteenth Century', *T.R.H.S.*, 4th ser., IV (1921),
166.
[5] The latter seems to have been the first general forest eyre of the reign:
D. M. Stenton (ed.), *Pleas before the King or his Justices 1198–1212*, III
(Selden Soc., LXXXIII, 1967), pp. lii–liv.
[6] *Pipe Roll 9 Henry II*, pp. 32, 36–40.
[7] *Pipe Roll 13 Henry II*, pp. 118–20, 162.

contains twenty charters of various sorts from Richard I to the abbey, a third of them concerned with forest privileges.[1] The earliest of these, from December 1189, was also the most comprehensive. The abbey and its men were granted almost complete exemption from forest jurisdiction in the Soke, and in the manors of vigorous assarting outside, Cottingham, Great Easton and Oundle. The abbey was to be allowed to enclose its assarts and its other land, both 'infra mariscum et extra', and it was granted 200 acres of assart in the Soke and 400 acres at Oundle free of all forest exactions.[2] The king reserved only his own hunting, and the regard of the woods of the knights and freeholders. In March 1190 there was a separate charter for the knights and freeholders, considered as a group, and apart from the abbey, for the first time.[3] Abbot Benedict was a friend of King Richard, and perhaps as a result the fine of sixty marks paid for these charters was not excessive.[4]

The price of John's confirmation of the same charters was 200 marks.[5] The abbey, however, did not for long enjoy the protection for which it had paid. In 1209 there was a major forest eyre, and the record of its proceedings survives for several counties, including Northamptonshire. Part of these proceedings have been printed, and some of the fines appear in the pipe rolls, but the bread and butter work of the regarders, the lists of waste and assarts, remain in manuscript.[6] The whole archive gives a strong impression, simply for want of anything dramatic, of the offensive pettiness of forest administration in the latter part of John's reign. Recognised privilege either brought fresh problems or else was ignored. Both the knights and the abbey had been allowed their own foresters: in 1209 the former paid £100 and the latter £200 that these foresters should not go to prison, since their woods had been badly kept.[7] The abbey manor of Eye was declared forfeit, and a fine of fifty marks claimed for its recovery, since a fawn had been found buried there.[8] At the other end of the scale, several villages paid sums varying from half a mark to two marks to be quit of suspicion of

[1] Swa. fos. 44r–50v.
[2] Swa. fo. 47r–v.
[3] Swa. fo. 47v.
[4] *Pipe Roll 2 Richard I*, p. 29.
[5] Swa. fo. 51r–v; *Pipe Roll 3 John*, p. 183.
[6] P.R.O. E. 32/62, 32/249. I am greatly indebted to Professor J. A. Raftis for drawing my attention to this material. The proceedings are in *Select Pleas of the Forest*, ed. G. J. Turner, (Selden Soc., XIII, 1901), pp. 1–6, and fines in *Pipe Roll 11 John*, pp. 37, 186–7.
[7] *Ibid.* p. 187.
[8] P.R.O. E. 32/249, m. 12r.

offences unspecified, and dozens of freeholders, as will be seen, paid for small assarts.[1] According to Swaffham's chronicle, 'the foresters and the beasts of the forests in those days lorded it over men, and there was nobody living within the forest bounds – be he rich or poor, or even religious – who was not wronged by them'.[2] There is more than enough material in the 1209 archive to support this judgement. It was presumably the continuance of such pressure which led all the free landholders in the Soke to offer 1220 marks for its disafforestation in 1215.[3]

According to the Peterborough chronicle it was the abbey, on its own, that was responsible for the disafforestation. Clearly, however, this was only part of the story. During the previous generation the knights and freeholders had occurred whenever the abbey did. In 1190 they had a charter separate from the abbey; in 1209 they were fined separately from the abbey; in 1215 they appear together with the abbey. We can see here how a community might grow up, in part as a result of royal pressure. It is as the natural leader of this local community that the abbot of Peterborough appears in 1215. How this group organised itself to pay the fine is shown in an exceptionally interesting group of documents in Swaffham's cartulary.[4] First the woodland had to be surveyed and valued. This was the work of four of the smaller landowners and a clerk, acting 'at the request of the lord Robert abbot of Peterborough, Roger of Torpel, Brian de la Mare, Richard of Waterville, and the other knights and freeholders of Nassaburgh . . . as was communally agreed'.[5] The survey of the woods survives, and lists a whole series of small parcels of woodland, scattered over the Soke, showing very vividly how the forest was being broken up.[6] The valuation survives too, and shows the knights and freeholders assessed in all

[1] P.R.O. E. 32/62, m. 3r–v.
[2] Sparke, p. 108.
[3] Swa. fos. 51v–52r, printed *Monasticon*, I, 392. The amount of the fine, 1220 marks, is given in Swa. fo. 243r (Appendix A. no. 3); as against the figure of 1320 marks given in Sparke, p. 108, and that of 200 marks to be found in Bazeley, 'The Extent of the English Forest in the Thirteenth Century', p. 148.
[4] Swa. fos. 120v–121v, 243r–v. Holt has some excellent remarks on parallel cases here (*Magna Carta*, pp. 52–5), while there is some useful information in the general survey of Miss Bazeley ('The Extent of the English Forest in the Thirteenth Century', pp. 140–72). But these seem the most precise set of records concerning the composition of the groups purchasing privileges, and the measures taken to apportion the fines. Because the Peterborough information seems unique in its detail, the relevant documents are given in full in Appendix A.
[5] Appendix A. no. 2.
[6] Appendix A. no. 1.

at £361 3s 1½d; the balance of the fine, £452 3s 6½d, was left to be met by the abbey.[1] The fine was to be paid over the next three years, in instalments of 720, 300 and 200 marks.[2] The group thus constituted in opposition to the king is found shortly thereafter concluding an agreement with the abbot and convent concerning rights of pasture.[3] Each party was granted the right to enclose and assart its own woodland, while the knights and freeholders were to retain their rights of pasture in the fen. Any dispute was to go to the arbitration of 'law-worthy men of Nassaburgh', and the document was sealed by six knights 'on behalf of all the knights and freeholders of Nassaburgh'.[4] Two of these six knights were not tenants of the abbey; this is a local, not an honorial group.

The list of assarts from 1209 gives for the first time a detailed picture of the work of reclamation in the Soke. These, admittedly, are the only forest proceedings to survive for the area, for the disafforestation removed the royal oversight. But even though this picture is static, we can still ask a fair range of questions of it – who was assarting, what was the size of holding, and what crops were sown?[5] There are seventy-eight entries in this list, and the total amount of land involved is 145 acres. Forty-two per cent of the land was sown with wheat and fifty-eight per cent with oats.[6] The parcels of land are small; five acres is a large holding, and amounts of half an acre and an acre are frequent. Several of the people mentioned have small holdings in more than one manor; thus Matilda of Scotendon occurs five times, holding three acres in Dogsthorpe, and parcels of two acres, one rood, half an acre, and one acre in Peterborough. The group seems remarkably homogenous, for these are freeholders,

---

[1] Appendix A. no. 2.   [2] Appendix A. no. 3.

[3] Appendix A. no. 4. The Statute of Merton tackled a social problem, but it was a problem far less pressing than it had been a generation before, and one that had largely to be solved by private agreement. For the law and its records on this point see Plucknett, *Legislation of Edward I* (Oxford, 1949), pp. 83–6, and Stenton, *Earliest Northamptonshire Assize Rolls*, pp. xxxi–ii. To say, as Powicke does, that this statute 'in the course of time effected a revolution in rural society as feudal relations gradually gave way to a harder doctrine of proprietary rights' (*Henry the Third and the Lord Edward*, p. 150), is to say a good deal too much; the chronology would seem to be against it, as also the fact that 'feudal relations' in rural society is a concept that needs to be handled with care – the custom of the manor and the common law were two distinct things (see, most recently, Raftis, *Tenure and Mobility*).

[4] 'pro omnibus militibus et francolanis de Nasso'.

[5] The information in this paragraph is taken from P.R.O. E. 32/62 m. 3; printed below Appendix A. no. 5.

[6] Elsewhere in Northamptonshire, where the two crops were sown, the proportion ⅓ wheat : ⅔ oats seems not uncommon: P.R.O. E. 32/249, m. 11, m. 13.

almost without exception. Ascelina of Waterville alone among the dozen or so most important tenants in the area occurs here. We know from the 1215 survey that the others had woodland, but they are not recorded as assarting in the Soke in 1209. At only one place, Longthorpe, does a village pay for an assart, half an acre sown with oats. A generation later, at the time of the surveys, it was only at Longthorpe that the customary virgaters were recorded as holding assart land. A much larger inroad into the pattern of free occupancy was made by the abbey itself. The abbot, the sacrist and the almoner between them held 42 acres out of the total of 145. One entry, indeed, serves to remind us that monks and freeholders were men of the same background. Salomon 'brother of the abbot of Peterborough' had eight acres of land in three parcels; it is possible that the family of Solomon of Werrington, prominent freeholders in the thirteenth century, was descended from him.[1] Seventy per cent of the land in the survey was held by free landholders, and the other thirty per cent by the abbey. Half of the abbey's land, the twenty-one acres in Westwode, seems to be its own assart; the other half, from the size of the parcels, probably represents land cleared by freeholders, and recently given to the abbey. Thus we see the abbey both assarting on its own and beginning to engross the clearances of its knights and freeholders.

Both these things appear very clearly in the dozens of charters from the Soke of Peterborough in Swaffham's cartulary, which show the abbey assarting and buying up recently assarted land. Abbot Robert of Lindsey (1214–22) formed a grange in the manor of Castor, which he granted to the cellary. It comprised:[2]

Omnia nova assarta nostra in Nasso Burgi, scilicet: Belasise cum omnibus pertinenciis, et Glintonhauue, et essarta de Estuude, et Franehauue de emptione nostra de Willelmo de Gimiges, et totum pratum de emptione nostra in Northburc.

The phrase 'our assarts' here covers a multitude of transactions. A good deal of woodland, in total at least a hundred acres, was bought for assarting.[3] Franehawe, mentioned in the charter to the cellary, amounted to twelve and a half acres in 1215,[4] and there was

---

[1] On this family see *C.N.*, p. lxii. Salomon was the brother of abbot Benedict: Swa. fo. 253r.
[2] Swa. fos. 104v–105r.
[3] In addition to the main transactions quoted, grants of small parcels of woodland in Castor will be found in Swa. fos. 208r, 222v, 223r, 232v, 236v 248r.
[4] This was bought from William son of Robert of Gimiges, Swa. fo. 231r.

also the whole of the woodland of Torold of Castor and his sub-
tenants, amounting to fifty acres.[1] Pasture was needed for the
plough beasts, and twenty compact acres were bought from Geoffrey of Northborough for forty marks.[2] The abbey was also assarting
from its existing holdings. Ralph Cordel granted 'unam rodam
terre et dimidiam in Heyninge in campis de Castre iuxta novum
assartum domini abbatis in australi costera' towards the foundation of Belsize.[3] Where there are new assarts there are presumably
old; the process was a continuous one. In 1248 William of Dover
claimed rights of common in 'illis culturis que iacent in territorio
de Eylisuurthe inter boscum Gileberti Francolani de Eylisuurthe et
Ketelis þuueyt Welle', which were referred to as being assarts.[4] Most
of the Castor charters refer to landlord assarting, for this was an
area of particular landlord enterprise. Yet there is equally clear
evidence of the transactions of the free peasantry. William the
clerk's grant of ten acres 'in territorio de Castre apud Basketiswelle'
was probably an individual assart, while the following grant of
Robert of Ailsworth certainly was:[5]

totum essartum meum in campis de Eylisuurthe, cum rifleto quod iacet
inter terram eiusdem abbatis versus occidentem et boscum eiusdem versus
orientem.

The charters would suggest, however, that the work of clearance
had not progressed far in this area when the abbey started work on
Belsize grange, and that it was itself responsible for clearing most
of the necessary land.

The picture on the neighbouring manor of Paston, with its
hamlets of Dogsthorpe and Cathwaite, was rather different. Each
of these place names is first found in the twelfth century. Marginally
the earliest of them is 'Bestwett iuxta Dodesthorpe', found in a
charter of abbot Martin of *c.* 1140, which survives (for no obvious
reason) only in a Ramsey cartulary.[6] It may well show how a good
deal of the twelfth-century assarting in this area took place, and for
this reason is worth quoting in full:

[1] See above, p. 67.
[2] Swa. fo. 224v.
[3] Swa. fos. 222v–223r. Around the same time Ralph Munioie gave:
'culturam que vocatur Languuang in Heyning, et abutat super ductum
aque de Rohaubroc, et dimidiam acram que abbutat super essartas
predicti abbatis' (Swa. fo. 248r).
[4] Swa. fo. 257v.
[5] Swa. fos. 236v, 230v.
[6] *Cartularium Monasterii de Rameseia*, I, 79 (where the charter is dated
1226–33).

Ego Martinus et totus conventus Sancti Petri de Burch concedimus
Acelino filio Walterii de Burgo et heredibus suis in feodum et hereditatem,
Adelildesholm cum bechio et maresio sicut ipse Acelinus illud cinxit cum
fossato suo; et viginti tres acras de terra lucrabili, que nunquam antea
lucrata fuerat in Bestwett iuxta Dodesthorp unoquoque anno pro decem
sol. pro omnibus servitiis et consuetudinibus.

A charter of 1155–75 contains the first mention of Cathwaite, when
two-thirds of its tithes were excluded from the endowment of the
rector of Paston, having previously been confirmed to the sacristy.[1]
The endowment of the sacristy seems to have been the work of
Martin of Bec, *c.* 1140; the Cathwaite assarts should probably be
dated to that time or shortly thereafter. Paston, the chief hamlet,
occurs slightly later, but when it does appear, in 1166–7, the whole
village (*tota villa*) was apparently assarting.[2]

The Cathwaite–Dogsthorpe area accounted for more than half
the 145 acres presented as assart in 1209. Further, it is probably
clearances of this period that are represented in the considerable
number of charters granting land to the abbey in the assarts of
Paston – a good number of its acquisitions can be dated to the period
1215–35. Thus William Puncun gave one and a half acres on the
sacristy's great furlong ('magna cultura sacristie'), which Simon
Anglicus had formerly held. John of Walton, in turn, gave
'totam terram meam in assartis de Pastona inter terram sacriste Burgi
et terram Willelmi Puncun'.[3] Assart land was also bought from the
Peverel and Tot fees.[4] Among Robert of Tot's grants were five
selions 'cum forario quod nominatur stibbinge Rogeri Grille', the
latter being one of his villeins, whose service he later transferred to
the abbey.[5] Abbot Robert created an enclosure of 40 acres from land
which he bought from freeholders in this area, and granted it to
Belsize Grange. Several of the freeholders are named, and their
charters can be identified.[6] It must be to this enclosure that Robert
of Tot refers in a charter granting the abbey:[7]

[1] *C.N.*, no. 514.   [2] *Pipe Roll 13 Henry II*, p. 120.
[3] Swa. fo. 180r, Franceys, pp. 96–7. John of Walton and William Punzun
are found together in 1209 (Appendix A. no. 5; for John see no. 23, for
William nos. 8, 22 and 24). The 'magna cultura sacristie' is perhaps no.
27.
[4] Franceys, pp. 47–8, 60.   [5] Swa. fos. 219r, 221r.
[6] 'Item emit et adquisivit terras apud Pastone, partem de Roberto Peverel,
partem de Roberto Tot, partem de Henrico clerico, et partem de aliis
francolanis; unde fecit fieri unam culturam circumfossatam, continen-
tem in se quadraginta acras, quod assignatum est apud Belasise' (Sparke,
p. 112). The charters of Henry the clerk and Roberto of Tot are identical
(Swa. fos. 224v, 218v).
[7] Swa. fo. 219r.

Boscum meum iuxta Estuude inter Coupuude et mariscum, cum tota terra absque omni retinemento; et siquid iuris habui in aliqua particula terre vel bosci vel infra novam fossatam quam dictus Robertus abbas fecit circa Estuude quietum clamavi eis.

The frontier here is moving towards Eastwood. We get confirmation of this *c.* 1230, when Richard of Waterville obtained recognition of rights of pasture in Castor and Longthorpe woods, in return for his remitting any rights in Eastwood.[1] The bulk of thirteenth-century reclamation seems to have taken place around Eastwood.

Half a century later, the sacristy formed a manor at Paston, and moved in to consolidate its earlier acquisitions in this area.[2] Here the amounts transferred are slightly larger, for tenants had frequently built up their own tenancies from parcels of assarted land, and these they granted to the abbey. Richard of Dene's grant of just under thirty acres shows this particularly clearly,[3] and the assart origin of a good deal of this land appears in Margery Gernun's grant of eight acres:[4]

Quorum quinque acre et una dimidia acra iacent iuxta le Thewytes iuxta terram persone de Pastona . . . in alio capite super Chirchestibbing et due acre et una dimidia acra in Tythestibbing iuxta le Theweytes iuxta terram Galfridi Miniuld ex una parte et abuttant uno capite super terram Roberti Peverel de Pastona.

The work of colonising Paston was the freeholders' enterprise, and in the abbey cartularies, particularly in Swaffham and the *Carte Nativorum*, we see their work at one remove.

Using the 1209 survey as a control, it is possible to be fairly precise about the origins of several of the assart holdings in these cartularies. Amongst the acquisitions of *c.* 1220 are two holdings of land 'inter Aileduledich et essartas Willelmi Guuitonis et Osberti de Estfeld'.[5] Since Osbert's son Berengar occurs in 1209, and since William's son occurs before 1200, these assarts can safely be dated to the last third of the twelfth century.[6] In the van of the assarting movement we find an early, indeed perhaps the first, rector of Paston, for this William Guito can only be the William Guito ap-

---

[1] Swa. fo. 205r. In 1247 Richard of Scotendon renounced his rights of common in Eastwood and Grimeshauue, in return for the confirmation of his rights in Westwood, and the destruction of an enclosure the abbey had made there (Swa. fo. 214r).
[2] This has been described above, pp. 67–8.
[3] Appendix D, note 7.
[4] Swa. fo. 166v.
[5] Swa. fo. 218v.
[6] Appendix A(5), no. 36; Swa. fos. 233v, 234r.

pointed between 1155 and 1175.[1] There are several transfers of land in Berengar's *stibbing* in the *Carte Nativorum*,[2] and he was only one among several of the tenants in John's day who gave their names to the land which they cleared. At the time of the surveys, *c.* 1231, the only freeholds which were clearly assart land were the following:[3]

Thomas tenet terram Odardi Coci per servicium coquine abbatis. Idem reddit p.a. ad quatuor terminos 16d. pro quarta parte terre que vocatur Socindonerstibbing.
Adam Swin reddit p.a. 32d. ad quatuor terminos pro 8 acris terre.
De terra Higgeney 20d. p.a. ad quatuor terminos.
De terra Simonis cementarii 18d. p.a. ad quatuor terminos. scilicet pro Warinstibbing.
De Alicia de Wengham 2d. pro dimidia acra in Neustibbing.

Adam Swin's is probably his own assart, but the others take us back at least a generation. Assarts of Higgeney and Richard of Scotendon were held by their widows in 1209. *Warinstibbing* is presumably the assart of Warin of Pecham, who held one and a half acres in Longthorpe, and along with his brother Roger had two acres in Dogsthorpe.[4] Now the payments in the surveys were at 4d an acre, so that Warin's Longthorpe holding was four and a half acres, three times the amount recorded in 1209. He and other tenants in this list were presumably clearing over a long period. We should perhaps multiply the 1209 figure of 145 acres three or four times to get a picture of the assarting movement in the first generation of the thirteenth century – this for Paston would give a figure of 450 to 600 acres.

---

[1] *C.N.* nos. 513–14. In Swa. fo. 249r–v, a tenant remitted his rights 'in terra que fuit Willelmi Witun sacerdotis quam idem W. elemosinarie Burgi pro salute anime sue legavit'. This is also assart land, for William of Upton granted the almonry four acres 'sub Estwode que iacent proxime essartis quas elemosinaria tenet de feudo Willelmi Witun' (Swa. fo. 227r). Further references to William's former property are in Swa. fos. 229r, 234r.

[2] *C.N.*, nos. 12, 50, 111–12, 114. *C.N.*, no. 27, a grant by Berengar and his brother of two acres 'in assartis', must come hard after the actual clearance, and be dated to the early part of the century.

[3] Surveys, fo. 183v.

[4] For the assarts of Richard of Scotendon see Appendix A(5), nos. 31, 54, 63, 65, 67; and for Warin and Roger of Pecham, nos 44, 73. *Swynstibbing* and *Higgeneyestibbing* occur in the *C.N.*, nos. 97, 99, 109. For William of Higgeney see Appendix A(5), no. 74; he had a house in Peterborough (Swa. fo. 179v). The Scotendon family were freeholders of some substance, with quite a large amount of property in the town of Peterborough, and land in Glinton and Paston. See the note to *C.N.*, no. 281, and also Swa. fos. 213v–214r, Franceys, p. 425, and *Curia Regis Rolls*, XI, no. 1703.

So far as can be gathered from these sources, the work of clearance started to gather pace again in the mid-twelfth century, and was at its peak in the period 1175 to 1225. By the 1250s the movement appears to be running down. The acquisitions of *c.* 1275 in the sacrist's registers seem not to be the assarts of the previous generation, but rather consolidated holdings from assarts made earlier. The *Carte Nativorum* also, showing transactions in free land in the second half of the thirteenth century, does not suggest that any of the holdings transferred were the creation of that period. These comments apply to the Soke of Peterborough.

Further from the abbey, in the Rockingham Forest, where the forest was deeper, and the abbey's control more spasmodic, the picture seems slightly different. At the end of the twelfth century the work of clearance appears less advanced. Perhaps in consequence, it continued for a good deal longer – to the beginning of the fourteenth century and perhaps beyond. Land was being cleared both at Cottingham and at Biggin Grange at the time of the earliest account rolls.

The forest eyres of Henry II show that the abbey was assarting from Oundle in 1163 and 1167.[1] A generation later, in the charter of 1189, it had confirmed to it an assart of 400 acres at Oundle.[2] This is the grange of Novum Locum, which in thirteenth century and later records is called La Biggin or Biggin Grange. It is described as the foundation of Abbot Benedict (1177–93):[3]

He also built Novum Locum, which was a purpresture made by Fulk of Lisours, the chief forester, on the abbey manor of Oundle. He obtained it in a case against William of Lisours. All that pertained to Novum Locum, namely nine carucates of land and the woods of Sywardeshawe and Frendeshawe, and all the rights of the church in that area, he either vigorously retained or else justly recovered by law or force of arms – for many saw the force of his arms in this transaction.

Fulk of Lisours was forester from the beginning of Henry II's reign;[4] and both he and his son were very reluctant to abandon the area which they had begun to clear.[5] These entries need to be interpreted, for it is unlikely that the abbey had cleared 400 acres in

[1] *Pipe Roll 9 Henry II*, p. 37; *Pipe Roll 13 Henry II*, p. 120.
[2] Swa. fo. 47r–v.
[3] Sparke, pp. 99–100.
[4] *The Great Rolls of the Pipe for the Second, Third and Fourth Years of the Reign of King Henry the Second, 1155–1158*, ed. J. Hunter (Rec. Com., 1844), p. 42.
[5] William of Lisours renounced his rights in this property in a final concord of March 1190, and was given 20 marks: Swa. fo. 173v.

ten years. What it probably did was establish this substantial clearing as a demesne manor directly farmed.[1] Sixty-six acres of meadow were bought in order to provide pasture for the plough beasts.[2] A large number of pasture rights had to be extinguished, but otherwise there is no evidence that this grange expanded by the purchase of free tenures.[3] These were virgin acres, and their clearance continued apace. In 1209 the regarders presented a further 'old assart' of eighty acres at Novum Locum, two-thirds of it sown with oats, the rest with wheat.[4] By the end of John's time the abbey must have cleared at least five hundred acres, and probably a good deal more. Agreements about noval tithes show the process continuing. In 1225 the rector of Oundle established his rights to tithes on lands cleared after 1215,[5] and in 1239 the rector of Benefield renounced any rights 'in decimis ultimi assarti in Syuuardeshauue quod nunc primo de avena seminatum erat'.[6] Shortly afterwards the regarders presented thirty and a half acres in the same place.[7] By the mid-century the pace seems conspicuously slower, but still in the early fourteenth century the accounts show assarts being made from the forest.[8] Biggin Grange was the abbey's largest manor, comprising at least a thousand acres by the late thirteenth century.[9] A vineyard was established here in 1308, and clerk who wrote the 1310 account decorated the heading for its entry with a vine.[10]

---

[1] This would be the suggestion of an interesting document, which records the gifts and purchases of a rich monk, Godman, in the last quarter of the twelfth century (Swa. fo. 272r–v). At Novum Locum he apparently bought oxen for seven ploughs, seed corn for a year, and gave a year's wages for the *famuli*.

[2] Swa. fo. 208v; the cost was 18 marks, and the land was held in fee-farm for 20s a year. The rent was faithfully paid by the bailiffs in the vacancy of 1210–14: *Pipe Roll 12 John*, p. 216; *Pipe Roll 13 John*, p. 271.

[3] 'Quieta clamacio multorum tenencium de communa pastura ibidem habetur set non registratur': Pytchley, fo. 95r. The only tenant recorded as renouncing rights in this area was Geoffrey Crassus (Swa. fo. 237r); perhaps related to this is a charter granting him 20 acres in Oundle (*C.N.*, no. 507, from 1194–9).

[4] P.R.O. E. 32/249, m. 11r.

[5] Swa. fo. 202r; the abbey gave him another parcel of land, Swa. fo. 97r.

[6] Swa. fo. 202v. On the subject of noval tithes see G. Constable, *Monastic Tithes from their Origins to the Twelfth Century* (Cambridge, 1964), pp. 105–6.

[7] P.R.O. E. 32/67, m. 12; *Chr.P.*, p. 138.

[8] The following entries occur in the 1307–8 a/c: 'in 14 acris in Frendeshawe assartandis ad terram faciendam 28s. In 3 quarentenis et 8 perticatis fossati faciendis circa Frendeshawe 29s. 4d. In uno vinario faciendo 2s.' (Fitzwilliam A/C Roll 233, m. 24d).

[9] In 1294 around 500 acres were sown, and around 400 acres leased out. Allowing for about 250 acres fallow this would give a figure of *c.* 1150 acres (Rockingham Compotus – Biggin Grange).

[10] Fitzwilliam A/C Roll 2389, m. 21r; see note 8 above.

Cottingham and Great Easton, on either side of the Northampton-shire–Leicestershire border, were contiguous manors and will be considered together. As at Oundle, the abbey paid fines for asserting in both places at the forest eyres of Henry II.[1] They are also mentioned in the charter of 1189.[2] But, unlike at Oundle, no retrospective grant was included, so that perhaps the main work of clearance in this area was only just beginning. In 1215 the disafforestation charter for the Soke carried with it license to assart a hundred acres at Cottingham and Great Easton.[3] This grant presumably was retrospective; certainly the work was completed by 1221, when the land was measured, and 107 acres found.[4] In the second quarter of the century abbot Walter was credited with clearing two carucates at Great Easton.[5] It is perhaps significant that in Swaffham's chronicle, Robert of Lindsey (1214–22) was the clearer and engrosser of the Soke, while Walter of St Edmund's (1233–45) was more remembered for his good works in the manors around the Rockingham Forest.[6] Rather more than at Oundle, though clearly less than in the Soke, there is the suggestion that the abbey was engrossing some free holdings. Certainly at Cottingham woodland was bought up for asserting. Thus part of Croppeshawe was bought between 1214 and 1222, while between 1233 and 1245 Geoffrey Wachet sold to the abbey, 'totam terram meam in Cropeshauue ... iacentem inter assartum domini abbatis quod vocatur Cropeshauue et viam que vocatur Prestgravesrode'.[7] For Great Easton also there are sundry purchases of woodland and agreements over rights of common.[8] As at Oundle, there is record of some activity at least until the early fourteenth century.[9]

By the middle of the thirteenth century, then, the movement of colonisation had ceased in the Soke, though it continued at a reduced pace in the manors around the Rockingham Forest. Woodland,

[1] *Pipe Roll 9 Henry II*, pp. 32, 36; *Pipe Roll 13 Henry II*, pp. 118, 162.
[2] Swa. fo. 47r–v.   [3] Swa. fos. 51r–52r.
[4] *Rot. Litt. Claus.*, I, 462; the abbey paid rent on the extra seven acres for the rest of the century (B. M. Egerton MS. 2733, fo. 178v).
[5] Sparke, p. 120.
[6] *Ibid.* pp. 108–20.
[7] Swa. fos. 234v, 183r–v.
[8] In 1239 the prior of Bradley and 'all the freemen of the neighbouring townships' remitted any rights they had in the abbey's 'parcum clausum et boveriam et assarta sua', in return for a confirmation of their rights of common in Great Easton: Swa. fos. 198v–199r.
[9] At Cottingham in 1286 the abbey paid for $8\frac{1}{2}$ acres of assart, and also for a *frussura* of 12 acres 'versus Rockingham' (*Chr.P.*, p. 138); in the 1300–1 a/c payment was made to a boy 'custodiente assartum versus castrum' (Fitzwilliam A/C Roll 2388, m. 16d.).

once so expendable, now becomes a very carefully guarded com-
modity indeed. The random sale of woodland was a grievance by
the mid-century, and it remained so for the rest of the middle
ages.[1] Among the constitutions of abbot William Hotot in 1248
there is the promise not to sell woodland without the consent of
the convent.[2] Fifty years later the chronicler praised abbot William
Woodford for saying that he would never sell woodland without
making a substantial charge, 'for he dared not use up the treasure
of his church'.[3] Complaints of the sale of woodland occur frequently in the fifteenth-century visitation records.[4] At least on this
estate, the movement from pasture to arable would appear to have
reached its limit by the end of the thirteenth century. By then, what
reclamation did take place was largely for pasture.[5]

That the fen frontier is considered after the forest frontier, therefore, is not just a reflexion of the smaller documentation; rather
because fen reclamation seems to have become more active as forest
reclamation declined. Yet the information on this second frontier
remains meagre. Peterborough was on the western edge of the peat
fenlands:[6] 'in them ploughing was difficult and undesirable. Until
the coming of the "drainers" of the seventeenth and eighteenth
centuries they formed the great pastures of the neighbourhood,
providing sustenance for many poor cottagers, and though far from
the evil condition which outsiders imagined them to possess, they
were subject to periodic freshes from the upland, and liable to flood
the arable.' The evidence would seem to show exactly this. There
was some reclamation for small holdings, but it was limited. The
greater part of the reclamation was for pasture.

[1] The Pipewell chronicler early in the fourteenth century severely criti-
cised the most recent abbots, who had been driven by debt to part with
their woodland on all sides. By contrast, he claimed, when the abbey was
first founded the monks and *conversi* tended the woodland as a mother
cares for her only son, letting no day pass without planting trees on the
land which they had bought (*Monasticon*, v. 434–7). It is remarkable to
find this Cistercian house, which could only have survived through land
clearance, presenting its twelfth-century history in so romantic a fashion.
[2] Swa. fo. 107r.
[3] Sparke, p. 152.
[4] In the visitation of 1446–7 this theme constantly recurs. The prior and
six others complained that the abbot was being over-prodigal with his
woodland, in the East and West woods of Peterborough, and at Fiskerton
in Lincolnshire: *Visitations of Religious Houses in the Diocese of Lincoln*, III
(Lincs Rec. Soc., 21, 1929), ed. A. Hamilton Thompson, pp. 287–96.
[5] M. M. Postan ,'Village Livestock in the Thirteenth Century', *Econ.H.R.*
2nd ser., XV (1962), 219–49. Note also Hallam's figures for South Lincolnshire in the thirteenth and sixteenth centuries: *Settlement and Society*,
pp. 195–6.
[6] *Ibid.* p. 2.

The manor of Eye is not recorded in *Domesday*, and probably it was then one of the appendages of Werrington.[1] Its development may be traced from the two sets of surveys. In 1125 there were thirteen half-virgaters here, and a couple of cowherds.[2] This in fact is a small fen colony. A century later there were fifteen full virgaters at Eye, together with twelve men with small holdings, and a cowherd.[3] In the accounts of around 1300 the twelve small-holders were classified as 'old cottars', and there were a further nineteen 'new cottars'.[4] These cottars' holdings can only have been gained from the fen, which would suggest that the work of reclamation had continued steadily. The same point would seem to appear from the figures for meadowland, although these are much more difficult to interpret. *Domesday* records no meadowland. In 1300 there was at least four hundred acres, and the place names of part of this suggest recent reclamation.[5]

The evidence for the manor of Glinton is of a similar kind. In the 1231 survey there were twenty-five small-holders there, who were described as cottars.[6] In the survey a century earlier there had been none at all.[7] *Domesday* records a hundred acres of meadow; in 1300 there were 165 acres sold – among them $9\frac{1}{2}$ acres in *le Newedik* and 40 in *le Inham*.[8] What was sold was surplus capacity, and there would have been many more acres in demesne. Werrington at the same time had 27 acres in *le Inham* and 42 acres in *le Newefrithede*.[9] Both Glinton and Werrington Inhams can be dated to before 1245.[10] We must think in terms of landlord and of peasant reclamation taking place right through this period, but there is not the material to provide any precise indication of chronology.

Within this area to the north and east of Peterborough there were two buildings which were described as 'granges'.[11] Oxney is

---

[1] *D.B.*, I, fo. 221b.   [2] *Chr.P.*, p. 165.   [3] Surveys, fo. 185r–v.

[4] Fitzwilliam A/C Roll 2388, m. 2d–m. 3r. The 'old cottars' owed nine days' work a year, while the 'new cottars' only owed three days' work at harvest time. The pattern of occupancy is a different thing altogether.

[5] *Ibid.*–$33\frac{1}{2}$ acres in the *Newemedwe* and 62 acres in the *Newefrithede*.

[6] Surveys, fos. 192v–193r.

[7] *Chr.P.*, pp. 162–3.

[8] *D.B.*, I, fo. 221b; Fitz. A/C Roll 2388, m. 7d–m. 8r.

[9] *Ibid.* m. 7r.

[10] Between 1233 and 1245 William Blakeman was given 'duas acras prati in Witheringtona Innome propinquiores Glintona Innome': Swa. fo. 239r. 'Inham' is a common name for assarted land: *P.N. Soc. Northants*, p. 246; Darby, *Medieval Fenland*, pp. 50–1; Hallam, *Settlement and Society*, p. 57.

[11] For monastic granges see the excellent survey of Colin Platt, *The Monastic Grange in Medieval England* (London, 1969), although his gazetteer unfortunately does not list sites in this region.

first described in the list of Ethelwold's purchases, when it was an island within the fen:[1]

The amount of woodland and open country and meadow at Oxney is 25 acres by measure, and outside the island 60 pieces of land which amount to 30 acres, and in the wood outside every third tree.

In 1125 it was clearly part of the vaccary at Eye, itself a colony. Its only inhabitant was a cowherd, his stock twenty-three cattle.[2] It is difficult to decide when this may be formally called a 'grange'; its establishment may not long have preceded the grant of a fair in 1249.[3] The other grange, Northolm, was not founded until the early fourteenth century. In 1304 and 1305 Abbot Godfrey was described as creating 'the manor of Northolm where no manor had been before, for it had lain as pasture. He also enclosed the meadow of Crane-more, which contained over two hundred acres of land.'[4] At the same time Professor Hallam has shown very clearly that such granges might actually be 'founded' up to a century after the enclosure of the fen in which they lay. And he has shown also that such colonisation on the part of the landlord very often represents the engrossing of previous peasant clearance.[5] They thus follow the pattern of the forest granges whose establishment has already been considered.

This material presents no single pattern for the estate. To the important question of which particular groups were engaged in reclamation, at which times, it provides no single answer. Rather it shows a different picture for each area, and observations have been made area by area, as far as the material allows. One question, raised at the beginning of the chapter, has not yet been tackled. This concerns the part played by the landlord, in this case the abbey of Peterborough, in the work of reclamation. Is it true, as Duby suggests, that 'because of the decisive part which the lords played, reclamation reflects a profound change in the pyschological attitude of the aristocracy'?[6] The difficulty here lies in separating the peasants from their lords. Landlord assarts were recorded in the Soke in Stephen's reign. At the same time the abbey was confirming

[1] Robertson, *Anglo-Saxon Charters*, p. 81.
[2] *Chr.P.*, p. 165.
[3] *Cal. Charter R. 1226–57*, p. 344.
[4] Sparke, p. 156; *P.N. Soc. Northants*, p. 234. The abbey was granted a fair here in 1306, *Cal. Charter R. 1300–26*, p. 66.
[5] *Settlement and Society*, pp. 35ff, 103. *Cf.* the establishment of a grange in Thorney Fen shortly after this date: Darby, *Medieval Fenland*, p. 50.
[6] Duby, *Rural Economy*, p. 72.

a freehold assart in Paston. In the forest eyres, in forest charters, the abbey and its knights and its freeholders invariably occur together. But between area and area they can be separated. In the Rockingham Forest, most conspicuously in the creation of Biggin Grange, landlord enterprise certainly was decisive, although sorting out the relative parts played by Peterborough and Fulk of Lisours in the foundation is more difficult. In Paston, on the other hand, the successors of the *Domesday* sokemen are assarting vigorously in the second half of the twelfth century, and the abbey's work in this area only adds cohesion and a certain amount of impetus to their enterprise. From here, on the southern borders of the Danelaw, assarting appears much more clearly as 'a small man's enterprise'. The abbey's activity changed colour to suit the countryside.

5 The Endowment of the Obedientiaries

Shortly after the Conquest the convent became established as a body separate from the abbot, and a number of departments emerged with separate responsibilities and separate endowments. The first sign of the split, here as elsewhere, comes in the reign of Henry I.[1] A charter from between 1107 and 1115 records an agreement made before the bishop of Lincoln and the abbot of Peterborough, between the monks of Peterborough and the abbey knights.[2] The knights were to give two-thirds of their tithes to the sacristy, and on their death a third of their goods towards their burial. The monks were a party to the agreement, the abbot witnessed it; this would seem to imply a firm division between the abbot's part and the convent's part at this time. There is a more explicit reference from 1117, when Pytchley was granted to Geoffrey Ridel for £4 a year – '40s. videlicet ad opus monasterii, et 40s. ad opus abbatis'.[3]

The reason for the division is difficult to determine. 'The primary cause', according to Professor Knowles, 'was the feudalization of the abbot's position'.[4] Spoliation during vacancies, it is suggested, should have been at least limited by this new expedient. Yet later it provided little protection, and it is difficult to believe that so naive an assumption was solely or even chiefly responsible for a change of this magnitude. This was, however, a time for churchmen to see divisions where before they had seen none. At exactly this time, under the influence of the reformed papacy, men were coming to separate the spiritual and secular functions of episcopal and abbatial office. Further, it was a period when the largest lay estates were subject to some measure of fragmentation. Like developments may well have come to give the convent the beginnings of autonomy. At the same time tithes came to be regarded as spiritualities, and the knights lost control over them.[5] For the abbey this was a major windfall. The poor documentation of the period may easily conceal

---

[1] Knowles, *Monastic Order*, pp. 404–6.
[2] Franceys, p. 147; printed in *Peterborough Local Administration*, ed. W. T. Mellows (Northants Rec. Soc., IX, 1939), p. 200.
[3] P.B.C., fo. 25r.
[4] Knowles, *Monastic Order*, p. 405.
[5] On the wider issues here see Constable, *Monastic Tithes from their Origins to the Twelfth Century*, pp. 83–98.

what was probably the most valuable single addition to the monastery's resources in post-Conquest times. What resistance there was
from the knights, most of it from Lincolnshire, was over by the
mid-century. At the dedication of Thurlby church in 1112 a knight
of Benceline de la Mare got her permission to grant his tithes to
the church, 'just as his peers did'. It possibly took a less spiritual
experience to bring round Guy Maufe, who 'in the year in which
king Stephen was captured' (1141) gave the abbey 'the tithes which
he had for long forcibly withheld'.[1]

The most important department was the sacristy, first mentioned
around 1100, and fully established by second quarter of the twelfth
century. Its initial endowment comprised the tithes of the knights
of the Soke, a number of churches, and a small amount of rent.[2]
Between 1132 and 1155 abbot Martin added to this the demesne
manor of Pilsgate,[3] the church of Castor,[4] and rents from a large
number of freeholders in and around Paston. A bull of Eugenius III
confirmed the sacristy's possessions in almost identical terms.[5] By
the middle of the century the sacristy was well established, and
several of the mid-century charters are concerned with its purchases.[6] The churches granted to the sacristy were mainly outside
the Soke, while the rents of freeholders were all within it. Pilsgate
and the area around Paston saw the sacristy's main expansion.[7] The
Pilsgate demesne was consolidated by the purchase of land and rent

[1] P.B.C., fos. 27r, 28r.
[2] Swa. fos. 99v–100r; printed in *Peterborough Local Administration*, pp.
200–1. There is a fuller list of the sacristy's rents, probably dating from
rather later, in glosses to Swa. fos. 17v–18r (and from there printed in
Hugh Candidus, pp. 171–2), but this does not distinguish the stages in
the endowment, and implies that it was all the work of abbot Martin.
[3] For some reason the abbey thought it necessary to obtain a confirmation
of this manor from Stephen (*Regesta*, III, 659), which may indicate
disputed title, and provide an additional reason for its grant to the
sacristy.
[4] The church had been granted back to the abbey in 1133 (P.B.C., fos.
25v–26r.)
[5] *Hugh Candidus*, pp. 116–18. The authenticity of this bull has been queried
by Douglas (*E.H.R.*, LXIV (1949), 538), but the difficulties of interpreting
these early feudal charters are not of themselves grounds for suspicion.
[6] In 1145 the sacrist bought the land of Aswart in Peterborough, 'ad opus
ecclesie et ministerium secretarii' (P.B.C., fo. 27r). There are other grants
to the sacristy *Ibid.* fos. 28r (*c.* 1150), 28v (1154), 28v–29r (1166).
[7] For the period up to the mid-century the main group of sacristy charters
will be found in Swa. fos. 177r–187r, and there are a few charters from
the third quarter of the century *Ibid.* fos. 160r–170v. A larger selection
of the sacristy's charters, and a more useful one since it includes the full
witness lists, is found in the early fifteenth-century sacrist's register. This
is now split into two: (1) Franceys; (2) B. M. Cotton MS. Nero, C.vii.
A guide to the contents of each of these volumes will be found in *Pytchley*,
pp. xxxvi, 156–7.

there and in Bainton, and at Pilsgate the sacrist held his court.[1] Paston, from being initially a complex of rents, had been constituted a demesne manor by the end of the thirteenth century.[2] The sacrist, along with the other obedientiaries, had property in the town of Peterborough, the bulk of which was acquired between *c.* 1190 and *c.* 1220.[3]

The almonry, the second of the two major departments, was the last department to be established. Initially its endowment seems to have comprised the church of Paston, granted between 1155 and 1175.[4] Abbot Benedict (1177–93) added the church of Maxey, two-thirds of the tithes of Paston, and a small amount of land and rent. Later, apparently, the same abbot granted rents from property in Peterborough and Lincoln, from the Southorpe fee, and from the Gargate fee in Warmington. The two fees of Sutton were granted to it in 1189, and this for a century was the almoner's only demesne manor. Before 1199 it acquired a further portion of the Gargate fee, and some land in Clapton, a village contiguous with Warmington. By 1210 abbot Akarius had added more property in Peterborough, and a small amount of assart land from Eastwood.[5]

With this initial endowment the geographical location of the almoner's property – his sphere of influence as it were – was fixed. On the basis of this, however, there was to be a fair degree of expansion and consolidation, especially during the first half of the century. It concentrated on the same areas.[6] A virgate in Sutton was first leased and then bought from Margaret of Gidney at a total cost of £24. There were several exchanges of land in the same area, and half a dozen small purchases. Ten further charters show the acquisition of just under sixteen acres in the neighbouring manor of Maxey. The purchase of land in Eastwood, which was confirmed in Akarius's charter, was only one of several in this area at the turn of the century; in five charters the almonry acquired twenty-eight

---

[1] Swa. fo. 179r.
[2] See above, pp. 67–8.
[3] Franceys, pp. 1–38.
[4] *Hugh Candidus*, pp. 129–30; on the endowment of the almonry see also Brooke, *William Morton*, pp. xix–xxv.
[5] The information in this paragraph is taken from the following charters. (1) Charter of abbot Benedict to the almonry (Swa. fos. 101v–102r); this does not mention Sutton, and is probably from before 1189. (2) King John's charter for the almonry, 1199 (*Early Northants Charters*, pp. 46–7). (3) Charter of abbot Akarius (Swa. fos. 102v–103r).
[6] The main block of charters relating to the almonry is in Swa. fos. 248r–262r. The later almonry register has not survived; *cf.* Brooke, *William Morton*, p. xxxi. References are given only for the more important of the documents mentioned in this paragraph.

acres in Eastfield, while another three charters granted unspecified amounts of land. A couple of tenancies were bought in Marholm, one of them for a couple of corrodies and four shillings a year.[1] A small sub-tenancy of the St Medard fee, a couple of messuages and twenty-four acres of land, was bought between 1245 and 1250.[2] There are eighteen charters relating to purchases in the town of Peterborough.

Outside the Soke of Peterborough, the almonry's main interests were in Warmington and Clapton. It was the only department actively engaged in the land market outside the Soke. A virgate was bought from Robert Gargate sometime in the 1180s,[3] and a further virgate and a half from the same fee before the end of the century.[4] Another half dozen transactions represent the consolidation of this property. From the Clapton family the abbey acquired two virgates, one of them described as 'large', thirty acres of arable and some meadow.[5] The main endowment of the almonry may therefore be dated to the last quarter of the twelfth and the first quarter of the thirteenth centuries. There were smaller purchases of land after this. The needs of the next half-century were met by the grant of Gunthorpe in 1277, and the purchase of related property, although this manor was later granted to the treasury.[6]

In the 1125 surveys the manors of Fiskerton and Collingham were assigned *ad vestitum monachorum*, an arrangement which may well go back to *Domesday*, and when a chamberlain's office was established these formed its initial endowment.[7] Abbot Martin confirmed these manors, and would have added further resources had he lived longer.[8] In fact, there was no increase in endowment until early in the thirteenth century, when Abbot Akarius added the manor of Thurlby, 'for the establishment of £40 a year is quite inadequate

---

[1] Swa. fo. 252r.
[2] Swa. fos. 261v–262r.
[3] Swa. fo. 260r–v; the abbey paid four marks for this.
[4] Swa. fo. 260r; cf. *Pytchley*, pp. 154–5.
[5] The main archive here is Swa. fos. 249v–250v. A final concord relating to one of these virgates makes it contain 150 acres (*C.N.* 502), but this can hardly be so. At some point along the line 'viginti septem acras terre et dimidiam' (Swa. fo. 249v) seems to have become 'septies viginti acras terre et decem' (*C.N.* 502). The 'large' virgate was not this but the other, and contained 45 acres: Swa. fo. 260r. The matter is mentioned lest any student of field systems attempts to foster this particular cuckoo.
[6] Brooke, *William Morton*, p. xxi.
[7] *Chr.P.*, p. 166. That a manor was described in *Domesday* as being *ad victum* or *ad vestitum monachorum* was more often than not, however, an added support to a disputed title (thus Aldwincle, above, p. 33, and Raftis, *Ramsey*, pp. 35–6).
[8] *Hugh Candidus*, pp. 122–3, 173.

for the responsibilities of the chamber'.[1] Abbot Robert of Lindsey increased this further. In place of the variable rent from Thurlby, which had proved difficult to collect 'because of the multiplicity of tenancies', he granted the fixed sum of ten marks.[2] He later granted a further ten marks from Fiskerton, Collingham and Scotter.[3] In the next abbacy the chamber was given another ten marks, making ninety marks in all.[4] The endowment of this office was thus increased by exactly a half in the first quarter of the thirteenth century.

The next endowment came a quarter of a century later, between 1246 and 1249, when the manor of Northborough was granted to it.[5] It was only with the late grant of this manor, his last major endowment, that the chamberlain acquired any sort of lordship. By this time the sacristy and the almonry had been actively engaged on the land market for the best part of a century. Perhaps less activity was necessary: the monks were probably more sensitive about clothes than about candles. A gloss to the Northborough charter, indeed, shows in interesting fashion their detailed solicitude, as well as demonstrating the way in which such changes in endowment were made. It starts by saying that the abbot and convent met in some 'neutral place' to discuss the needs of the abbey, goes on to state that the brethren are frequently less well clothed and shod than is proper, and finishes by calculating the precise value of Northborough in garments of various sorts and in footwear.[6]

The initial endowment of the cellarer was the manors of Fletton and Alwalton, opposite Peterborough on the Huntingdonshire bank of the Nene. As with the office of chamberlain, it was probably created in the mid-twelfth century,[7] and it did not receive any further endowment until the early thirteenth century. The major increase here was in the abbacy of Robert of Lindsey, when there were three grants during a period of eight years (1214–22).[8] The first charter granted the manor of Gosberton and two mills. The

---

[1] Swa. fos. 103v–104r.
[2] Swa. fos. 105v–106r. The chamber certainly had had no profit from Thurlby in the intervening vacancy: the 1210 Pipe Roll records payment of the original £40 only (*Pipe Roll 12 John*, p. 215).
[3] Swa. fo. 105r.
[4] Swa. fo. 106r.
[5] Swa. fo. 108r. This was a sub-tenancy of the Torpel fee, and had been acquired and partly consolidated during the previous abbacy.
[6] Swa. fo. 108r.
[7] Abbot Martin (1132–55) is recorded as having wished to increase its endowment (*Hugh Candidus*, pp. 122–3).
[8] Swa. fos. 104v–105v.

second granted the 'aids' from Fletton and Alwalton,[1] and a wide variety of rents and dues – £8 from the abbot's chamber, rent charges on the manors of Tinwell and Castor, two mills in Paston, and fisheries in Whittlesey Mere and elsewhere. At the same time the abbot promised to increase the endowment still further should the number of monks grow beyond seventy-two.[2] When after 1216 the number increased to eighty, a further charter transferred to the cellary the bulk of the property recently assarted and acquired in the Soke. This, it was estimated, would provide fifty measures of wheat, sixty of barley, and eighty of oats. The history of this department shows most clearly of all the continuing adjustment to changing circumstances, and the principles on which it operated. New monks had to be supported by new land: abbot Robert's charter is a very precise logistical exercise.

The heads of the two largest and most outward-looking departments, the sacrist and the almoner, acted with a considerable degree of independence. They seem to have been individually responsible for consolidating their own particular areas, and for purchasing their own land. The latter practice may have been unusual, but the Peterborough charters are quite explicit:[3]

pro hac mei donacione ego Normannus recepi de pecunia ecclesie predicte de Burgo per manum sacriste 20 solidos esterlingorum.

pro hac mea clamancia Alexander de Hauderness tunc sacrista eiusdem ecclesie in magna necessitate mea mihi dedit coram multis viris discretis et fidedignis 40 solidos esterlingorum.

pro hac autem abiuracione dedit mihi Simon de Kancia tunc sacrista 10 solidos et unam summam siliginis.

pro hac autem quieta clamacione et relaxacione Ricardus de Folckingham tunc elemosinarius unam summam frumenti mihi caritatem contulit.

Independent purchasing very likely goes back to the original foundation of the departments. In 1145 the sacrist redeemed a mortgage for 42s, 'by the counsel of Martin the abbot of the same

---

[1] Up to this time it must be presumed that the cellary had received the agricultural profits of this manor, but not tallage or the other profits of lordship.

[2] The community had grown slightly during the previous century, for in 1125 the number of monks was 60 (*Chr.P.*, p. 167). We are told that abbot Martin increased the number by 20 (*Hugh Candidus*, p. 173), but the existing number was not stated.

[3] Franceys, pp. 105–6, 110–11, 17–18; Swa. fo. 210v. Numerous other charters have similar clauses: for the sacristy, Franceys, p. 13, Swa. fos. 167v, 177r, 205v, 212v; for the almonry, Swa. fos. 221r, 234r–v, 254v, 260v.

church and of the senior brethren'.[1] By the end of the century there
is no mention of the abbot's consent,[2] and the autonomy of each
obedientiary is very clear. In a case from John's time the sacrist
even appeared in his own right before the *curia regis*, and not as the
abbot's attorney. He was forced to withdraw before the case was
concluded, 'because he could not proceed without the abbot', but
it must have been the common law, not canon law, which gave him
pause.[3] So much independence was perhaps unusual, and certainly
it was against the Rule.

The first evidence of visitation in our period, and the only set of
injunctions to survive from it, come from bishop Hugh of Wells in
1231.[4] The injunctions are in no sense concerned with administrative reorganisation, but rather show the points of tension between
abbot and convent, and suggest that if anything departmental
autonomy and not abbatial autocracy was the chief problem. The
abbot was henceforth not to contract debts with Jews or other
usurers without the consent of the convent, nor was he to pledge
any of the goods of the abbey in respect of such loans. The document soon gets onto more specific matters, and the chief disputes
seem to have been between the abbot and the sacrist. Here there was
compromise. The tallage from Pilsgate manor, the sacrist's chief
profit from secular lordship, was diverted towards building operations of the abbot's choosing. But the sacrist's right to the chattels
of deceased knights of the honour was left largely intact, and his
responsibility for entertaining the abbot at Pilsgate was limited to a
moderate amount once a year. The injunctions continue:

Nonetheless he and all the other obedientiaries shall when asked give all
honour and reverence and aid to the abbot humbly and devotedly, from
the things pertaining to their offices both inside and outside the monastery. If an obedientiary should wish to convene any ecclesiastical or lay
person for acquiring or revoking the rights and goods of his office, he
shall do so at his own expense. And he shall do this only so far as is neces-

---

[1] P.B.C., fo. 27r. A reference to abbot Martin in the chronicle, 'multas
alias per se et per monachos suos adquisivit' (*Hugh Candidus*, p. 123),
gives the same impression.

[2] In just the same way, references to the lord's consent to the alienation
of knightly tenancies disappear in the second half of the twelfth century.

[3] *Pleas before the King or his Justices, 1198–1202*, I, ed. D. M. Stenton
(Selden Soc., LXVII, 1953), nos. 2384, 2840; *Rotuli Curie Regis* (Rec. Com.,
1835), II, 214.

[4] Swa. fo. 94r–v. *Cf.* C. R. Cheney, *Episcopal Visitation of Monasteries in
the Thirteenth Century* (1931), p. 14 and note. The text shows that the
visitation was conducted by the bishop in person.

sary, and shall in no way aggrandize himself, save with the abbot's counsel and the convent's approval.

In all this the strength of the obedientiaries is taken for granted, and from the bishop they got tacit recognition of their right to order their own affairs.

It would appear to have been only in 1248 that the central administrative organs of the abbey were reformed.[1] It was then ordained that two monk-wardens should be appointed, and two receivers to administer all the revenues from the abbot's estates. One of the receivers was to be a monk, the other one of the abbot's chaplains. The profits of the liberty were to be the responsibility of the monk, who was to account for what pertained to the king at the Exchequer. An annual balance sheet was to be presented. 'We seem to have here a system of centralized receipt and the offices of abbot's receiver and convent treasurer in embryo.'[2] The system of centralised receipt, however, does not seem to have lasted. It may be that it was 'premature': it may well be, on the other hand, that the ordinance was frustrated by a purely local set of circumstances.

It is noteworthy that the very quarter-century which saw most of the 'centralisation' in other monastic houses,[3] found Peterborough at its weakest, and its abbots in a vulnerable position. William Hotot, the abbot who issued the injunctions of 1248, was deposed in the following year, accused, if Matthew Paris is to be believed, of dilapidation and of gifts to his kinsmen.[4] His debts in 1248 were estimated at 411 marks.[5] The next abbot, John of Caux, who was for a time royal treasurer, left debts of over seven hundred marks.[6] Individual incompetence can be only a partial explanation for such

[1] Swa. fo. 107r–v, which gives the date; printed in Sparke, p. 126. For commentary see D. Knowles, *The Religious Orders in England*, I (1948), 58, and Brooke, *William Morton*, p. xxi. The glosses to Swaffham's cartulary link these ordinances with the 1231 injunctions of Hugh of Wells but seventeen years separates the documents and they have little in common.
[2] Brooke, *William Morton*, p. xxi note 2.
[3] The best survey of this is in R. A. L. Smith, 'The *Regimen Scaccarii* in English Monasteries', reprinted in his *Collected Papers*, ed. D. Knowles (London, 1947), pp. 54–73. *Cf.* also his *Canterbury Cathedral Priory* (Cambridge, 1943), pp. 14–28, and Knowles, *Religious Orders*, I, 55–63.
[4] *Matthaei Parisiensis Chronica Majora*, ed. H. R. Luard, V (Rolls Series, 57, 1880), 84–5. There may be another side to this story, for in 1248 he owed £120 to Richard of Hotot his brother (Vesp. E.22, fo. 41r).
[5] *Ibid.*
[6] Sparke, p. 132. John seems to have cut a poor figure both on the national scene (T. F. Tout, *Chapters in the Administrative History of Medieval England*, I (1920), 299), and within his own monastery; he was forced in his anniversary charter to apologise for the paucity of his endowment of the convent (Swa. fo. 32r; copied with patronising commentary into the chronicle, Sparke, pp. 130–2).

debt; undoubtedly able abbots who followed found themselves in even worse case. The burden of royal and papal taxation increased steadily towards the mid-century and thereafter.[1] In 1248, the abbot agreed that the convent should not be required to contribute to papal taxation unless they were specially mentioned in the grant of the tax; there had been no hint of such pressures in 1231.

Within a few months of Robert of Sutton's accession in 1263, the abbey became involved in the civil war of Henry III's reign.[2] Walter of Whittlesey's chronicle is highly eloquent on the house's misfortunes.[3] The knights of the honour, who were 'against the king at Northampton', claimed their lord had led them there. Whatever the truth of this, the abbot had to fine with the king on numerous occasions as proof of his loyalty. He paid for peace, he paid for love, he even paid 'for perfectly recovering his love'.[4] He also had to pay protection money to de Montfort, and to several other magnates. At the same time, the local gentry took the opportunity to confiscate several of the more distant demesne manors: Thurlby, Tinwell, Collingham, Fiskerton and Scotter.[5] The whole business brought very considerable strain, and the chronicle gives the enormous sum of £4324 18s 6d as the total of the abbey's payments on account of the war.[6] To keep afloat the abbot, on whom the burden of this 'extraordinary' expenditure fell, raised loans from merchants and exploited his most ready form of capital, his woodland.[7] Most significant here, he was forced to borrow heavily from the various obedientiaries. It is difficult to work out reliable figures from the chronicle, but certainly he must have borrowed at least £500 over the period, the greater part of it from the sacrist.[8] He left a debt of 3000 marks in 1274,[9] and his

---

[1] John of Caux had been required to pay 570 marks to the king and 540 marks to the pope: Swa. fo. 32r.

[2] The conflict is well brought out in its Northamptonshire setting in R. F. Treharne, 'The Battle of Northampton', *Northamptonshire Past and Present*, II (1954–9), 73–90.

[3] Sparke, pp. 134–42. *Cf.* Raftis, *Ramsey*, p. 115 note 66: if this was a period of 'disruption and loss in farm profits' at Ramsey, the chaos on the Peterborough estates must have been far greater.

[4] Sparke, pp. 135, 138, 139 ('pro amore eius perfecte recuperando').

[5] *Ibid.* pp. 136, 138–9.   [6] *Ibid.* p. 140   [7] *Ibid.* pp. 140–3.

[8] He obtained a loan of £13 6s 8d from the convent treasury (*Ibid.* p. 141), while in the cartulary there is a recognition of a loan of 80 marks from the convent in 1270, 'ad liberandum nos de manibus mercatorum' (Swa. fo. 32v). He seems to have obtained loans from each of the major obedientiaries, usually effected by these officers not taking up parts of their statutory endowment. Clearly in such a situation the power of the convent did not grow less.

[9] This is the figure given in the contemporary chronicle (*Chr.P.*, p. 20); Whittlesey gives it as 2000 marks (Sparke, p. 150).

successor was forced to postpone his arrival for a year as an economy measure.[1]

The 1248 injunctions were not taken very far. Weak and circumscribed abbots could do little against the powerful vested interests of the individual departments. An indication of this is provided by the history of the central treasury. If such an office was established in the mid-century, it certainly did not survive. A convent treasury on a smaller scale was established later, however, and for it a certain amount of charter material has survived. It was possibly created shortly before 1277, when it was granted the chief rent from the newly acquired manor of Gunthorpe.[2] After this, a large percentage of the small gifts and purchases of land, the acres which had once gone to the sacristy or the almonry, now came to the treasury.[3] This gave the treasurer a kind of 'reserve fund',[4] but there was nothing approaching a major reorganisation, and the independent position of the major obedientiaries remained secure.

It must be emphasised that the history of administrative reform in a house shows its *economic* position only to a very limited extent. The reforms were designed to remove any threats to the monastic discipline, and nothing more. This point comes out clearly when the history of reform at Peterborough is compared with that of the neighbouring house at Ramsey. What seems to have happened at Ramsey was that the problems of inflation and expansion of numbers came upon a community by no means either stable or well run. In consequence, around 1202, Hubert Walter issued a constitution for the house which effectively put all external affairs in the hands of two monks and a steward. And the endowment of the obedientiaries, which at Peterborough was provided for under the existing system without undue stress, demanded at Ramsey a large degree of reorganisation.[5] At Peterborough there was no change until the mid-

---

[1] He told the convent he was required at the Council of Lyons, and went off for the summer to the Isle of Wight (*Chr.P.*, p. 20).

[2] Swa. fo. 165r: initially 15 marks were allocated to the treasury, and 5 to the abbot's chamber. Whittlesey's statement that abbot Robert of Sutton borrowed £13 6s 8d from the 'tesaurarie conventus' in 1270–1 is possibly, but far from certainly, anachronistic (Sparke, p. 141).

[3] The last of the charters which were added on spare folios of Swaffham's cartulary, from *c.* 1270 to *c.* 1280, were beginning to record grants of this kind: Swa. fos. 162v, 163v.

[4] Brooke, *William Morton*, p. xxi note 2. R. A. L. Smith cited Peterborough as one of the abbeys where the word *scaccarium* came into general use in the late-thirteenth century (*Collected Papers*, p. 59). Only one mention of the word from this period has been found (Vesp. E.22, fo. 110v), and the reference is almost certainly to the building known as the abbot's chamber (Mellows, *Local Government*, pp. 132–3).

[5] Raftis, *Ramsey*, pp. 98–102.

century; then what was legislated for was not radical, and far more was attempted than was in fact achieved. For such reasons purely administrative changes are possibly the least rewarding aspect of the relations between abbot and convent.

The basic problem was how the monastery could survive, and even possibly expand, on the basis of fixed resources. The problem was particularly acute for the departments. The fragmentation of the monastery's resources between the abbot and the convent made for inflexibility, and was an added source of weakness in a time of rapid change. Initially it was spiritualities, above all tithes, that provided for the various departments that acquired a competence in the first half of the twelfth century. The smallest of the surviving demesne manors were also hived off, Pilsgate to the sacrist, Alwalton, Fletton and Gosberton to the cellarer. The more important departments also inherited fixed rent charges on some of the larger demesne manors.

Differently endowed, the abbot and convent had to react differently to the inflation of the late twelfth century. What happened to the abbot is well known – direct management and strong lordship (both of them equally important in the accounts of 1210–12) at least made up for the erosion of fixed rent incomes.[1] The departments were a good deal less strong; they had little lordship,[2] they were smaller, and founded on a motley of fixed rents, spiritual and secular. They were almost a new foundation within an established house, and had all the disadvantages of the new Benedictine foundations of the twelfth century.[3] They could only continue as they had begun. The greater part of Swaffham's cartulary is taken up with small charters of the period *c.* 1175 to *c.* 1225, and these gains went to the departments almost without exception. In their scale, and in their work of consolidation over a small area, the departments invite comparison with the abbot's knightly tenants. In this context the strength of the convent is less than surprising. The sacristy or the almonry, no less than the Hotot family of Clapton, was founded upon land, and had its own interests and its own traditions.

---

[1] See further below, pp. 145–6.
[2] The abbot held tenaciously to the profits of lordship in Pilsgate, and with Fletton and Alwalton alienated them a good deal later than the manor.
[3] R. W. Southern, *Western Society and the Church in the Middle Ages* (Harmondsworth, 1970), pp. 232–3.

6   'Carte Nativorum'

The market for freehold land has been considered above only insofar as the abbey itself was directly engaged in it. A document of unique value, however, the *Carte Nativorum*, makes it possible to study another facet of this market, one in which the abbey was engaged indirectly inasmuch as it claimed to control the property dealings of its villeins.[1] What follows in this chapter is not a complete analysis of the document. It attempts to present as fully as possible, however, the material on a number of issues which the document raises. I shall discuss first the abbey's attitude to the property dealings of its villeins, and then the nature and origins of the land transferred, the chief problem here being to decide whether or not this was customary land. The status and substance of the men active in the market are considered: how far and in what way were these the charters of villeins? I shall then move on from the document to consider some of the uses to which this land was put. This involves an examination of inheritance patterns, especially among the more prosperous sections of the villein community. The general problem is the relationship of this land to the network of customary tenures. Finally, I shall discuss land occupation alongside land ownership, and examine some evidence of property development. The cartulary at each point is considered alongside related texts, in particular the account rolls, which contain a good deal of supplementary information, and are indispensable for its proper study.

First, the attitude of the abbey administration to the land market. The document is a creation of the abbey, and so we have first of all to look through the abbey's eyes. Before examining any modern interpretation, it will be best to see what can be gained from the documents themselves.

A gloss to three of the charters is intended to explain how they

---

[1] *Carte Nativorum. A Peterborough Abbey Cartulary of the Fourteenth Century*, ed. C. N. L. Brooke and M. M. Postan (Northants Rec. Soc., XX, 1960). Professor Postan's section of the introduction to this volume is a wide-ranging and stimulating essay on the whole question of the peasant land market; some of its premises, however, are questioned in Paul R. Hyams, 'The Origins of a Peasant Land Market in England', *Econ. H.R.* 2nd ser., XXIII (1970), 18–31.

came to be included in the collection; it could as well serve for the rest.[1]

Item hic sunt tres carte per quas Willelmus et Willelmus nativi abbatis filii Willelmi filii Galfridi de Undele nativi eiusdem emerunt de liberis hominibus liberam terram et pratum in Undele, et que capte sunt in manu domini Ricardi abbatis anno eiusdem vicesimo, eo quod nativi sui ea adquisierunt, et postea eisdem tradita est, tenenda ad voluntatem domini, solvendo per annum eidem de novo redditu obolum.

This, in a short space, makes six points, all of which are important. (1) These men were the abbot's villeins; (2) the land they bought was free land, and (3) had been bought from free men. (4) It was therefore seized, and (5) subsequently re-granted to them to hold of the abbey at will. On its re-grant (6) they were charged an increment of rent. In all this the abbey's attitude would appear to be both clear and consistent. It insisted that villein transactions in free land be enrolled, and that when such land had been acquired by charter these charters be surrendered. At least theoretically these free tenancies were held at the lord's will; although it was not possible to carry the principle right through, and probably the main point thus guarded was that the rent was not a customary one. On entry to such land the tenant paid a fine, while on initial enrolment he invariably paid an 'increment of rent' or a 'new rent'.[2] Several entries emphasise that this land was outside the customary framework, and that thus its rent could be increased. It was therefore in the abbey's interests to keep the distinction between villein land and free land as clear as possible, and every relevant entry in the accounts makes this interest clear. Each of these points is considered in turn.

The fact of the surrender of charters is implied by the very existence of the cartulary, although this is only occasionally mentioned in the accounts. But in 1300–1 John Smith paid an increment of 1d for an acre of land which he had bought 'by a charter which remains in the abbey', while there are two similar entries in the fragment of account for the western group in 1294–5.[3] It is tempting to suggest

---

[1] *C.N.* 442.

[2] The phrases used are 'incrementum redditus' or 'novum redditus'. The principle is stated very clearly in the entry which follows: 'Et de 4d. de Isabella et Johanna filiabus Willelmi atte Kirkegate de incremento redditus 2 acrarum libere terre quas dictus Willelmus adquisivit. Ita quod quelibet acra solvet per annum 2d. cum redditu 1d. prius soluti pro eisdem' (Fitzwilliam A/C Roll 233, m. 9r).

[3] 'Per cartam que remanet in abbacia', Fitzwilliam A/C Roll 2388, m. 6r (= *C.N.* 154); 'per cartas que resident apud Burgum', Rockingham Compotus, under Great Easton (= *C.N.* 418–22); 'per tres cartas que sunt apud Burgum', Rockingham Compotus, under Oundle (= *C.N.* 439–41).

that on its more distant manors in 1294–5 the abbey was asserting a point that it had made rather earlier in the case of nearer manors. How much earlier it is impossible to say, for the compilation of a new rental in 1295–6 means that this information does not appear in later accounts.[1] But certainly by this date the surrender of charters and their collection at the abbey were well-established. There is some evidence to suggest that, within each section, series of charters were entered in the order in which they were seized.[2]

If charters were not surrendered and sales were discovered then the land was seized, since in theory it was forfeited to the lord.[3]

Item hic sunt quinque carte per quas Robertus Pacy de Eston . . . et Emma Godyer nativi abbatis de Burgo adquisiverunt 6 acras et dimidiam, et dimidiam rodam terre in Eston, sibi et heredibus suis . . . que quidem terra capta est in manu domini abbatis anno domini Ricardi abbatis decimo nono in plena curia tenta apud Eston anno supradicto.

Another of the important glosses in the cartulary amplifies the point that such lands were regranted to the tenant to hold at will: 'Memorandum quod hec est una carta Johannis filii Johannis Rose de Irtlingbur' (per quam) emit unam rodam et dimidiam terre arabilis, que capte sunt in manu domini eo quod nativus, et retradite sunt eidem Johanni tenende ad voluntatem domini.'[4] The question of tenancies at will is crucial to this discussion, for from it the other points follow. Clearly in the case of Robert Pacy the abbey is objecting to free land having been acquired hereditarily, by charters which contained the words 'sibi et heredibus suis'. 'We know what their meaning is – they imply enfranchisement and a freehold estate of inheritance.'[5] This is what made a charter 'vicious'.[6] The abbey had to insist on tenancy at will, for uncertainty of tenure was the nearest the law got to a conclusive proof of villeinage, and such clauses in charters, rather than the transactions themselves, threatened certainty. In objecting to them the abbey was asserting the principle

---

[1] The date is given in Fitzwilliam A/C Roll 2389, m. 18r; the rental has not survived.
[2] Of the Glinton archives listed in *C.N.*, p. xiv, nos. iv, v and vi follow one another in the *redditus assisus* section of the 1309–10 Glinton account roll (Fitzwilliam A/C Roll 2389, m. 8d–9r). This suggests that Glinton archives i–iii came in before the rental of 1295–6 was compiled.
[3] *C.N.* 424.
[4] *C.N.* 388.
[5] P. Vinogradoff, *Villainage in England* (Oxford, 1892), p. 71; see also P. R. Hyams, 'The Origins of a Peasant Land Market in England', pp. 24–5.
[6] *Court Rolls of Chalgrave Manor, 1278–1313*, ed. M. K. Dale (Beds Hist. Rec. Soc. 28, 1950), p. 43; cited *C.N.*, p. xliii.

that such land lay outside the network of customary tenures, and was held on quite different conditions. It could not be allowed to descend according to the same laws. This appears very clearly when the two forms of holding are juxtaposed in a single tenancy.[1]

Et de 16s. quadrante de Galfrido filio Radulphi Pridil pro relevio unius mesuagii 5 acrarum et dimidie terre et dimidie acre prati quondam predicti Radulphi. Et de 20s. de eodem pro 3 acris libere terre tenendis in tota vita sua quas pater eius adquisivit, solvendo per annum 1d. de novo redditu pro eisdem.

Et de 10s. de Johanne filio Augustini pro fine medietatis unius mesuagii et 3 acrarum terre que fuerunt Reginaldi filii Stephani. Et de 10s. de Galfrido Fraunceys et Emma uxore eius pro fine alterius medietatis dictorum mesuagii et terre, faciendo servicia et consuetudines. Et de 6s. 8d. de predictis Johanne, Galfrido et Emma pro tribus acris et 1 rode libere terre, tenendis ad terminum vite eorum pro 18d. per annum, quorum 15d. sunt de novo redditu. Basilia relicta Reginaldi filii Stephani capit de domino 1 acram libere terre tenendam ad terminum vite sue, et solvit 1d. de novo redditu, et nichil dat premanibus.

The abbey occasionally modified this position. Thus several of the entry fines for the larger archives of free land make no mention of holding at will: men like John of Walton of Eye and Simon le Western of Glinton leave entries of a distinctly more proprietary air.[2] But it was proprietary with reservations, for coupled with it was the insistence that the rent charged was uncertain, and liable to be changed every time the holding changed hands. For this reason the free land was kept distinct.[3]

Et de 4d. de incremento redditus 4 acrarum libere terre quas Robertus atte Strete et Agnes uxor eius tenent ad voluntatem domini que solebant reddere 8d. per annum.

Et de 10s. de Agnete relicta Thome de Eketon de fine pro 1 cotagio et 2 rodis terre ei pertinentibus et una acra dimidia et una roda libere terre et 3 acris et dimidia de sokagio, et solvet per annum 2d. de incremento redditus pro dicta libera terra.

Free land and customary land are invariably kept apart.[4]

---

[1] Fitzwilliam A/C Roll 2389, m. 9r, m. 7d.
[2] *Ibid.* m. 3d (quoted below, p. 114), m. 8d.
[3] *Ibid.* m. 8d; Fitzwilliam A/C Roll 2388, m. 8r.
[4] This is the distinction made by the documents. By customary land here I mean land held in villeinage, for the standard villein obligations. The term 'villein land', as used by Professor Postan, includes free land held in addition to customary holdings.

It would not seem that the land market on the Peterborough estate was connected with any blurring of the distinction between free and customary land. This distinction, we are rightly told by Professor Postan, 'so clear in theory was often blurred in practice',[1] and impressive evidence is quoted in support of this proposition. But estates differ, and at Peterborough it does not appear to have been so. A clear distinction, in fact, seems to have been the one basic principle to which, in a time of great mobility of property, the abbey administration clung. To discover why it clung to it we have only to look at the accounts; the abbey's reward for its solicitous care may be seen both in the fines for land and in the ever-increasing rent roll.[2] On each manor, in each account, the rent item grows steadily.[3]

It may not have been only financial considerations that lay behind this concern to keep free land and customary land apart. An interesting history may lie behind the diplomatic of the charters themselves. In these charters the principle of substitution instead of subinfeudation becomes established around the middle of Edward I's reign. At exactly this time the abbey administration begins to confiscate the charters, and to regrant the land on rather different terms. An effort to get behind the diplomatic to social change will provide no clear answers. The study of the law, however, is 'one of the best means that we have for estimating the social process'.[4] And it is not impossible that the abbey's confiscation of charters was in some way connected with the legal activities of Edward I's government.

The forms of *Quia Emptores* are reproduced in villein charters very quickly indeed after the statute. This perhaps shows not so much the quickness of any 'reaction' as that feudal society was a single entity; that Edwardian legislation tackled problems, common to each level of this society, which individuals were beginning to solve for themselves.[5] One consequence of this, relevant here, was

---

[1] *C.N.*, p. xliv.
[2] The entry fine, and an increase of rent, are invariably required on this estate. At Ramsey on the other hand, Professor Raftis concludes that fines were charged only where the lord's licence had not been obtained: 'no evidence has been found that the lord always exacted a licence fee with this permission' (*Tenure and Mobility*, p. 82).
[3] At Glinton the rent 'charge' based on the 1295–6 rental was £7 5s 2½d, while the total amount of rent collected in 1309–10, swelled by the extra rent for free land, was £9 2s 10¾d. Fitzwilliam A/C Roll 2389, m. 8d–9r.
[4] Vinogradoff, *Villainage in England*, p. 44.
[5] In the edition, charters with subinfeudation clauses are dated to before 1290, and those with substitution clauses to after that date (*C.N.*, p. xvii; the changes in form here may be seen by comparing charters 93, 94 and 95). This is a sensible way to solve problems of dating which otherwise

that in insisting on substitution the abbey frequently extinguished the rent obligation to the freeholder from whom the property had been acquired. At least some of these rights were respected, and a separate section of the account rolls carefully records the halfpennies and pennies which the abbey therefore paid out.[1]

What exactly lay behind the abbey's attitude is far more difficult to determine. It was suggested above, however, that it may have insisted on tenancy at will because of the threat of freedom in the clause 'sibi et heredibus suis'. Dr Hyams' work on villeinage makes a number of points which may be important in this connexion. The *favor libertatis* of thirteenth-century records, he says, perhaps existed as 'a climate of opinion especially keen to prevent the conviction of innocent freemen as villeins'. But 'by 1300, professional lawyers had arrived on the scene in force; their subtleties are well attested by the earliest yearbooks'. And so the 'bias' of this legislation changed.[2] It may be that fear of the lawyers, instigated in the abbot's mind by lawyers themselves,[3] and perhaps buttressed by the case law of the 1280s, lies behind the confiscation of these charters. Until that case law is investigated the suggestion that follows can only be hypothetical, but certainly it is not conspicuously anachronistic. The abbey feared that clever lawyers might drive a coach and horses through formulae that custom had enshrined. This, after all, was what the king was doing to the landlords at this time;[4] the peasants would do it next. Then indeed the landlords' world would have collapsed, and this is what the preambles to the Edwardian statutes would have us believe.

Basic to the argument so far is the assumption that essentially the *Carte Nativorum* shows one of the facets of the market for free land in the Soke of Peterborough. This point must now be considered more fully. It is especially important that the two questions of the

would be completely intractable. Even with a pattern thus imposed, however, several charters stand outside it (*C.N.*, p. xvii note 2). It is not impossible that further study might show others to do so, and this might serve to put *Quia Emptores* within a history of change in conveyancing practice, rather than have it solely an originator of change.

[1] Thus *C.N.* 383 was seized by the abbey, and regranted as a tenancy at will, 'reddendo inde domino abbati de Burgo per annum de novo redditu 1d., unde unus obolus debet solvi Ricardo filio Stephani per manum prepositi abbatis' (*C.N.* 388). This was paid in the *redditus solutus* section in each of the surviving accounts between 1294–5 and 1309–10.

[2] P. R. Hyams, 'Legal Aspects of Villeinage between Glanvill and Bracton' (Univ. of Oxford D.Phil thesis 1968), p. 391.

[3] On the retaining of lawyers by the abbey see Chapter 7.

[4] D. W. Sutherland, *Quo Warranto Proceedings in the Reign of Edward I, 1278–1294* (Oxford, 1963).

status of the parties and the nature of the land transferred be kept apart, and these are considered separately on the basis of two samples from the text. The section relating to the manors of Boroughbury and Eye will be analysed to try to gain some indication of the nature of the land. Then, for an indication of the status of the men, the smaller group of Castor charters will be considered, since these can be extensively supplemented by charters from this manor in the Fitzwilliam collection.[1]

What was the nature of the Boroughbury land? In the 1309–10 account for Eye, John of Walton paid a fine of 3s 4d for 'nine acres of free land which he bought by various charters, and he shall pay 6d a year as a new increment of rent'.[2] This archive can be identified.[3] It comprises nine charters, and includes land which is described as lying in the 'assarts towards Eastwood', within the 'assarts of Paston', in *Stibbinges* and in *Apeltre*. This provides evidence from this estate for a phenomenon which elsewhere is extremely well documented; that land recently reclaimed was free and freely held.[4] With this in mind we can consider the group of 115 charters which appear in the Boroughbury and Eye section. Of these 24 may be excluded from the sample straight away: 12 of them deal with messuages only, or with other property in the town of Peterborough, 6 contain meadowland only, and at least another 6 are duplicates. There remain about 91 charters seemingly concerned with arable land.

At least 53 of these 91 charters have place-names which hint at recent reclamation – *Stibbinges*, *Thweites* and 'assarts' in Paston; Berengar's *stibbing*, *Bethweyt*, *Stibbing* and *Thwaites* in Peterborough; Higgeneye's *stibbing*, Swyn's *stibbing* and *Holestibbing* in Longthorpe.[5] Much of this land is in the Peterborough hamlets of Dogsthorpe, Newark and Garton. There were customary tenancies in the first and last of these, but there were also large amounts of former woodland recently reclaimed,[6] and the majority of the

---

[1] The samples are *C.N.* 8–122, 352–378; these comprise roughly 40 per cent of the charters of the Soke.

[2] Fitzwilliam A/C Roll 2389, m. 3r–d.

[3] *C.N.*, p. xiii (no. ix); this is the land sold in charters 79–87.

[4] R. H. Hilton, 'Gloucester Abbey Leases of the late Thirteenth Century', *University of Birmingham Historical Journal*, IV (1953–4), 1–17; cf. *C.N.*, pp. xlix–l, and the references there cited.

[5] These are among the entries under these places in the Index to the *C.N.* Land variously described as lying 'beneath' or 'towards' Eastwood is included within this category.

[6] Surveys, fos. 181v–183r. The first mention of each of these hamlets comes from the twelfth century (*P.N. Soc. Northants*, pp. 226–7).

Dogsthorpe entries refer to land in 'the assarts towards Eastwood'. A smaller number of charters can be identified as free land by other means; in five instances the grantors can be identified as free men,[1] and in a further six a presumption of freedom can be worked out by association.[2] There remain 27 charters, little more than a quarter, which cannot be clearly identified as free land. At the same time no evidence has been found that any of this land was unfree; that is to say, that it represented fragments of customary tenures.

The status of the parties must now be considered. This is the most complicated question of all. The manor taken for the sample is Castor, for here the abbey cartulary can be supplemented by, and checked against, an independent body of material, the Fitzwilliam charters.[3] When the two sources are examined the comparative limitations of the monastic cartulary are immediately apparent; it has twenty-eight charters for Castor, as opposed to 147 in the Fitzwilliam collection from the reign of Edward I alone.[4] The cartulary shows only a minute fraction of the market for free land in this area, essentially the archives of only three men. There are three account rolls from between 1300 and 1310, a period to which a fair number of charters in each collection may be dated, and so they might be expected to provide supplementary information also. And yet they seem to show a quite different world. In practically no instances are the parties the same; where they are it is because some of the customary holdings, right through the period for which accounts survive, were held by free men.[5] In this perspective the Castor charters are now examined, taking first the grantors of land, and then the smaller number of grantees.

---

[1] *C.N.* 46, 49, 75, 99 and 101.

[2] Charters 31 and 119 can be shown as free by reference to the latter, 71 and 118 by reference to neighbouring tenants, and 74 and 113 from place-names.

[3] This is one of the largest sections in the valuable collection of charters in the Fitzwilliam muniments, which are now deposited in the Northamptonshire Record Office.

[4] There are 637 charters from the manor for the period up to the sixteenth century.

[5] E.g. the 1309–10 account, Fitzwilliam A/C Roll 2389, m. 5d. Surveys of this land a generation later will be found in *C.N.* 551 and 553. However unreliable the 1322 account as to the obligations of tenancies and as to the value of the land (Sparke, pp. 175–216; *cf. C.N.*, p. xxviii), I would not altogether discount its statements as to the amount of demesne and the number of customary holdings. Under Castor it records: 'Item sunt 7 virgate terre et dimidia que solebant esse (in) manibus bondorum, et nunc sunt in manibus liberorum tenentium pro voluntate domini propter impotenciam bondorum' (Sparke, p. 176).

The twenty-eight documents in the cartulary have sixteen different grantors; of these thirteen are definitely free men, while none can be identified as unfree. Probably the most substantial of these men was Ralph, son of Robert Abovetown.[1] The cartulary has two grants by him, which comprise two acres.[2] The Fitzwilliam archive has fourteen alienations, involving seventeen acres of arable and two acres and a rood of meadow.[3] In addition an unspecified amount of land was granted to Geoffrey Russell, one of the abbey's stewards and one of the men who had acquired substantial holdings in Paston on the dissolution of the Tot fee there.[4] The total amount involved in Robert Abovetown's archive was probably around twenty-five acres. There is no means of telling what percentage of his holding this may have represented, especially since his father certainly, and probably he also, held land elsewhere.[5] In eleven cases the payment is mentioned, and the amounts total £13 11s 0d.[6] There are grants to thirteen different families. On the credit side there are two items; the first of them a grant to him of six acres and miscellaneous land in Castor, and the other a grant of four acres and a rood by the rector of Castor.[7] Each of the grantors of land in the cartulary will be found also in the Fitzwilliam collection, and in each case primarily as a grantor.[8] While the charters of the *Carte Nativorum* form but a small fraction of the total charter material available for this manor, this fraction does not appear to be unrepresentative. The two collections supplement one another.

It has been suggested that the land dealt in here was free land. So analysis would seem to confirm, what *a priori* would be expected, that in the first instance the majority of the grantors were free men. Where the grantors were not free it must be that this was a transfer in the second or third generation, rather than that the

---

[1] Fitzwilliam Charter 53 was witnessed by 'domino Radulpho Aboveton'.
[2] *Ibid.* 353 and 366.
[3] *Ibid.* 132-3, 135-44, 215-16.
[4] *Ibid.* 139.
[5] Robert Abovetown, Ralph's father, held land in Pilton (twelve miles from Castor), which he granted in 1272 to the Hospitallers of Armston: Buccleuch Charters, B1. 376.
[6] This sum was paid for land totalling 11 acres and 2½ roods. The average price of land would thus appear to be between a pound and two marks for an acre of arable, while the price of meadowland was rather higher.
[7] Fitzwilliam Charters 105, 146.
[8] This point is demonstrated more fully in my thesis, as cited, pp. 275-80, which assembles all the evidence from the two collections on those who appear as principals in the *C.N.*

holding was necessarily customary land.[1] It is noticeable that in the valuable summaries of the main archives, the conspicuous sellers of land were all of them free men.[2] And several of these names – Walton, Peverel, Puttock and Blakeman – will already be familiar to those who have read the earlier chapters of this book. The village land market on this estate, the market of the *Carte Nativorum*, must be seen as but one facet of the market for free land, of which it formed a part.

While, however, the charters confiscated stretched back over several generations – most of them go back as far as the woodland clearances of the freeholders of the Soke – the tenant from whom they were confiscated was at the very least a villein. To this extent the document is rightly called *Carte Nativorum*, for these were the charters which villeins held. And yet the Castor archives were the archives of free men. This is, to say the least, extremely interesting, for it questions the document's title, and serves to complicate what might have seemed one of its least complicated facets.

That these were freemen there can be little doubt. The two main archives in this section are those of Reginald and William, the sons of Walter.[3] These were both free men. William the son of Walter was definitely free, since he was one of several men witnessing a charter of July 1311 who were described as 'liberis hominibus de Castre'.[4] Reginald the son of Walter witnessed several charters around the same time,[5] and must be presumed free for the same reasons. Sons of both men occur in the next generation, and they also show the same signs of freedom.[6] We are thus faced with a problem: both the main archives of the Castor section of the cartulary were the archives of free men, and the land was clearly freehold. It has been shown earlier that in the late thirteenth and early fourteenth centuries most of these charters were confiscated, and that their recipients can be shown from other manorial sources – as well as from the frequent glosses to the text – to have been villeins. This was not the case here. From the account rolls of

[1] Thus the fact that Richard of Crowland's father was a villein does not prove anything about the nature of the land Richard transferred, *cf.* *C.N.*, p. xiii.
[2] *C.N.*, pp. xiii–xvi.
[3] Castor archives i and ii, *C.N.*, pp. xiv–xv.
[4] Fitzwilliam Charter 224.
[5] *Ibid.* 119, 221, 226.
[6] *Ibid.* 243, 275, 315, 346 (for Reginald); 119, 128, 309, 334, 362 (for John).

Castor, indeed, we might have suspected that no villein market for freehold existed.[1]

The gloss to the first of the charters of William son of Walter states: 'Geoffrey Ridel. William Cordesti (has this land) with this William's daughter in marriage. A day has been fixed for discussion concerning the land and meadow.'[2] Now the settlement of the marriage which is referred to here has survived.[3] In it William son of Walter gave to William son of Roger Cordel, with his daughter in marriage, a messuage with appurtenances in Ailsworth, five and a half acres of arable land, and three roods of meadow. Cordel is seemingly the largest of the freeholding families in Castor,[4] and so the property is unlikely to have come into the abbey's hands in this generation.[5] When then was it seized, and why? In most cases the reasons for the seizure of property are stated in a gloss to the relevant charter; the tenant might be a villein, or the wife of the grantor might be a villein.[6] But how this tenancy came into the abbey's hands must be a subject for conjecture. This manor is particularly complicated because several freeholders farmed villein land of the abbey at this time.[7] Perhaps Reginald son of William was one of these, and the abbey administration suspected that it was small parcels of such land that he was acquiring. This is possibly why the three sets of Castor charters were seized.

Our problem here is clearly that of abbey administration in the 1340s. In a village with a large body of freeholders – the majority of whom did not hold of the abbey, and some of whom leased custo-

[1] There are no additional entries for free land in the *redditus assisus* section of the accounts up to 1310, such as occur frequently in the other manors of the Soke.

[2] *C.N.* 360.

[3] Fitzwilliam Charter 221.

[4] Members of this family are sometimes described as *dominus* in charters (e.g. *Ibid.* 17), and in 1337 a life tenancy of 40 acres made provision for a younger son (*Ibid.* 357).

[5] It is highly unlikely that the abbey administration, even in the Soke of Peterborough, was insisting on the registration of free land bought and sold by free men.

[6] *C.N.* 378, 370.

[7] Note the description of certain of the boundaries in Fitzwilliam Charter 221: 'et abuttat super terram que Galfridus Bretoun tenet de domino abbati de Burgo', 'iuxta terram que Radulphus Hert de Eyleswrthe tenet de domino abbati de Burgo'. Ralph Hert was reeve of Castor in the accounts between 1300 and 1310, and he was among those who held virgates at farm of the abbey at both these dates. A Cecily Bretoun was another who held a virgate at farm. Fitzwilliam A/C Rolls, 2388, m. 5d, 2389, m. 6r. The references to 'terram que X tenet de domino abbati de Burgo' are possibly to land thus held; certainly this phrase has not been found in any other charter of the period. Some parts of this property were in the literal sense close to villeinage. Further than this we cannot go.

mary land from it – the problem of keeping the distinction between customary land and freehold was obviously immensely difficult. It was a problem which, perhaps for this reason, seems to have been tackled here far later than elsewhere on the Soke, and certainly it was never satisfactorily solved. In this case it is tempting to conclude that the Castor section of the *Carte Nativorum* reflects nothing so much as the monastery's enthusiasm.

This, it must be stated at once, is clearly exceptional; Castor is an exceptional manor. The archives from the other manors in the Soke – Boroughbury, Walton, Werrington and Glinton – are much larger, and here there can be little doubt that these are villein archives, and the title of the document therefore means exactly what it says. Something of the substance of these villeins can be gathered from the documents themselves, and this information can be supplemented from the account rolls. These would suggest that in large part the cartulary contains the archives of the more prosperous sections of the villein community, and that what they show is a Peterborough 'kulak' class enriching itself at the expense of a section of the freeholding community – a class from which it has been suggested that the abbey was profiting too. In the accounts several of the larger families can be studied in some detail, and it is this material to which I shall now turn. I shall discuss the use made of the free land in family settlements; as already stated, the most important problem here is the relationship between this land and the network of customary tenures.

The aristocrats among the Boroughbury villeins at this time were the families of Gere and le Wro. Their joint archive is the largest item in the cartulary; it shows Mabel and Simon Gere acquiring free land in the last quarter of the thirteenth century, and then in and shortly before 1305 using this land to endow two sons and a daughter.[1] William, the elder son, had three acres of arable and one of meadow; Walter, the younger son, had five acres of arable and one and a half acres of meadow;[2] Agnes married Simon in le Wro, reeve of Boroughbury, and had from her parents three and a half acres of arable and one of meadow.[3] The total amount of land disposed of here was fifteen acres.

The court and account rolls show something of the background

---

[1] Boroughbury archive i, *C.N.*, p. xiii. Charters 28–37 show the acquisition of Simon Gere's holding, and nos. 16–19, 119–22 its dispersal.
[2] *C.N.* 16–18.
[3] Fitzwilliam A/C Roll 233, m. 1d. Simon in le Wro's archive is *C.N.* 116–22.

to these transactions. In particular they show, what the charters will
never show, the customary holdings to which these small amounts of
free land were appended. One of the relevant holdings appears in
the accounts. In 1307–8 Mabel and Simon Gere surrendered a virgate for the use of Hawisia in le Wro and Richard her son.[1] The
Geres were granted a house and two half-acres for their lifetimes.
Hawisia was the sister of Simon in le Wro; she had married in 1300,
so that Richard in 1308 must still have been a child. The form of this
agreement suggests that in 1308 the family with the capital was le
Wro. But it would seem that by then both sons were already provided with customary tenancies. The youngest almost certainly was,
for he married Matilda daughter of Reginald of Warmington.
Matilda farmed a customary virgate in 1300–1, and shortly thereafter was due to start to perform services.[2] The elder brother's holding is not recorded, but in the 1320 court rolls he appears frequently. He turned up late to work for the lord, and when he came
he worked badly. In 1335 he paid to educate one of his sons.[3] It was
the more prosperous members of the community who acted in this
way. We must presume, therefore, either that the virgate Simon
Gere disposed of in 1307–8 was a second customary holding, or that
William Gere had earlier married a widow. The latter is perhaps the
more likely.

If the Gere family is important in the court rolls between 1320
and 1340, however, it is the le Wro family which is pre-eminent. In
1320 Simon in le Wro occurs frequently in both the Boroughbury
and the Longthorpe court rolls. He sent colts to do the lord's ploughing, and kept his horses to do his own work. He turned up late, dis-
obeyed the bailiffs and was generally uncooperative.[4] Fines for
these offences amounted to three shillings. This perhaps was part of
a wealthy villein's conspicuous expenditure; it demonstrated his
importance both to the abbey administration and to his fellows. In
this cause he probably counted two or three shillings a year as money
well spent.

---

[1] Fitzwilliam A/C Roll 233, m. 1d.
[2] *C.N.* 17; Fitzwilliam A/C Roll 2388, m. 1d.
[3] 'Willelmus Gere male messuit bladum domini, 3d. . . . Willelmus Gere
non venit tempestive ad opus suum, 3d.' (Peterborough D and C Muniments, Court Rolls, Box 1a); Fitzwilliam Court Roll 139.
[4] 'Simon in le Wro misit pullanos pro opere domini faciendo, et tenuit
equos suos in opere proprio, per quod opus domini fuit minus bene
factum. Ideo in misericordia, 18d. . . . Simon in le Wro non venit tempestive ad opus domini, 6d. . . . Simon in le Wro quia inobediens domino
et ballivis operandi et respondendi in omnibus, 12d.' (Peterborough D
and C Muniments, Court Rolls, Box 1a).

Simon's nephew Richard seems to have found other uses for similar sums. In 1341–2 he had by far the largest archive of free land in Boroughbury,[1] and every surviving source for the previous twenty years seems to record his acquisitions. In the account of 1334–5 he paid 2s, 'for an inquest to be made concerning an acre of meadow which he bought from John Defec, and for entry to a cottage which he bought from Reginald Walby'.[2] Each of the three fragments of court rolls from this period records his purchases: he paid a 12d fine in 1335 to purchase an acre of free land from Alice of Stanton, 2s in 1336 for an acre and a half 'beneath Eastwood', and 18d in 1340 for half a messuage of land.[3] Various glosses to the cartulary entries make it possible to trace other parts of his archive. Three separate acres in the assarts 'next Eastwood' have glosses referring to Richard, which perhaps identifies them as the three acres 'apud Estwodebrigg' which he held in 1341–2.[4] In 1339 he held land which Robert Alred had held in 1317, and also part of the land which Simon Gere had given to his son Walter.[5] Together this material gives a good impression of the enterprise which lay behind the twenty acres he and his mother held in 1341.

Richard's holding was made up of numerous small parcels of free land, scattered over a wide area, and was quite separate from his customary holding. How was this land exploited? He was engaged in buying up cottages, as were several other of the more prosperous Boroughbury tenants. The cottage can hardly have been for his own occupation; they must have been bought for speculative purposes, and were intended to be rented out. The arable also was probably not farmed by Richard but leased by him, with anything over and above the fourpence an acre owed to the abbey as his own profit. Such men were no less rentiers than their lords. Some of the archives which follow raise similar questions, and I shall try to answer them in a later part of this chapter.[6]

The next family to be considered is that of Alred. None of its dealings appear in the cartulary, but by a fortunate accident its

---

[1] *C.N.* 554.
[2] Peterborough D and C Muniments, Account Rolls, Box 1a.
[3] Fitzwilliam Court Rolls 139, 138; Fitzwilliam A/C Roll 2390. The first of these entries was registered in court in April 1335, while the relevant charter is dated December 1334 (*C.N.* 73); the transfer had been made just after the previous half-yearly court.
[4] Compare *C.N.* 21–3 and 554 (p. 216). Another gloss relates to two further acres in the same area, *C.N.* 92.
[5] Compare *C.N.* 69 and 70; *Ibid.* 17 (gloss).
[6] See below, pp. 119–22.

settlements in two generations appear in the account rolls. As above, there is particular emphasis on the part played in these settlements by the free holdings. The first set of entries is from 1309–10.[1]

Et de 6s. 8d. de Matilda relicta Roberti Alred ut possit tenere unum liberum cotagium de herede Johannis de Bringhirst per servicium 15d. per annum, et eciam 2 acras et dimidiam libere terre quas dictus Robertus adquisivit, reddendo per annum de novo redditu 3d. ad Pascham et ad festum sancti Michaelis.

Et de 20s. de Rogero filio Roberti Alred ut possit tenere unum cotagium de tenemento Horebore et 3 acras terre in le Stibbing in tota vita sua, faciendo inde ut prius.

Et de 66s. 8d. de Roberto filio Roberti Alred pro fine unius mesuagii et unius virgate terre que quondam fuerunt predicti Roberti, faciendo serviciis et consuetudinibus.

The transfer of land in the next generation is found in the account roll for 1333–4.[2]

Et de 2s. de Johanne filio Roberti Alred pro ingressu habendo in una acra terre et 3 rodis libere terre quas Robertus Alred quondam tenuit.

Et de 12d. de Johanne filio Roberti Alred pro ingressu habendo in uno cotagio in Neuerk.

Et de 13s. 4d. de Roberto Sewale pro ingressu habendo in uno mesuagio et una virgata terre que Robertus Alred quondam tenuit, faciendo inde ut prius.

Et de 11s. de Alicia relicta Roberti Alred pro ingressu habendo in uno mesuagio et una virgata terre et 1 acra et 3 rodis libere terre quas Robertus Alred quondam tenuit.

In the first set of entries we see that, in addition to his customary virgate, Robert Alred had two cottages and five and a half acres of free land.[3] A cottage and two and a half acres of this land provided a tenancy for his widow; on her death they evidently reverted to the eldest son. What remained of the free land, a cottage and three acres, provided a holding for the younger son, while the customary virgate descended to the elder. By the next generation, the second Robert had acquired another virgate, which on his death came to Robert Sewale. The main holdings descended slightly differently this time.

---

[1] Fitzwilliam A/C Roll 2389, m. 1d.
[2] Peterborough D and C Muniments, Account Rolls, Box 1a.
[3] The three acres which went to his younger son were acquired in 1300–1, and in the same year he paid 13s 4d to have a further son 'put to letters' and that he might remain to take orders (Fitzwilliam A/C Roll 2388, m. 1d).

The family virgate remained with the widow, who kept a half of the
free land as well. The son retained the other half, and a cottage
in Newark. The court roll of 1337 carries the story a stage further.[1]

Johannes Alred dat domino 2s. pro ingressu habendo in dimidia acra
terre de qua Robertus Alred obiit seisitus, et iacet subtus curia Alicia
in le Wro, tenendo per servicia et consuetudines.

Robertus filius Simonis filii Galfridi de Eye dat domino 40s. pro ingressu
habendo in uno mesuagio et una virgata terre que Alicia Alred tenet,
tenendo per servicia et consuetudines, et ut possit ducere eandem Aliciam
in uxorem.

The widow married again. In addition to his cottage, acre and three
roods, her son obtained another half acre of land, presumably a part
of his mother's acre and three roods of 1333–4. There the information for this family ends. Whether the son subsequently obtained his
father's holding is not clear, but very likely he did not. Certainly his
father had been considerably more fortunate. In each generation the
appendages to the customary holding are used to provide tenancies
for the younger members of the family.

The villein aristocracy was a closely integrated one.[2]

Et de 46s. 8d. de Simone Sweyn de Carton pro ingressu habendo ad
Johannam filiam Johannis de Walton tenente unum mesuagium et una
virgata terre que Robertus de Cranewell reddit in manu domini, faciendo
serviciis et consuetudinibus. Et eciam ut idem Simon et Johanna possint
tenere ad terminum vite eorum unam acram terre quam Johannes de
Walton adquisivit per cartam et eis dedit. Et eciam ut possint tenere unam
acram prati quam Emma Sweyn eis dedit, quam quidem quondam Ricardus Sweyn et Emma uxor eius adquisierunt per cartam. Reddendo
inde annuatim pro terra et prato 3d. de novo redditu, scilicet ad Pascham
et ad festum sancti Michaelis, per plegios Johannis de Walton et Simone
in le Wro.

Simon in le Wro, a member of the Boroughbury aristocracy, is here
a pledge to a marriage settlement involving two of the more important families in Eye. John of Walton had one of the two virgates held
at farm on this manor in 1309–10, while elsewhere in the same
account he paid 3s 4d for nine acres of free land which he had bought
by charter.[3] His daughter held a virgate which Robert of Cranewell
had surrendered, probably for a consideration which is not mentioned. As subsidiary endowment each family added little: John of

[1] Fitzwilliam Court Roll 138.
[2] Fitzwilliam A/C Roll 2389, m. 3d.
[3] *Ibid.* m. 3r; John also farmed a virgate at Longthorpe in 1307–8 (Fitzwilliam A/C Roll 233, m. 4d).

Walton made over one acre from his nine, while the Sweyn family added an acre of meadow which they had previously acquired. Neither family alienated any portion of a customary holding.

The dealings of two reeves of the manor of Boroughbury provide final examples of the place of freehold in relation to the network of customary tenures. The two families are those of John Palfrey of Eye and Richard Hunne. In the last decade of the thirteenth century John Palfrey acquired six and a half acres of assart land in Paston.[1] One and a half acres of this formed the portion of his daughter on her marriage to Simon Abbot, a customary tenant of Boroughbury.[2] The Abbots were a family of substance, and one of them was reeve of Boroughbury in the 1340s. Two further acres were sold to the ubiquitous Richard in le Wro.[3] The rest of the tenancy was in 1340 attached to the family's customary holding, when John Palfrey's wife fined for it as follows:[4]

Alicia que fuit uxor Johannis Palefrey dat domino 4 libros pro ingressu habendo in uno mesuagio una virgata terre et tribus acris libere terre que (vir eius) quondam tenuit, tenendo per servicia et consuetudines, et super hoc Ricardus filius ipsius Johannis Palefrey remisit eadem Alicia totum (ius suum ad) totam vitam ipsius Alicie de predictis tribus acris libere terre.

The high fine – a rare example of a fine of over five marks – is explained by the extra non-customary land, and by the substance of the parties.[5] The fine is interesting for two further reasons. In the first place because John's son Richard had already fined for his father's land in 1337, presumably in the father's lifetime.[6] It would seem that such a surrender and admittance did not extinguish the widow's full right for her lifetime.[7] On her death the holding remained to her son or her son's heirs.[8] Second, whatever had been the theory of a generation earlier, this record speaks of the son's *right* to his father's free land. The widow retained this along with the

[1] Boroughbury archive x, *C.N.*, p. xiii and Charters 88–95.
[2] Fitzwilliam Court Roll 139; *cf. C.N.* 88 gloss.
[3] *C.N.* 92.
[4] Fitzwilliam Court Roll 140.
[5] For a consideration of entry fines see below, pp. 182–8.
[6] Fitzwilliam Court Roll 138.
[7] Raftis, *Tenure and Mobility*, pp. 36ff., and J. Z. Titow, 'Some Differences between Manors and their Effects on the Condition of the Peasant in the Thirteenth Century', *Agricultural History Review*, x (1962), pp. 1–13. It is also possible that this is a second customary holding. At Winchester no tenant might possess more than one of these (*Ibid.* p. 7), and it would seem that this was true of Peterborough also.
[8] Raftis, *Tenure and Mobility*, p. 49.

customary holding as a matter of grace, and for her lifetime only. She presumably had no right to alienate.[1]

In 1307, and for at least a quarter of a century thereafter, one of the joint reeves of Boroughbury was Richard Hunne. In 1314 he married, and took over a customary virgate; he paid no entry fine, and he was allowed to farm the land for 24s a year.[2] In the following year he acquired a substantial part of the free land left by Robert atte Grene when he died. Robert's widow succeeded to his customary tenancy, and his two sons between them had an acre of his free land. Richard Hunne had a further three acres and a rood of this land, in addition to an acre which Robert had earlier surrendered to his use.[3] A powerful reeve was in a position to put a number of pressures on a family, but the most obvious one is financial, and it seems very likely that the atte Grene family was in debt to him.[4] In the 1333–4 account Richard Hunne is clearly extremely well established, and he had a lease of eighteen acres of demesne land in addition to his customary tenancies.[5] His son inherited a similar position; in 1340–1 he had two virgates, one of which he had acquired in that year on his marriage to Agnes daughter of Richard Abbot.[6] Another text of the same period shows how the father's free land had been divided. The eldest son, Richard son of Richard Reve, had two and a half acres, while William and Reginald had an acre each. A fourth son, John, had been sent for education in the abbey in 1320.[7] The information here is taken from the survey of 1341–2.[8] In many ways this is the key document in the collection, for it is intended to sum up the material earlier recorded. Around 1300 the market for free land was clearly fluid, and a wide variety of people were engaged in it. Two generations later the major families had engrossed the lot;

---

1 The reasons for this provision perhaps appear in the gloss to Charter 89, which suggests that the mother had sold the land, and that the sale was being contested at the time the *Carte Nativorum* was being compiled.
2 Fitzwilliam A/C Roll 247.
3 Fitzwilliam A/C Roll 248.
4 The widow paid only 3s 4d, a very low fine for a full holding, which is further evidence that the family was badly off.
5 Peterborough D and C Muniments, Account Rolls, Box 1a.
6 Fitzwilliam A/C roll 2390.
7 'Ricardus Hunne habet licenciam ex gracia domini Godefridi abbatis ponendi Johannem filium suum ad litteraturam, et ut possit permoneri ad sacros ordines clericales' (D and C Muniments, Court Rolls, Box 1a). There is of course no guarantee that such a provision was invariably followed by a clerical career. A John Hunne, indeed, was fined in 1337 for bad ploughing (Fitzwilliam Court Roll 138). Perhaps this was a different man; perhaps a frustrated vocation.
8 *C.N.* 554.

eight families, all of them powerful and inter-related, account for all of the land.[1] These are the Peterborough 'kulaks'.

What have so far been considered are customary virgates and the freeholds attached to them. Most of the manors in the Soke of Peterborough, in particular Glinton and Werrington, and a few of the manors elsewhere, also contained quite a large number of socage tenancies. I shall now consider whether or not these tenancies descended by the same rules as governed the descent of other customary tenures, and what part free land played in relation to them.

A socage and a free holding are combined in the following entry from Werrington in 1300–1.[2]

Et de 30s. de Osberto Griffin de fine pro 1 mesuagio et 12 acris terre de sokagio et pro 1 acra libere terre quam dictus Osbertus emit de Willelmo filio Walteri. Et solvet 1d. annuatim de incremento redditus pro dicta acra terre que prius reddidit 1d.

The basic holding here is identical with that which Ralph Griffin had held seventy years earlier,[3] a fact significant in itself since in many places sokeland was subject to partible inheritance. Interesting also are the additional details about the Griffin family which may be found in the cartulary. A daughter of Ralph Griffin had been given an acre and a half of land which her father had previously acquired, and to this she added a further acre shortly before 1290.[4] Her brother John purchased land totalling an acre and a rood. The cartulary, however, shows only a small part of John's archive, for in 1307–8 his son inherited from him five acres and a rood of free land.[5] There is no way of telling the precise relationship of Osbert to these other Griffins. All we know is that Osbert had the customary holding, which suggests that here again the *Carte Nativorum* entries relate to a daughter and a younger son. This entry also shows that, with regard to free land, those who held socages were subject to the same rules as the other customary tenants.

On a slightly smaller scale is an entry in the Werrington account for 1307–8.[6]

Et de 23s. 4d. de Matilda uxore Willelmi Russell, Galfrido, Ricardo et Alicia pueris suis, ut possint tenere unum cotagium et tres acras de sokagio

---

[1] The families were Gere, le Wro, Abbot, Hunne, Alred, Papley, atte Grene and Poper of Eye.
[2] Fitzwilliam A/C Roll 2388, m. 7r. At the same time Osbert surrendered a toft and a croft, on which he had presumably been living up to this time.
[3] Surveys, fo. 189v.
[4] *C.N.* 207–12.   [5] *C.N.* 226–8; Fitzwilliam A/C Roll 233, m. 7d.
[6] *Ibid.*

et unam acram et dimidiam libere terre ad terminum vite eorum. Et sciendum quod predicti Ricardus et Alicia tenebunt et habebunt dictam acram libere terre in tota vita eorum, et dabunt singulis annis de incremento redditus 1½d.

On the surface the cottage and the sokeland seem to have descended to the widow and the three children jointly. The settlement which lay behind this, however, is probably shown by the entry in which the two youngest children were granted the free land for their lifetimes. It is likely that the sokeland was not divided, and remained to the elder son.

It would thus appear that the rule of primogeniture applied to the inheritance of socage tenures by males. As would be expected, however, land was divided between females. There is an example of this from Glinton in 1321, when the socage of Reginald Heriz was divided between his four daughters. In the following entry these as a group – three daughters and their husbands, and one unmarried daughter – paid 30s for entry into fifteen acres of free land, paying an increment of rent of a penny an acre.[1] But this freehold was a single tenancy for accounting purposes alone, for in the next entry one of these acres was surrendered to the use of William son of Simon le Western.

Outside the Soke of Peterborough the abbey manor with the greatest number of socage tenures was Great Easton in Leicestershire, and here the picture is rather different. The socages were smaller; sometimes at least they would seem to have been divided between males; and they were bought and sold. On each of these points, Great Easton provides a contrast with the manors nearer the abbey.[2] At Werrington the smallest of the socages were of three or four acres. At Great Easton in 1294–5 the first two socages recorded were (1) a quarter of a toft and of a rood of land and a quarter of a rood of meadow, and (2) three roods of land and a third of a rood of meadow. At times it was the youngest son who finished up with such holdings.

Et de 16s. o¼d.[3] de Petro, Ricardo et Johanne filiis Ricardi Page pro relevio unius cotagii et 3 rodarum terre de socagio que fuerunt Ricardi patris

---

[1] Peterborough D and C Muniments, Court Rolls, Box 1a.
[2] The information for this manor is taken from the three main account rolls: Rockingham Compotus; Fitzwilliam A/C Rolls, 233, m. 30r, 2389, m. 28r.
[3] The fine of 16s o¼d which appears here seems to have been the standard fine on this estate for a socage tenure, whatever its size. The same amount was occasionally paid for entry to burgage tenancies in Oundle; e.g. Fitzwilliam A/C Roll 2389, m. 20r.

eorum. Et de 2s. de Johanne filio Ricardi Page qui est de etate 8 anno-
rum pro relevio 2 partium dicti tenementi quas predicti Petrus et Ricardus reddiderunt in manu domini.

This entry, however, suggests that the land had descended as a
joint holding, and other entries suggest that such holdings might
be partitioned. There is no direct evidence here, but it is difficult
otherwise to account for the absence of complete socages of any size.
In the first two entries in the 1309-10 account, Ralph son of John of
Yaxley paid 5s for half of a part of a socage which had belonged to
John his father, while Thomas son of Hulle paid 16s 0¼d for part of
a socage which had belonged to Ernold his brother. Finally, the
purchase of socage tenures is openly admitted on a number of
occasions. Amicia Roy paid 20s relief for nine roods of socage that
William Hobyn had acquired, while Richard of Britwell paid two
marks for half a socage which had been surrendered 'for a certain
sum of money that Richard had paid' to the previous tenant.[1]

It is not possible to be certain why there were these differences
between manors. It may be that we should start with partibility, and
suggest that seigneurial pressure was responsible for enforcing a
change in inheritance patterns on those manors that lay closest to
the abbey. But it would seem more likely that we should start with
impartibility, and look for differences in differing obligations towards the demesne. And we find that at Glinton the sokemen each
owed ten works a year, making a total of 160 works, all of which
were performed, while the services of the Great Easton sokemen
were commuted.[2] For as long as they owed necessary services, the
abbey would preserve the integrity of its socages as far as possible.

At a number of places above it has been suggested that not all the
land a man acquired was necessarily intended for his own occupancy. There is quite a lot of material on this point. There are in
the first place a number of fines by which a man took up land 'super
quam possit edificare', with license to build. This of itself does not
prove that the land was not intended for the owner's occupancy.
The fine is frequently a large one, however, and often there is
further information on the men concerned. The majority of these
men are not smallholders emerging from the rural proletariat, but
rather substantial freeholders, or men who already possessed a

[1] The transfer of customary holdings in the Soke of Peterborough may
have involved cash transactions, but this is nowhere stated.
[2] Fitzwilliam A/C Roll 2389, m. 10r (Glinton), m. 29d ('de opera soke-
mannorum nichil quia taxantur in denariis'; Great Easton).

customary holding. Thus an entry from Irthlingborough in 1307–8 shows Hugh of Kettering being given license to build on two roods of land which had been surrendered to his use.[1] Now Hugh leased considerable quantities of demesne land from the abbey during this period; in 1300–1 he had eight acres 'of the furthest-off and worst demesne land', which he held at will,[2] and in a later account he paid ten shillings to bake his bread 'in his own courtyard on the outskirts of the village'.[3] Such a man was certainly not building for himself. And in the earliest surviving account for Irthlingborough, Henry the clerk paid 2s for a cottage which had belonged to Thomas Smith.[4] Henry's son held a virgate freely of one of the abbey knights, and other land as well;[5] he also is unlikely to have bought to occupy. The same point can be made with regard to a couple of entries in the Great Easton section of the same account, in which John the vicar and Robert Pacy each paid 3s 'for a plot of land on which he had built'.[6] Both these men held other property. Robert Pacy held half a virgate at farm at this time,[7] while the *Carte Nativorum* contains an archive of several of his purchases of free land.[8] And the vicar presumably had at least a roof over his head; in 1307–8 his son paid an increment of rent for seven acres of free land of his father's gift.[9] A couple of smiths are also found building on new land, although they may simply have been expanding their business.[10] These examples could be added to.

For whom were all these men building, if they were not building for themselves? There are a number of possible explanations. They

---

1 Fitzwilliam A/C Roll 233, m. 25d.
2 'Et de 2s. de Hugone de Keteringge ut possit tenere 8 acras de remotiora et peiora terra tocius terre dominice ad voluntatem domini' (Fitzwilliam A/C Roll 2388, m. 14d). This provides a good example of a landlord explicitly leasing worn out demesne land; *cf. Ely*, p. 121, and J. Z. Titow, 'Land and Population on the Bishop of Winchester's Estates (1209–1350)' (Univ. of Cambridge Ph.D. thesis 1962), pp. 29–30.
3 Fitzwilliam A/C Roll 233, m. 26r.
4 Rockingham Compotus, under Irthlingborough.
5 Black Book, fo. 156r.
6 Rockingham Compotus, under Great Easton.
7 *Ibid.*
8 *C.N.* 417–24.
9 Fitzwilliam A/C Roll 233, m. 29d.
10 In 1294–5 Robert Smith of Cottingham paid 2s for an oven and a smithy and all the houses which Stephen Smith surrendered to the lord, 'una cum una placea super quam edificavit, tenendo ad voluntatem domini' (Rockingham Compotus, under Cottingham). In 1300–1 at Kettering, Thomas Smith of Barton paid 2s 'pro fine unius placee super quam possit edificare, que quidem placea continet in longitudine 40 pedes, et in latitudine 16 pedes, et dabit domino per annum de novo redditu 12d.' (Fitzwilliam A/C Roll 2388, m. 15r).

may have provided tenancies for younger members of their families. On occasion they may have provided holdings for their own labourers.[1] More often than not, however, the land and building must have been leased on the village land market.

This impression of entrepreneurship is strengthened by examples of the manorial administration apparently doing the same thing. At Kettering in 1294–5, a total rent of 39s was paid for nine acres and a rood of land, newly leased upon *le Newelond*, and there is reference also to some tofts newly leased out.[2] Other entries may show related development. On the same manor in 1281–2, eighteen cottars paid an increment of rent of 7s 4½d, while in a later roll the 'chief tenants' (*capitales tenentes*) paid rents totalling 5s 2d for fifteen shops newly farmed out.[3] This succession of entries from the one manor suggests that these were not random concessions, but development and leasing according to policy. The reasons for this policy are not difficult to find. By the time the last set of cottages was leased the the rent for them was running at 4s an acre, as compared with the shilling or so normal for undeveloped land at this time.[4] The abbey was but one landlord among many. Ralph of Thorney, one of the abbey bailiffs, is also found building upon land which he had acquired, and leasing other land as tenancies at will.[5] There are a number of similar entries from the western group of manors, in particular from such places as Cottingham,[6] Great Easton and Irthlingborough, which seem to show a movement away from demesne

---

[1] Note here the nine cottages which Henry de Bray either built or acquired in Harlestone between 1295 and 1306: *The Estate Book of Henry de Bray*, ed. D. Willis (Camden Soc., 3rd ser., XXVII, 1916), pp. 49–51. These he must have built either for his own labourers (as suggested by E. W. Watson in a review of the above, *E.H.R.*, XXXIII (1918), 100), or to lease.

[2] Rockingham Compotus, under Kettering; Fitzwilliam A/C Roll 2388, m. 15r. The 1294–5 account for Kettering was printed by C. Wise, *The Comptus of the Manor of Kettering for A.D. 1292* (Kettering, 1899), and the extract quoted will be found on p. 3 of this edition.

[3] B.M. Add. Ch. 737; Fitzwilliam A/C Roll 233, m. 26d. The phrase *capitales tenentes* is an interesting one, for there was a large cottar population on this manor (*cf.* Postan, *Cambridge Economic History*, I, 624).

[4] This is another part of what seems a determined attempt to increase the size of the abbey's rent roll. The rent 'charge' in the 1281–2 fragment for Great Easton was £10 18s 8½d, while the rent total was £11 8s 8d. In 1294–5 the 'charge' was £14 5s 0¼d, and in 1300–1 it was £15 2s 4d. The amounts for leases for meadowland were increasing at an even greater rate.

[5] *C.N.* 483; see below, p. 138.

[6] Part of the Cottingham account in 1300–1 reads: 'Et de £6 2s. 9½d. de firma toftorum cum firma 2 acrarum terre affirmatis ... et de 3s. de 3 cotagiis de novo levatis et affirmatis' (Fitzwilliam A/C Roll 2388, m. 16r).

cultivation at this time. It may be that what we have here represents a specific reaction to a fall in agrarian profits.[1]

The picture of the peasantry buying land for development may thus be supplemented by the picture of the abbey leasing developed land. Further, the abbey itself was clearly prepared to buy land for speculative purposes should occasion arise. It has already been noted that the abbey bought rents from Peverel before 1289, and from both Blakeman and Puttock between 1295 and 1300.[2] Land was involved as well as rent. The 1300–1 account from Irthlingborough shows half an acre of land, bought from Henry the clerk, being leased for 5s, while the same amount came from three roods of meadow that had been bought from Richard son of Stephen.[3] Both the men concerned were freeholders, and the latter held at least five virgates of land.[4] The abbey was also prepared to buy cottages. It had two cottages in Cottingham which it had bought from Thomas Gonel, each of which was worth 2s a year.[5] And the same kind of entrepreneurship must lie behind several of the rents paid out in the Boroughbury accounts of this period. In 1307–8 among the rents paid (*redditus solutus*) there was the entry, 'in rent to the convent cellarer for the new cottages at the end of town 6d'. The total amount owed was 14d, but 8d was subtracted since the cellarer owed this amount under another heading.[6] Here the abbot was collecting rent due to one of the obedientiaries, and then passing the money on. And it must be probable that he was doing more than this; that more than fourteen pence was collected from these properties, the balance remaining as the abbot's profit. The abbot did not only buy land and rent from his freeholders, he may even at times have bought property for speculative purposes from some of the monastic departments.

The evidence so far is limited, and suggestive rather than conclusive on the general matter of development. But it is something that any positive picture can be got from four or five scattered account rolls. The general conclusion can only be the obvious one: that rising land values reflect the pressure of population upon land. We would seem to have here some interesting examples of the way the abbey administration and the prosperous tenantry were capitalising on the consequent demand.

---

[1] See below, pp. 150–4.   [2] See above, pp. 64–5.
[3] Fitzwilliam A/C Roll 2388, m. 14r.
[4] Black Book, fo. 156r; Vesp. E.22, fo. 49r; *C.N.* 388.
[5] Rockingham Compotus, under Cottingham.
[6] Fitzwilliam A/C Roll 233, m. 1d, m. 2r.

In conclusion, it must be stressed that the land market considered here has to be seen within the perspective provided by the chapters on freehold and on colonisation. The *Carte Nativorum* show something of the part played by freehold land in the village land market, and some of the uses to which this freehold land was put.[1] If this chapter makes a positive contribution it must be on this point alone. Otherwise the suggestions it makes are negative. Perhaps the most important of them is that here the land market does not seem to have been in any way connected with the break-up of customary tenures. Elsewhere this was certainly so,[2] but there is no evidence that even in the early fourteenth century the Peterborough administration had gone even part of the way towards abandoning the principles that such land was impartible and inalienable. The chronicle would appear accurate in stating that when the abbey was unable to obtain villein tenants for certain of its customary virgates in Glinton and Castor, these were farmed in their entirety to free men.[3] They were not split up but maintained intact;[4] in 1340, when they were surveyed at least half a century after they were first leased, the amount of land in them varied hardly at all.[5] Indeed, in providing a framework whereby inequalities of economic position could at least in part be worked out outside the network of customary tenures, the market for free land may have guarded against fragmentation. The examples, admittedly, are taken from the villein aristocracy; those with under half a virgate would probably not have had much slack of this sort. The point cannot be taken too far.

A second suggestion arises from the first. The uniqueness of this cartulary, and its undoubted major importance, could perhaps lead to more being made of it than is in fact is there. It is limited in that it shows chiefly the aristocracy of the four manors closest to the abbey. Its inadequacy for the village of Castor, and the care with which consequently it must be used, has been demonstrated in some detail.

---

[1] This, as Postan states (*C.N.*, pp. xlix–l), is the least studied aspect of the village land market. It was ignored by Homans (as Powicke pointed out in *E.H.R.*, LVII (1942), 501–2), and more recently its consideration has been deferred by Raftis (*Tenure and Mobility*, p. 83 note 96).

[2] *C.N.*, p. xlv.

[3] Sparke, p. 176.

[4] In 1300–1 none of the Castor virgates were split up, in 1307–8 five and a half virgates were, and in 1309–10 three and a half. The entry for 1309–10 reads: 'Et de 50s. de 3 virgatis terre et dimidia terre native existentis in manu domini affirmatis per parcellas' (Fitzwilliam A/C Roll 2389, m. 5d). Such grants were revocable.

[5] *C.N.* 551, 553.

Further than five miles from the abbey its lordship could effect only a fairly spasmodic supervision. The charters from outside the Soke are by comparison very few, and seem to show the assertion of a principle rather than the establishment of any tenacious or continuous control.

The number of the charters, further, can easily give a false impression of the total amount of land involved. It is a large archive that amounts to more than five acres, and the twenty acres of le Wro are the acquisitions over two generations of a family which was clearly exceptional. The biggest archive thus represents less than a customary tenancy of average size. In considering any family it is necessary to start with its customary holding, and this the *Carte Nativorum*, by its very nature, ignores. It is these tenancies which are of primary importance, the focus of a loyalty which was immediate as well as atavistic, since for all these families their customary tenancies were the main source of their economic position.

From the cartulary we are led to consider the attitude of the peasantry to the land they held. To study this from documents which reflect lordship is a hazardous exercise, but there is no other way. Only one thing is really clear, and that is the position of the free land within the context of family settlements. Again and again, whenever these families can have any life breathed into them at all, the document appears as a register of daughters and of younger sons. Enough of the records have been quoted, perhaps, to make this point clear, and the list could have been very much further prolonged. With a family such as Alred the same land is being used for this purpose over a couple of generations; more often than not we see only the one generation, and more often still this has to be guessed at. The peasantry here were endeavouring to satisfy ambitions and obligations born less of manorial custom than of observation of a wider world; that their younger sons should have some small independent position; that their daughters should have a dowry, even were it only half an acre of land.[1]

The dynamic which had led to this situation and which kept it in being is less easy to determine. This is the final question the material raises, and it provides no satisfactory answer. To what extent the attitude to the family holding was the result of pressure from the

---

[1] On the other hand, G. C. Homans, *English Villagers of the Thirteenth Century* (1941), Book II on 'Families' (espec. Chs. X and XIV), treats these as desires that had existed from time immemorial.

lord, to what extent the expression of the attitude of the peasantry to land which it regarded as its own, it is impossible to say. In the material these two things cannot be distinguished. One explanation would be that they are not in fact distinguishable, that seigneurial interest and family feeling were in this matter one.

Towards the end of the twelfth century, we see on the larger estates the same changes in administrative technique and personnel that had taken place in the royal government at the beginning of the century. When abbot Samson of Bury, 'banished from his private counsels all the great men of the abbey, both lay and literate, without whose advice and help it seemed that the abbey could not be governed', he incurred the displeasure of Glanvill, and indeed caused something of a sensation.[1] A generation later he would not have done so. Then, indeed, the dichotomy implied by the phrase 'both lay and literate' was ceasing to apply. In John's time the educated layman was still a rarity. But in the second half of the thirteenth century literacy was more broadly based. A list of the abbey's clerks in 1296 contains eighteen names, and their fees amounted to £35 13s 4d;[2] slightly later a son of the greatest wool merchant of the day occurs among them, and several younger sons of the more prosperous Peterborough villeins.[3] Without these men we would have no accounts, and no means of looking in detail at the village society from which many of them came.

The administrative machinery which the abbey constructed on this basis was, by comparison with that of the early thirteenth century, highly complex. For this reason, the temptation to consider the period 1200 to 1350 as 'the age of high farming', and then to read the conditions of 1300 back to 1220, is one that should be resisted. One indication of the 'managerial revolution' is the change-over from a 'feudal' to a 'professional' steward. On examination this becomes a rather complex movement. Gilbert of Barnack spans the new order and the old. He married a daughter of the previous, hereditary, steward, and his free tenancy was converted to a knight's holding.[4] The next steward, who occurs in John's reign, is master Geoffrey Gibbuin, a clerk. He ceased to act for the abbey

---

[1] *The Chronicle of Jocelin of Brakelond*, ed. H. E. Butler (Nelson's Medieval Texts, 1949), pp. 26–7.
[2] Vesp. E.22, fo. 6r.
[3] See below, p. 159, and above, pp. 111, 113, 116.
[4] See above, p. 33.

when a vacancy occurred in 1210. For the next half century his successors were not masters; and it was only in the civil war that another of them was appointed to this office, Robert of Sheffield, who occurs between 1266 and 1294. It was probably around the time that he was appointed that accounts for the manors began to be kept. Perhaps the real administrative revolution at Peterborough came not in the late-twelfth but in the mid-thirteenth century. As to John's reign, it seems almost as though professionalism had outrun its social background.

It is only when we first have account rolls, late in the thirteenth century, that it is possible to get a complete picture of the administration of the estate. Then the chief place was occupied by a couple of monk-wardens. It was they who had the ultimate responsibility for the estate as a whole. Alongside the wardens, but clearly on a slightly lower rung, there was the lay steward, whose office had recently been defined as that of 'steward of the liberties'. Alongside also, there were local landowners linked to the abbey by the ties of family and neighbourhood; some of them were judges, and received an annual retainer from the abbey for their services. The estate was divided into three groups of manors, roughly corresponding to (1) the Soke of Peterborough, (2) Northamptonshire and (3) Lincolnshire.[1] Each of these groupings was under the control of a lay bailiff. From the 1260s certainly, and perhaps earlier, the abbey had been run by an administrative system basically similar to that outlined. But within this period there was a great deal of change; in the sixteen years for which we have really detailed evidence, 1294 to 1310, there are marked shifts in the balance between the various offices.

In the accounts of 1294–5 and 1300–1 the activities of the monk-wardens can be followed. They clearly had general oversight of the manors, as their counterparts had at Canterbury.[2] Occasionally they presided over the manorial courts. In 1294–5 one of them leased an acre of demesne land in Warmington; in 1300–1 another ordered ditching at Eye, and supervised the impounding of pigs at Glinton.[3] All extraordinary expenditure had to be authorised by them. In 1300–1 Simon of Freston made small payments to the *famuli* on practically all of the manors; he paid a shepherd at

---

[1] Table 6.
[2] Smith, *Canterbury*, pp. 100–10.
[3] Rockingham Compotus, under Warmington; Fitzwilliam A/C Roll 2388, m. 3r, m. 8r.

Glinton and a man picking peas at Fiskerton; he bribed a park-keeper at Fotheringhay, and tipped a minstrel when the Bishop of Lincoln visited Fiskerton.[1] Here the strictly manorial functions are beginning to shade off. The same man went with the lay steward to the 1301 parliament at Lincoln,[2] and further took time off in the middle of the harvest season to go to the general chapter.[3] He attended the fairs at Stamford and Boston.[4] The wardens clearly had a very general commission indeed.

It may well have become too general. In 1302, shortly after his accession, Godfrey of Crowland reorganised the system, and the office of monk-warden disappeared for the rest of his abbacy. In the place of the two wardens there stood one man, described as the abbot's steward.[5] The change must have been partly one of name, for Peter of Ketene was a warden in 1300–1, and steward in 1302, and there seems no reason to suppose his responsibilities were much changed.[6] But this abbot may well have taken a particularly active part in the running of his estate, and probably more was now left to the lay steward and the bailiffs. Certainly no monk is as ubiquitous in the 1307–8 and 1309–10 accounts as Peter of Ketene had been in 1300–1. Probably at the same time, abbot Godfrey established a general receipt. In 1300–1 there were two men receiving both cash and grain in roughly equal quantities. One of them was the abbot's receiver, the other the cellarer, receiving that part of the produce allotted to the convent. In 1307–8 only one man, Robert of Spalding, received cash. Clearly we have here the abbot's receiver, at last occupying the position enjoined by abbot William of Hotot over half a century earlier.[7] There is evidence of other reorganisation at the same time. The four previous groupings of manors were reduced to three. The sheep-farming activities were in part centralised, for the sheep of the home group were removed from the control of individual reeves and accounted for separately. The accounts therefore show, just as their existence reflects, an administration which was continuously subject to change.

---

[1] *Ibid.* m. 2r, m. 4r, m. 10d, m. 21r.
[2] *Ibid.* m. 21r.
[3] He was thus bound at Kettering, when a quarter of malt was brewed to speed him on his way (*Ibid.* m. 15r); his commission is in the register (Vesp. E.22, fo. 58v).
[4] Fitzwilliam A/C Roll 2388, m. 17d, m. 21r.
[5] Vesp. E.22, fo. 48r.
[6] John of Cambrai was described as steward in 1288 (Black Book, fo. 260v), and as warden in 1291 (*Chr.P.* p. 148).
[7] See above, p. 95.

I shall discuss the organisation of the estate in the next chapter. This chapter will concentrate on the lay officers – on what sort of men they were, and what sort of work they performed. The material for each individual will be taken all together, and an attempt will be made to consider his life and work as a whole. With the chief office, the lay stewardship, this is particularly difficult.[1] In the first half of the thirteenth century charter evidence predominates; we see the stewards chiefly in their own land dealings and as official witnesses to the dealings of others. The individuals can be seen more clearly than their duties. And since several of these men had their landed base outside the estate, we can hope to see only a fraction of their land dealings.

Geoffrey Gibbuin, the first clerk to hold this office, was the steward of abbot Akarius. Between 1201 and 1210 he occurs chiefly, although not entirely, on behalf of the abbey.[2] After 1210, when Akarius died, he occurs as the attorney of several lords.[3] During this period he had the wardship of Geoffrey of St Medard, which he is said to have bought from the abbot for £100.[4] This may have been a device to keep property out of the king's hands during the vacancy. It should not be presumed that this amount of money was beyond him, however, for he seems to have had a fair amount of property in the Buckinghamshire–Oxfordshire area.[5] This was the base from which he acted, and to which he returned. Sometime between 1204 and 1219 he bought an estate in Willen for forty marks, to acquit the tenant of his debts to Jews. He gave this to the Benedictine priory of Snelshall; he acted for this and other religious houses in the area; and he died at Oseney in 1235.[6]

On the three men after Geoffrey Gibbuin there is little material.[7]

---

[1] A list of the stewards of this period is in *C.N.*, pp. 226–7.
[2] See the references in *C.N.*, p. 226; also *Curia Regis Rolls*, I, 398, 422, II, 136, 245, III, 337, V, 127; *Pleas before the King or his Justices 1198–1212*, ed. D. M. Stenton, IV (Selden Soc., LXXXIV, 1967), no. 2914; *Memoranda Roll 10 John*, ed. R. A. Brown (Pipe Roll Soc., new ser., XXXI, 1957), pp. 49, 59–60.
[3] Stenton, *Pleas*, IV, no. 4551; *Curia Regis Rolls*, VI, 270, 397–9, 403.
[4] *Ibid.* VI, 151, VII, 144–5.
[5] A. B. Emden, *A Biographical Register of the University of Oxford to A.D. 1500*, II (Oxford, 1958), p. 761, and the references there cited.
[6] *Ibid.*; *Curia Regis Rolls*, VII, 9–10, XI, no. 2369, and *passim* until Vol. XIV, no. 492; *Cartulary of Snelshall Priory*, ed. J. G. Jenkins (Bucks Rec. Soc., IX, 1952), nos. 7–8; *Curia Regis Rolls*, XV, no. 1636.
[7] There is enough to rescue a couple of them from the italics of the printed list (*C.N.*, p. 226). Simon of St Edmund occurs in three charters (Franceys, pp. 43, 156, 158); 'dominus Rogerus de Noville' occurs once as steward, in a charter which cannot be firmly dated (Franceys, p. 181).

Richard of Saltfleetby, the next steward, takes us to south Lincoln-shire, from where a large number of the abbey's clerks early in the thirteenth century seem to have come.[1] Richard was almost cer-tainly a clerk, for a man of this name was presented by the master of the Gilbertines to the church of Thrussington in 1224.[2] He was among the tenants of half a fee in Osbournby, and from his Peter-borough connexion we find him holding land in Upton and Castor.[3] Of Thomas of Ufford, steward of William Hotot, more is known, for he was based more firmly within the estate. He was a free tenant of the abbey, but what he had inherited was but a small part of his substance at the time of his death. He can be seen consolidating his estate, acquiring 'parcels from divers men in Ufford to hold of the chief lords of the manor of Torpel'; and his son was to be one of those to profit from the dissolution of the Milton fee.[4]

What these men did on a small scale the next steward, Geoffrey Russell, did on the large. His antecedents are unknown, his suc-cessors undistinguished among the lesser gentry of the Soke,[5] but in his time he lived in another world. Between 1250 and 1263 he was steward of the abbey; shortly after this he is found as steward to Isabella de Fortibus; after 1271 he was steward of the palatinate of Durham, and between 1278 and 1281 steward of Wallingford.[6] At the end of his lifetime he occurs as a royal justice.[7] If he ceased to be steward of the abbey, he continued to assist it, and he con-tinued to buy property in the Soke of Peterborough.[8] Some of the land which had come to the abbey from the Milton family was granted to him in a fee-farm in 1254;[9] shortly after 1263 he ac-

---

[1] *Rotuli Hugonis de Welles*, ed. W. P. W. Phillimore, 3 vols. (1912–14).
[2] *Ibid.* II, 293–4.
[3] *Book of Fees*, p. 1029; Fitzwilliam Charters, nos. 4, 7, 1537.
[4] *C.Inq.P.M.*, IV, no. 47; Swa. fo. 34v; Pytchley, fo. 107r.
[5] Fitzwilliam Charters, nos. 267, 845–6.
[6] Denholm-Young, *Seignorial Administration in England*, pp. 70, 75.
[7] *Cal. Close R. 1272–9*, p. 398; *Cal. Patent R. 1272–81*, pp. 340–1.
[8] He witnessed a writ of abbot Robert of Sutton in 1266, after Robert of Sheffield, who was his successor as steward (Franceys, p. 160). The last of his transactions that can be dated is the purchase in 1279 of land in Paston (P.R.O. CP. 25 (1) 174/52/60). A man granting land in the same area to the abbey in 1261 had to exclude 'illam partem quam prius vendidi domino Galfrido Russell tunc senescallo Burgi de eadem terra' (Swa. fo. 264v). On the other hand what looks like a grant by Geoffrey Russell to the abbey (headed 'Galfrido Russell de quodam mesuagio in Burgo') turns out to carry the gloss, 'istud mesuagium emptum fuit de denariis Ade quondam ballivi de Castre per diligenciam istius Galfridi Russell tunc senescaldi de Burgo' (Swa. fo. 188r). In such records private and official dealings become almost impossible to distinguish.
[9] *C.N.* 543, the date being given by Pytchley, fo. 110r.

quired part of the Tot fee in Paston.[1] At a time when the abbey seemed to be short of money to invest in land, its chief servants had particularly good opportunities for their enterprise. When his career is compared with those of stewards earlier in the century, his increased opportunities become clear; and this shows in turn the increase in the demand for professional skills at this time.

Geoffrey was succeeded by Robert of Sheffield, who seems to have acted as steward for the best part of thirty years. Unlike his predecessors, little is known of his private substance, but there is a good deal about the duties of his office, found in the chronicle, the proto-registers and the earliest accounts. He represented the abbey in cases arising under the Dictum of Kenilworth. A few years later, in 1275, we find him in the hundred court, successfully claiming the abbot's jurisdiction in a murder case. It was he who held the inquisition on the death of a knight of the honour who did not hold of the king.[2] At the same time he was constantly with the abbot, frequently present when his knights did homage, and the normal chief witness both to the abbot's charters and those of private individuals.[3]

The earliest steward's commission to survive is that for John of Oundle, appointed guardian of the abbot's liberties in 1298.[4] Now we begin to see in more detail the rewards such men could expect. Shortly after his appointment, seemingly, he was granted the lease of ninety acres of land at Biggin Grange; in 1300 the new abbot revoked this lease, but gave him 60s a year until he could find a benefice for him, and he continued a farm of thirty acres at Biggin.[5] In 1304 he was presented to Scotter in Lincolnshire, one of the abbey's most valuable churches, worth £30 a year in 1291.[6] The account roll of a couple of years later shows that he owned two and a half burgage tenancies in Oundle, and also that he farmed a customary virgate there for 32s.[7] There are some interesting men in these accounts. When Walter Langton, Edward I's treasurer, started to build up an estate in Northamptonshire, it is not surprising that he turned to Peterborough's chief lay officer. Certainly John of

[1] Vesp. E.22, fo. 38r.
[2] *Rotuli Selecti*, p. 161; *Chr.P.*, pp. 21-2, 41; Black Book, fo. 235v; *Pytchley*, pp. xxiv-xxv.
[3] See the instances cited in *C.N.*, p. 227; also Fitzwilliam Charters, nos. 46-7, 79, 82, 84, 1550, 1555-6, 1565.
[4] Vesp. E.22, fo. 37v.
[5] Fitzwilliam A/C Roll 2388, m. 11r; Vesp. E.22, fo. 59r.
[6] *Ibid.* fo. 79r; *Taxatio Ecclesiastica Angliae et Walliae auctoritate Papae Nicholai IV* (Rec. Com., 1802), p. 75a.
[7] Fitzwilliam A/C Roll 233, m. 22r-d.

Oundle was one of Langton's stewards also: in May 1305 he is recorded as carefully counting out 50s owed to the bishop.[1] He served at least two masters, and it is impossible to say how many of his numerous dealings in the Northamptonshire Feet of Fines were his own.

This may not have been ideal from the abbey's point of view, and perhaps as a result the commission of the next steward, Robert of Thorpe, was rather more precise. He was to serve the abbot and convent to the exclusion of all other lords, and to give all manner of service, counsel and aid when occasion required. In return he was to receive 100s a year from the abbey, until he had been given lands, tenements and rents in Stamford, or elsewhere, to the value of this amount.[2] This Robert came from a family with strong roots in the Soke. While they remained freeholders, they had built a manor house at Longthorpe, as well as the adjacent church. As lords of a village, although not knights, they have been considered alongside other gentry families in the thirteenth century.[3] By service they grew further still. Robert started in the abbey's service as a clerk,[4] but he started from a secure base, and he had an open cheque to buy property worth way above what was then thought of as a knight's substance. He acquired a considerable amount of property in Longthorpe and Castor, and he had a lease of 56 acres at Biggin Grange.[5] More substantially, between 1315 and 1322 he acquired two-thirds of the manor of Marholm.[6] The house the family lived in still survives, and the wall paintings in the principal room 'give the most vivid impression of civilised life in a manor house'.[7] On one wall they painted the coats of arms of the knights of Peterborough barony, who had long been in effect and now were in reality their peers. On another wall, the story of the Three Quick

[1] A Beardwood, 'The Trial of Walter Langton, Bishop of Lichfield, 1307–1312', *Trans. of the American Philosophical Soc.*, new ser., Vol. 54, part 3 (1964), pp. 33–4; *Records of the Trial of Walter Langeton*, ed. A. Beardwood (Camden Soc., 4th ser., 6, 1969), pp. 11, 24, 148, 170.

[2] Vesp. E. 22, fo. 116v.

[3] See above, pp. 50–2.

[4] Fitzwilliam A/C Roll 2388, m. 17d; P.R.O. CP. 25 (1) 176/60/489; Vesp. E.22, fos. 26r–50v, *passim*.

[5] His holdings of the abbey are listed in Vesp. E.21, fo. 79r–v, which shows that around 1300 he bought part of the Meynil freehold in Longthorpe; in 1311 he bought nine solidates of rent in Castor (Fitzwilliam Charter no. 1361); and the grange tenancy was farmed for 28s a year (Fitzwilliam A/C Roll 2389, m. 21r.).

[6] Fitzwilliam Charters, nos. 1063, 1079–80, 1085–9, 1096.

[7] N. Pevsner, *The Buildings of England: Bedfordshire and the County of Huntingdon and Peterborough* (Harmondsworth, 1968), p. 186.

and the Three Dead daily reminded the family of the dangers of immersion in secular affairs.[1] Robert of Thorpe is the last steward in the period considered. He represents the epitome of the steward's office, both clerk and local landowner, and he took the rewards of both.

Amongst the most important of the steward's professional colleagues were local lawyers. In abbot William of Woodford's register there is a list of fees paid to six men, the abbey's annuitants on the bench around 1296. Hugh of Cressingham and John of Berewyk each received 66s 8d, William Inge and John de Insula 40s, and Henry Spigurnel 20s.[2] Behind this list of justices we must imagine the increasing complexity of the common law, and in particular the war against the landowning class represented by the *Quo Warranto* proceedings.[3] As in John's reign, the abbot had to deal with a needy and ever-inventive royal administration, which had to be met on its own terms. As in John's reign, he had to broaden the scope of his professional advice. The practice of paying justices was not necessarily corrupt; but bribes were certainly offered at times,[4] and at the very least such relationships involved tensions.[5] Something of these may be seen in considering the abbey's relationship with a man whom contemporaries recognised as honest, Elias of Bekingham, who in 1289 was one of the very few serving judges not removed for corruption.[6] In 1269 he was presented by the abbey to the church of Northborough, and certainly by 1280 some cases involving the abbey were coming before him.[7] In 1281 he was presented to Warmington, one of the three most valuable churches in the abbey's possession.[8] Six years later he was the abbey's agent in the Southorpe transaction, and seems to have been sufficiently wealthy to lend it a large part of the capital required.[9] He acted for it

[1] E. C. Rouse and A. Baker, 'The Wall Paintings at Longthorpe Tower, near Peterborough, Northants', *Archaeologia*, XCVI (1955), pp. 1–57.
[2] Vesp. E.22, fo. 6r; printed in *Select Cases in the Court of King's Bench under Edward I*, ed. G. O. Sayles (Selden Soc., LV, 1936), p. cxliii.
[3] Sutherland, *Quo Warranto Proceedings in the Reign of Edward I*.
[4] The 1307–8 account records a payment of 13 marks to the justices, 'in dono justiciariis de Trailbaston per abbatem £8 13s. 4d.' (Fitzwilliam A/C Roll 233, m. 14d), and there is a long account in Whittlesey's chronicle of entertainment offered the justices a generation later (Sparke, pp. 226–9).
[5] The two sides to this question are argued by G. G. Coulton (*Five Centuries of Religion*, II (Cambridge, 1927), 367) and G. O. Sayles (*Select Cases*, I, pp. lxxvi–iii).
[6] E. Foss, *The Judges of England*, III, 52–3; *D.N.B.*, IV, 85b–86.
[7] Bridges, II, 530; *Chr.P.*, pp. 35, 39.
[8] Bridges, II, 481; *Taxation of Pope Nicholas*, p. 39b.
[9] *Pytchley*, pp. 62–72; *cf.* Sayles, *Select Cases*, I, p. lxxviii.

also in acquiring property in Polebrook in 1285; he was frequently among the witnesses to homages; he was granted expenses in the account roll of 1294–5.[1] He seems to have built up a small landed estate of his own in the Nene valley.[2]

Cressingham and Berewyk, to whom the largest fees were paid, take us towards less reputable territory. Little is known of their dealings with the abbey, for they were men at the ends of their careers. But what brought them into contact with it is easy to surmise. Both were servants of Queen Eleanor. Hugh of Cressingham was Eleanor's steward by 1290, having previously been steward of the bishop of Ely. A man much loathed, he died at Stirling Bridge in 1297, and bits of his skin were distributed around Scotland in token of its temporary liberation.[3] John of Berewyk was Eleanor's treasurer, and also one of her executors.[4] Queen Eleanor was a dynamic and important landowner in this area, and her servants would naturally come into contact with those of the abbey. It might indeed be possible to go beyond this, for such pensions might well be calculated to secure a certain amount of mutual understanding.[5]

John de Insula and Henry Spigurnel were each members of Northamptonshire families. Spigurnel, the junior of those retained, had been a professional advocate until he was appointed to the bench in 1295.[6] De Insula, his senior, was a member of an important Northamptonshire administrative dynasty.[7] In 1301 and 1307 he was involved in what looks very much like speculation in the Soke, in Paston and Etton.[8] Such men as these might possibly have brothers in the monastic community. Very likely they had relatives there. If only lists of the monks survived, many relationships of this

[1] CP. 25 (1) 174/54/155; *Chr.P.*, pp. 144–5, 149–50; Rockingham Compotus, under Kettering and Tinwell.
[2] In 1304 he sold 20 acres of land in Tansor to John of Oundle (CP. 25 (1) 175/59/450), and a man described as his *serviens* is found buying land in the neighbouring manor of Hemington in 1295 (Buccleuch Charters, BI. 253).
[3] Miller, *Ely*, p. 267; Tout, *Chapters*, v, 238–9, 271–2; Foss, *Judges*, III, 82–3; G. W. S. Barrow, *Robert Bruce* (London, 1965), p. 125.
[4] Tout, *Chapters*, II, 42, 83, v, 238–9; Foss, *Judges*, III, 237–8; *C.Inq.P.M.*, v, no. 397.
[5] A famous letter of archbishop Peckham declares that Eleanor's clerks were 'of the stock of the devil rather than of Christ' (*Registrum Epistolarum Johannis Peckham*, ed. C. T. Martin, III (Rolls Ser., 77, 1885), 937–8); see further Tout, *Chapters*, v, 236–8, 270–2, and Richardson, *English Jewry under Angevin Kings*, pp. 107, 220.
[6] Foss, *Judges*, III, 301–3; Sayles, *Select Cases*, I, pp. lxii–iii, 154; *Documents Illustrating the Rule of Walter de Wenlock*, ed. B. F. Harvey (Camden Soc., 4th ser., 2, 1965), p. 32 note 19.
[7] Denholm-Young, *Collected Papers* (Cardiff, 1969), p. 176 note 2.
[8] CP. 25 (1) 175/59/403–4, 175/61/504, 506.

sort would become a good deal clearer, and at the same time less 'official'.

One point in this connexion is raised by the pension paid to Roger of Hegham. Clearly he was much more closely tied to the abbey than the other lawyers considered;[1] and in 1300 his relationship with it was formalised. He undertook to give the abbot and community 'counsel and aid in all cases touching the house, however and whenever he could help them'; in return he was to receive the substantial fee of £10 a year.[2] Now the terms of this grant are interesting. They are very similar, for instance, to those in the oath taken by a man on joining the large and formal council of the archbishop of Canterbury in the late-thirteenth century.[3] Can this be taken to imply, as has been suggested, that Peterborough had a formal council at this date?[4] It is just possible, but if so it seems strange that there is no other record of it. It is more likely that the abbot took advice in a much less formal way. Thus when abbot Godfrey took a homage at his grange at Eye in 1301 the senior witnesses were a judge, Humphrey of Waledene, and a neighbouring landowner, John Spigurnel.[5] Later, in 1342, what looks like the abbot's council was convened in a case against the abbot of Swineshead concerning marshland in Gosberton:[6]

And the first day of the assises at Lincolne was on Wednesday, being the morrow after the feast of S. Peter ad vincula: at which time there came thither Gilbert de Stanford, then Celerer to the Convent, John de Achirche bailiff of the said abbot's manors; together with Sir John de Wilughby Lord of Eresby, Sir John de Kirketon, and Sir Saier de Rochford, knights, John de Multon parson of Skirbek, as also divers others of the said abbot's counsel.

---

[1] The account rolls between 1294–5 and 1307–8 frequently record his expenses; he attended the parliament at Lincoln on the abbey's behalf in 1301 (Rockingham Compotus, under Oundle; Fitzwilliam A/C Roll 2388, m. 11r, m. 14d, m. 19r; *Ibid.* no. 233, m. 20d, m. 25r, m. 26r); he also frequently witnessed homages (Vesp. E.22, fos. 26r–48r, *passim*).
[2] *Ibid.* fo. 62r; printed Sayles, *Select Pleas*, I, p. cxliii.
[3] Smith, *Canterbury*, p. 72 note 6.
[4] This was suggested by Miss Levett, but she quoted no reference: A. E. Levett, *Studies in Manorial History* (Oxford, 1938), p. 24.
[5] Vesp. E.22, fo. 47v. Waledene 'had long been familiar as a bailiff of Queen Eleanor and an active royal agent' (Tout, *Chapters*, v, 239 note 4; Foss, *Judges*, III, 309–11); John Spigurnel was perhaps the elder brother of Henry Spigurnel (Foss, *Judges*, III, 301).
[6] Dugdale, *Imbanking and Draining*, p. 234, from Peterborough D and C MS. 6, fos. 153r–156r. The last phrase appears there as, 'et aliis quampluribus de consilio nostro' (fo. 153v); later the abbot is described as appearing 'cum domino Johanne de Wylughby et aliis de amicicia et consilio suo' (fo. 154v).

These were all Lincolnshire men, and a formal council would have had to have been more broadly based than this. More likely, this represents an *ad hoc* group of men familiar with 'the customs of Holland'.[1] For this reason, on this occasion, they became the abbot's councillors.[2]

It is probable that Roger of Hegham was the chief judicial officer of the abbey, known elsewhere as the *legistre*.[3] Either before or shortly after his first connexion with the abbey, he bought the small abbey fee of Helpston, in various parcels, between 1290 and 1294.[4] Helpston, a couple of miles off the main road north, must have been a useful manor for a busy justice, especially one with a private practice in the area. He was in it often enough to witness several charters; he had a bailiff to administer the property in his absence; and he presented a relative to the church when it fell vacant in 1297.[5]

The bailiffs operated on a different level, and over a more limited area. They come into clearer focus, for their activities were confined to the estate, and the fullest documents we have, the account rolls, are properly speaking their records.[6] In the accounts of the late-thirteenth century the bailiffs, like the stewards, were subordinate to the monk-wardens. It was the wardens who held the manorial courts, gave the *famuli* their annual bonus, and the like. When the wardens were superseded early in the fourteenth century, such duties as these came to the bailiffs. They mainly acted within their own group of manors. Bernard of Castor, the bailiff of the 'northern' group between 1300 and 1310, had the most extensive of these. The farthest distant of the manors he controlled, Walcot, lay eighty miles from the abbey. In 1307–8 he made at least five journeys around his manors; he handed over money to the receiver at Boston fair, probably the proceeds from the sale of grain; and he went to the gaol delivery at Lincoln, to claim the cases due to the abbey.[7] In

---

[1] *Ibid.* fo. 153v–'consuetudinibus patrie de Heylond'.
[2] The references quoted as proving the existence of a council at Ramsey are open to similar objections: Levett, *Studies*, pp. 24, 27.
[3] *Walter de Wenlock*, p. 28 note 3.
[4] *Pytchley*, pp. 148–9; Bridges, II, 514. The Helpston family seems rather weak at this time; there had been several alienations previous to this (Fitzwilliam Ch., nos. 808, 810–11), and others followed (CP. 25 (1) 175/57/342, 175/58/360, 365). The last of these, in 1928, was a further sale to Roger of Hegham.
[5] Fitzwilliam Ch., nos. 822, 835; a grant of a messuage and 14 acres of land to his bailiff is *Ibid.* no. 830; *The Rolls and Register of Bishop Oliver Sutton*, ed. R. M. T. Hill, II (Lincs Rec. Soc., 43, 1950), 138.
[6] D. Oschinsky, 'Notes on the Editing and Interpretation of Estate Accounts', *Archives*, IX (1969–70), 84–9, 142–52.
[7] Fitzwilliam A/C Rolls 233, m. 17r.

1294 the bailiff of the Great Easton group collected the tenth of that year, levied by contributions from each of the manors, and took it to Oxford.[1] Wool sales were centralised under them in a similar fashion. The bailiffs of the 'home' and 'western' groups, along with the stock-keeper, supervised the collection of the wool clip from the whole estate.[2] The bailiffs therefore had responsibilities to the estate as a whole, as well as the task of supervising in detail the work of the manors in their group.

The bailiffs were paid on the same scale as the other abbey clerks, receiving fees of between twenty and forty shillings a year. This may seem low compared with the hundred shillings of the steward, and even with the twopence a day paid to the bailiffs of the bishops of Ely, for they were at best two-manor men.[3] But we must remember the entries in the 'expensa forinseca' section of the accounts – these were men living on a not unsophisticated form of expense account. More important, perhaps, were the opportunities offered to forceful men by the very fact of their holding office. An examination of the careers of two of the bailiffs at the time of the main accounts, between 1300 and 1310, shows this very clearly.

Richard of Crowland, bailiff of the property in the Soke of Peterborough, was the more important of the two. He was a nephew of abbot Godfrey of Crowland, by whom he was appointed.[4] By the time of his death in 1346 he had built up a considerable estate. His main holding was the quarter-fee of Walton, which he bought in 1305.[5] Later he acquired the Cathwaite portion of the Barnack fee, for his lifetime,[6] and a small amount of the Torpel fee, the bulk of which was purchased by Robert of Thorpe.[7] Just as we found John of Oundle, as steward, farming a customary holding in Oundle, so Richard of Crowland farmed two customary virgates at Boroughbury.[8] He could presumably sublet the holdings, either in parcels or as a whole, at a profit. He also had a substantial amount of property in the town of Peterborough,[9] and bought an impressive

---

[1] Rockingham Compotus, under Great Easton and Tinwell.
[2] See below, pp. 158–9.
[3] Miller, *Ely*, p. 255.
[4] *Pytchley*, p. 142, where it is stated that his promotion was 'contra voluntatem conventus'.
[5] B. M. Add. MS. 25288, fo. 59v; *Pytchley*, pp. 142–3.
[6] *Pytchley*, p. 125 note.
[7] Fitzwilliam Ch., nos. 1080, 1181.
[8] Fitzwilliam A/C Roll 2388, m. 1r–d, m. 2d.
[9] CP. 25(1) 175/62/16, 29.

list of cottages to build a house in Westgate.[1] In the first quarter of the fourteenth century he seems ubiquitous.[2] For the last generation of his life the sources are less abundant, and probably in any case the main spate of his activity had passed. The records of his later years conjure up the picture of a small country gentleman, and this is probably not far from the truth. He had a town house and a country house, to which he retired. In 1345 he describes himself as 'manens in Walton', and in the following year he died there 'in mansione sua'.[3] He must have been around eighty by then;[4] probably few remembered that his father had been a villein, and even the convent had forgotten their disapproval.

Ralph of Thorney, the bailiff of the 'western' group, was a man of the same kind. In 1299 he leased the tithes of Eye from the sacristy, along with certain neighbouring property.[5] But the headquarters of his group of manors was Warmington, and this seems to have been the centre of his estate. Shortly after 1315 he bought two-thirds of the Gargate fee there from William of St Lucy.[6] By the time of his death in 1333 his estate comprised nearly three hundred acres; an extent was made a couple of years later, and 'gives a remarkable picture of an estate largely built up by piecemeal acquisition'.[7] The land had been bought from at least eighteen different people, and probably a good many more. Not only does the extent show how he acquired his land, it shows also how a careful tenant might improve it. He built on land which he held from the nuns of Stamford, and then leased the cottages to tenants at will. Divers cottages in Warmington were farmed for thirty shillings. We know too that on the manors of his group he could expect to lease parcels

---

[1] 'Item memorandum quod Ricardus de Croylande perquisivit diversa cotagia de quibus fecit mansum suum ad finem de le Westgate. Videlicet de Roberto de Thorpe omnia cotagia cum croftis que quondam fuerunt Roberti Hoket usque ad magnum solarium. Item solarium et aulam usque ad coquinam que fuerunt Simonis Aubry de Pastona, qui fuit clericus in ista domo. Item tenementum Henrici de Wytheringtona in quo edificatur coquina. Item tenementum Willelmi de Stauntone, in quo edificantur porte. Item tenementum Petronille Durant, in quo edificantur solarium et celarium cum crofto adiacente.' (Pytchley, fo. 107r). In 1335 he granted to Simon Aubrey of Paston, mentioned above, two messuages and two tofts, and an acre and a rood (Franceys, pp. 92–3). This looks like an exchange; and this would date the building of his town-house.
[2] Red Book of Thorney, fo. 66r; Fineshade cartulary, fo. 18r.
[3] Franceys, pp. 32, 322.
[4] He had held land in Castor in 1285. Fitzwilliam Ch., no. 84.
[5] Franceys, pp. 119–20.
[6] Vesp. E.21, fo. 78v; *Pytchley*, pp. 126–7.
[7] *C.N.*, p. xix and no. 483; the date of his death is in Franceys, p. 307.

of demesne on favourable terms.[1] His position in the abbey administration, involving regular contact with the area over a long period,
must surely have been the determining factor in the acquisition of
this estate.

The range of skills, and the number of people, required to do the
abbey's work expanded considerably during the thirteenth century.
Clerks, stewards, bailiffs, attorneys, legal advisers, as well as friends,
were all required wholesale by comparison with the previous
century. But on the evidence of this chapter no single group of
these men can be considered simply as salaried officials. The
'landless bailiff',[2] after all, is a legal fiction, forced on us by an
administration which lost sight of him as he crossed the village
boundary. Just as Langton's wealth was used to create a huge landed
estate in the East Midlands, so a lawyer's fees had also to be invested
in land. Patronage had its repercussions on the land market in the
thirteenth century as in every other. Justices might be itinerant,
but they came from a base in one area and might build up holdings
in others; their place in the commonwealth cannot just be seen in
official terms. The point has wider implications. For there is a temptation to make men's dealings with one another official, and to
categorise them – simply because we have official sources. Funda-
mental to this chapter have been the ties of friendship, family and
interest which joined together the abbey and the local community.

[1] Fitzwilliam A/C Roll 233, m. 22d.
[2] T. F. T. Plucknett, *The Medieval Bailiff* (London, 1954), p. 25.

8   The Organisation of the Estate

At Peterborough, as on many estates, the reign of Henry I provides
the fullest documentation of the whole of the twelfth century, a
circumstance which suggests a high level of efficiency in local estate
management. The *Descriptio Militum* was the basic text for the
chapter on Norman feudalism. The surveys of the Peterborough
manors, from rather later in the reign, are no less basic to an examination of the monastery's landed resources and the exploitation of
its estates.[1]

Just as there was careful planning in which properties the abbey
retained in demesne and which it subinfeudated, so there was a careful division of function between the various demesne manors. Each
of the manors provided a 'farm', a specified amount of cash or of
grain, on which the community of monks depended for its main-
tenance. The various farms are listed in Table 3.[2] Various groupings
of manors can be clearly distinguished from this table, and they are
further distinguished by Table 4, which shows the burden of labour
services on the main villein tenancies. This is the result, not just of
differing estate function, but of different degrees of manorialisation.
These in turn reflect the geography of the different regions. There
is a further indication of the same divisions in Table 5, which shows
the number of plough teams in demesne, and the number of oxen
per plough. The first of these tables might be taken to indicate the
estate structure, the second the social structure, and the third the
geographical structure. An examination of each table in more detail
will show how closely these three things were intertwined.

It can be seen from Table 3 that there were two kinds of manor in
1125, one of which provided cash only and the other both cash and

---

[1] *Chr.P.*, pp. 157–68.

[2] The rents from the manors in the left-hand column amount to £247 18s 4d,
out of the total of £284 13s 4d given in the text (*Ibid.* pp. 166–7). Rents
from various individuals amount to £35 15s 0d, the chief items being £20
from Ascelin of Waterville for the farm of Irthlingborough, Aldwincle
and Stanwick, and £10 from the reeve of Stamford. This leaves a discrepancy of £1 between the figures and the total. The full sum is recorded
as being *de firmis maneriorum*, even though a small part of this was not
strictly manorial rent.

Table 3   *Farms of Peterborough manors 1125–8*

Fiskerton	£20		
Collingham	£20		
Scotter	£22		
Walcot	£4 10s 0d		
Gosberton	£5 13s 4d		
Thurlby	£3		
Kettering	£26		
Tinwell	£15		
Cottingham	£12		
Great Easton	£12		
Pytchley	£12		
Irthlingborough Aldwincle and Stanwick	£20	from Ascelin of Waterville	
Oundle	£11	8 measures of wheat	8 measures of malt, one cow, and 300 loaves
Warmington	£10	12 of wheat	8 of malt
Pilsgate	£14		
Peterborough	£30		
Eye and Oxney	£5		
Longthorpe	£1 15s 0d	4½ of wheat	4½ of malt
Werrington	£2	4 of wheat	4 of malt
Glinton	£5	8 of wheat	8 of oats
Castor	£6	12 of wheat	8 of malt
Etton	£6	4 of wheat	3 of malt, 1 of oats
Walton	£1	4 of wheat	4 of malt
Fletton	—	4 of wheat	4 of malt
Alwalton	£4	4½ of wheat	4½ of malt
		Totals rent	£284 13s 4d
		value of grain	£97 12s 0d
			£382 5s 4d

Table 4   *Labour services from full tenancies 1125–8*

Manors where full tenancies owed three days' service per week

Kettering
Oundle
Warmington
Pytchley

Pilsgate
Etton
Longthorpe
Glinton
Castor

Manors where they owed less than three days' service per week

Tinwell	2 per week
Cottingham	2 per week (3 in August)
Great Easton	2 per week
Collingham	1 per week
Thurlby	2 per week (4 in August)
Fiskerton	2 per week
Scotter	2 per week

Alwalton
Werrington   } Ploughing service in respect of teams, and work
Peterborough   } 'according to the custom of the manor'
Gosberton

Eye   Nil

Fletton
Irthlingborough } No information
Aldwinckle
Stanwick

grain. This division is explained by the chronology of the monastery's endowment, and by the geography of the estate. At Peterborough these two things were as one, for the abbey's sphere of
influence spread outwards, and the manors farthest from the abbey
were those which it had most recently acquired. The more distant
manors sent cash only, as did all the property outside the Soke of
Peterborough, with the exception of Oundle and Warmington.
Within the Soke, Boroughbury provided cash, as did the two fen

hamlets of Eye and Oxney, and Pilsgate, the most distant of the demesne manors in this area. The other manors in the Soke sent grain, and this was their chief contribution, for their cash renders amounted to only £21 15s 0d. The grain sent was valued at £97 12s 0d. Since both Oundle and Warmington sent grain, it seems clear that the pattern of food rents goes back to the tenth century, when these two manors were acquired.

The pattern of villein obligation reflects this division of function within the estate.[1] It will be seen from Table 4 that, with the possible exception of Werrington, no manor which owed a food-farm had a customary obligation for a full tenancy of under three days a week. The amount of week-work required remained at three days; Eye was brought into line, as it developed, as were Peterborough and Werrington, if indeed they departed from it at this date. The Lincolnshire tenants, and those of the manors on the scarp-top, had a smaller but still significant customary obligation.[2] The pattern of villein obligation, and the whole pattern of estate management up to the Black Death, are thus clearly visible by the end of the first quarter of the twelfth century.

Although the Peterborough demesnes lay on a wide variety of soils they were in an area dominated by the heavy clays. The figures for oxen per plough-team, given in Table 5, show this very clearly. Of the twenty-six demesne manors of the abbey, seventeen had eight oxen to each plough. Three of the exceptions, Great Easton, Cottingham and Tinwell, were on the lighter limestone soils of the Lincolnshire uplands. Alwalton and Fletton lay south of the Nene, in northern Huntingdonshire. Each of these manors had six oxen to each plough. Two of the four manors in the northern group, Thurlby and Scotter, also fell below eight, as did the manors of Peterborough and Pytchley – each of these places had seven or a fraction more. The bulk of the property, near the Nene and its tributaries, lay on the western edge of the claylands, a stronghold of the eight-ox plough.

The information from 1125 shows also that the abbey managed to maintain the value of its demesne property after the conquest, despite the fact that nearly half the estate was subinfeudated by 1086. The demesne manors were valued at £167 13s 4d in 1086, while the

---

[1] The figures are considered in detail in Lennard, *Rural England*, pp. 378–82.

[2] The two days a week service owed by the Lincolnshire manors was a light burden for the estate, but for the county this was a heavy manorialism indeed: Stenton, *Lincs Domesday*, p. xxvii.

Table 5   *Plough-teams 1125–8*

	Ploughs in demesne	Number of oxen	Oxen per plough-team
Collingham	2	16	8
Fiskerton	3	24	8
Gosberton	4 oxen		
Thurlby	1	7	7
Scotter	4	24	6
Tinwell	2	12	6
Cottingham	2	12	6
Great Easton	2	12	6
Kettering	4	32	8
Oundle	3	24	8
Warmington	4	32	8
Aldwincle	2	16	8
Irthlingborough	2	16	8
Stanwick	2	16	8
Pytchley	4	30	$7\frac{1}{2}$
Pilsgate	1	8	8
Longthorpe	2	16	8
Werrington	2	16	8
Etton	2	16	8
Glinton	3	24	8
Castor	4	32	8
Walton	2	16	8
Eye	1	8	8
Peterborough	4	29	$7\frac{1}{2}$
Alwalton	2	12	6
Fletton	2	12	6

total estate was valued at £317 11s 0d. In 1125 the demesne manors were worth £284 13s 4d, and the grain liveries brought the total to £382 5s 4d. In two generations the abbey had made up its losses consequent upon the Norman settlement. This is perhaps the most remarkable of the abbey's managerial triumphs in the period studied. The fixed rents, the value of farms and direct payments, remained stable for the next century.[1]

1125	£284 13s 4d
1176	£281 6s 10d
1211	£303 10s 0d

[1] *Chr.P.*, pp. 166–7; *Pipe Roll 23 Henry II*, pp. 104–5; *Pipe Roll 13 John*, p. 271.

The total amounts accounted for in the three years for which vacancy accounts have survived were as follows.[1]

1176 (year)	£394 6s 3d
1210 (6 months)	£1000 15s 2d
1211 (year)	£808 17s 2d

It will be observed that while in 1176 the rent item was the preponderant part of the total received by the vacancy commissioners, thirty-five years later the same item was comparatively insignificant. Behind the variation in these figures lies the change from indirect to direct management. The phenomenon is well known,[2] and the Peterborough evidence is not particularly remarkable, but it seems well to establish the chronology as closely as possible.

In 1176 all the manors seem to have been farmed. The abbacy of abbot Benedict, between 1177 and 1193, sees the beginning of direct management on this estate. Among the earliest of the manors so managed, and perhaps serving as a model for the rest, was Biggin Grange, carved out of the Rockingham Forest in the area to the north and west of Oundle.[3] The next surviving vacancy account, from Michaelmas 1210, shows all the manors under direct control. The work of recovery had been a long process, as it could only be, with a group of farmers of varying rights and varying influence. Robert of Neville had farmed Collingham in Nottinghamshire, and only surrendered it for a payment of £40 cash and a pension of £10 a year.[4] Walcot in Lincolnshire, the farthest distant manor, was only recovered in 1210 by the vacancy commissioners themselves; they seem to have seized the property, and forced the tenant to take a pension of £5 a year.[5] Under the Angevins the Lincolnshire manors proved the most difficult to control, just as they had been in Norman times.

Comparing the figures for 1176 and 1211 it will be seen that the value of the monastery to the crown, and potentially presumably to the monks, had more than doubled in the intervening period. Out of total receipts of £808 in the latter year, the crown at least could take

---

[1] *Pipe Roll 23 Henry II*, pp. 104–5; *Pipe Roll 12 John*, p. 215; *Pipe Roll 13 John*, p. 271.
[2] The most recent examination is in Edward Miller, 'England in the Twelfth and Thirteenth Centuries: An Economic Contrast?', *Econ.H.R.*, 2nd ser., XXIV (1971), 1–14.
[3] See above, pp. 81–2.
[4] Swa, fo. 272r–v; *Pipe Roll 13 John*, p. 271. In 1185 he was the only lay tenant holding a church of the Templars, at Ashby de la Laund in Lincolnshire (Lees, *Templars Surveys*, p. clix).
[5] *Pipe Roll 13 John*, p. 271.

£520 profit. Two new factors made these figures possible, direct management and strong lordship; the latter, dependent on the former, was no less important than it. In 1211 again, manorial profits (sale of grain, wool, stock and pasture) amounted to £236 10s 0d, while seigneurial profits (sale of justice, and tallage) amounted to £251 17s 2d.[1]

THE EARLY FOURTEENTH CENTURY

It is the best part of a century before the abbey's own records provide figures sufficiently detailed to be compared with those for the royal administration in King John's time. I shall consider both the organisation of the estate and its total value as they were in the early fourteenth century, before turning to the more detailed examination of individual topics which the account rolls permit.

The Peterborough manors in the earliest account rolls are arranged in four groups, which divide upon lines that can be seen in the early twelfth century surveys. Each of the groups was under the control of a bailiff. The central group comprised the manors of the Soke of Peterborough, and this was usually referred to as the 'home' group. The smallest, the 'northern', comprised the Lincolnshire manors and Collingham in Nottinghamshire. All the manors in Northamptonshire, with the exception of Cottingham, formed a 'western' group. Cottingham, Great Easton and Tinwell, the three manors in the Limestone belt, together with Torpel, Upton and Lolham when these were leased of the crown, formed a last group. This has been called the 'scarp-top' group; the manors in it are in some way distinguished in both Tables 4 and 5. This last group was disbanded between 1301 and 1307, its manors in the Soke going to the home group, and the others going to the western. From Peterborough the abbey administrators went in two directions, north and south-west. The staging manors were Thurlby to the north and Warmington to the south, and the accounts show a considerable amount of movement through each of these places.[2]

The amounts of cash and grain sent to the abbey also followed very closely the pattern of 1125. The cash liveries are shown in Table 7.

---

[1] It is impossible to calculate what percentage of the seigneurial figure would have been collected by *the abbey* at this period.

[2] For more information on Peterborough's network of communications see my note in *Local Maps and Plans before 1500*, ed. P. D. A. Harvey and R. A. Skelton (O.U.P., forthcoming).

Table 6   *Groups of manors 1300–1*

Group	Bailiff	Manor
	Walter	Town of Peterborough
Home	Richard of Crowland	Boroughbury Eye Longthorpe Castor Walton Werrington Glinton
Northern	Bernard of Castor	Thurlby Collingham Scotter Walcot Fiskerton
Western	Ralph of Thorney	Warmington Oundle Biggin Grange Ashton Stanwick Irthlingborough Kettering
Scarp-top	Robert Fayifox	* Great Easton * Cottingham * Tinwell † Torpel † Upton † Lolham

By the time of the next account, in 1307–8, manors marked † had been transferred to the home group, and manors marked * to the western group.

It will be seen that the bulk of the cash came from the northern group; and most of this was from the two large manors of Fiskerton and Scotter. In 1300–1 the cash from this group represented 60 per cent of the total cash liveries, in 1307–8 it was 52 per cent, and in 1309–10, when both the home and western groups put large amounts of money into improvements, the figure was 78 per cent. In both 1300–1 and 1307–8 the amounts sent by the other groups were fairly stable; from the home group rather over 15 per cent, and from the

Table 7   *Cash liveries*

	1294–5 £	1300–1 £	1307–8 £	1309–10 £
Home group	missing	158	132	63
Northern group	missing	620	417	568
Western group	75	c. 245	248	93
		1023	797	724

western between 24 and 31 per cent. In 1309–10 the figures were 9 and 13 per cent respectively. The surpluses, especially from the western group, might be transferred to other uses; in 1307–8 various of the Northamptonshire manors transferred £51 to Biggin Grange, and they sent £178 there in 1309–10.[1]

The grain liveries were no less important, and here a greater responsibility lay upon the manors closer to the monastery. While the surplus from the northern manors was sold, that from the home and western manors was sent to the abbey. In the 1300s this arrangement was clearly of long standing, for a document from the vacancy of 1263 states.[2]

If in any year it is possible to get 140 measures of all kinds of grain from each plough of the 57 ploughs in Nassaburgh and the western areas and also Thurlby . . . then all the grain from Fiskerton, Collingham, Scotter and Walcot may be sold, save for seed-corn, and the labourers' corn, and the expenses of the abbot and other visitors. In such a year it should not be necessary to buy more than 206 measures of any sort of grain.

The later account rolls reflect this carefully organised stability. The value of the grain sold was relatively small, amounting to £121 in 1301, £129 in 1308 and £199 in 1310 (a year of very high prices). So far as the amounts sent to the monastery is concerned, only one set of liveries was not stable, and that was oats. The amount of oats sent to the monastery fell in fifteen years by almost a half, from 985 quarters in 1295 to 526 quarters in 1310. Yet the real decline had

[1] The liveries were not the only payments made out of manorial revenues, although they were much the most substantial. Contributions to royal and papal taxation were assessed on each manor, and rendered separately. Various pensions and corrodies and occasional payments also came out of manorial receipts.
[2] Vesp. E.22, fo. 42r.

come earlier, for the 1295 figure included 561 quarters sent by Kettering, all of which had been bought.[1] The amount of wheat sent remained fairly constant, between 1100 and 1400 quarters. So also, if their figures are taken together, did the amounts of barley and drage. Peas were sent from a few manors, but the amounts were small.[2] An estimate of the cash value of each set of liveries is given as part of Table 8. Two figures are given for grain, one adjusted and the other unadjusted. The unadjusted figure is on the basis of the price at which each grain seems most frequently to have been sold, in Lincolnshire, in the same year. The adjusted figures are taken from the decennial averages of Thorold Rogers.[3] Both sets of figures are thus impressionistic.

Table 8   *Cash and grain liveries*

Date	Cash liveries £	Grain liveries		Total	
		Adjusted £	Un-adjusted £	Adjusted £	Un-adjusted £
1294–5	not known	915	789	—	—
1300–1	1023	778	665	1801	1688
1307–8	797	898	754	1695	1551
1309–10	724	868	1368	1592	2092

The table does, however, provide a clear indication of the respective values of cash and grain liveries. The picture varies as the price of grain fluctuates. At the same time in two of the three accounts the value of the grain was greater than that of the cash; in 1310, with high grain prices, the value of the grain was almost twice that of the cash sent. A comparison of these figures with those for 1125 is instructive. In 1125 the value of the liveries was around £350, and little more than a quarter of this was accounted for by grain. In the three accounts between 1300 and 1310 their total value was

[1] The 1295 figure of 985 may be compared with the 1263 estimate that 1048 *summas* were required (*Ibid.*).
[2] Between 30 and 50 quarters of peas came from the home manor of Boroughbury, and any further supplies needed were purchased.
[3] Prices in 1301 and 1308 were rather below, and in 1310 were considerably above, the decennial averages found in J. E. Thorold Rogers, *A History of Agriculture and Prices*, I (1866), 245. See also the 50 year averages found in W. Beveridge, 'The Yield and Price of Corn in the Middle Ages', reprinted in *Essays in Economic History*, ed. E. M. Carus-Wilson, I (1954), 20.

around £1600 to £1800, and of this figure half was grain and half cash. More manors sent grain in the early fourteenth century than had done so two centuries earlier. In 1125 only Oundle and Warmington among the western group had sent grain: between 1300–10 all the manors in the group did so, including Cottingham and Great Easton, both of which were twenty-five miles away. In respect both of manors covered and of the relative value of the grain sent, the abbey was more dependent on grain liveries in the early fourteenth century than it had been in the early twelfth. At neither date was the abbey responsive to the market. On the one hand it was buttressed against changes in market prices, on the other it missed their opportunities.[1]

ARABLE FARMING

As well as the general figures that have just been considered, the account rolls naturally provide detailed evidence of the abbey's farming techniques and methods of estate management. The surviving Peterborough account rolls, however, have major limitations. Only three of them cover the whole estate; they span less than ten years; and no two of them are consecutive. They will show organisation at a point of time, but they are unlikely to show change over time, and when they do it is difficult to put this change in any perspective.

For the study of the abbey's arable farming these limitations are particularly serious. The lack of consecutive rolls means there can be no proper examination of yields. What can be studied is the total amount of demesne sown, and the area sown with each crop. Figures for total acreage are presented in Table 9. The fragmentary accounts mean that for all the manors in the western group the time covered is extended to fifteen years, and for three manors to nearly thirty. There seems to be marked change in total acreage on four manors within the estate. The largest manor in the northern group, Fiskerton, seems to have increased its acreage, and so perhaps did Scotter. In the western group three of the manors at least declined. In the manors of the home group, over the decade for which accounts survive, the amount of change is not marked. The manors on the fen edge – Werrington, Glinton, and Eye – seem to have expanded

---

[1] Canterbury Cathedral Priory, for instance, was much more closely geared to the market (Smith, *Canterbury*, pp. 131–3), but the relevant Canterbury manors were at least twice as close to London as were those of Peterborough.

Table 9   *Acreage sown*

Home group	1281–2	1294–5	1300–1	1307–8	1309–10
Boroughbury			560	551	502
Eye			255	210	293
Castor			381	277	322
Walton			195	219	184
Werrington			155	174	195
Glinton			189	183	196
Longthorpe			261	238	246
(Torpel)			186	c. 160	124
(Upton)			186	154	88
Western group					
Warmington		265	287	280	265
Ashton		186	175	158	154
Oundle		236	180	233	162
Biggin Grange		c. 500	482	468	440
Stanwick	150	157	163	160	144
Irthlingborough	179	156	159	96	95
Kettering	272	260	283	275	264
Cottingham	262	c. 275		255	224
Great Easton		375		276	263
Tinwell			114	138	123
Northern group					
Collingham			151	184	149
Fiskerton			294	309	337
Scotter		154	186	164	196
Walcot			64	66	59

overall, while the other manors in the group seem to have declined slightly. The home manor of the abbey, Boroughbury, which presumably was run with more than average care, can be studied over a longer period because of a number of fragmentary accounts.[1] They suggest an effort to keep up the demesne acreage, but over the long-term they show a decline.

In some of the farthest flung manors of the western group the effort to maintain demesne cultivation was being abandoned. It is

---

[1] In 1292 the demesne sown was 562 acres, it was 560 in 1301, 551 in 1308, 502 in 1310, 536 in 1313 and 484 in 1315: Fitzwilliam Account Rolls, 2387, 2388, 233, 2389, 247 and 248.

only for this group that a detailed examination of manorial organisation is attempted. Appendix B sets out manor by manor the
crops sown. Of the nine manors for which there is information from
1294–5 to 1309–10, one manor (Kettering) showed a slight increase,
one manor (Warmington) was stable, and the other seven manors
showed a decline. The total acreage sown on these nine manors was
2408 acres in 1294–5 and 2012 acres in 1309–10, a decline of 16.5 per
cent overall. Within these figures there are considerable variations.
The amount sown with various crops may change drastically even
where total acreage remains fairly stable, while on a few manors the
total decline is very marked indeed. A major factor both in reorganisation and in overall decline is a slump in the amount of oats
sown. In 1294–5, 732 acres were sown with oats, but by 1309–10
this figure was down to 529 acres, a decline of 28 per cent. The
decline in oats was 203 acres in an overall decline of 396 acres.

Table 10   *Distribution of crops sown in the western group*

1294–5:			*1309–10*:		
Wheat	34 per cent		Wheat	32 per cent	
Barley	10		Barley	15	
Oats	30		Oats	26	
Drage	15		Drage	12	
Rye	5		Rye	6	
Peas	6		Peas	9	
	100			100	

Examples of reorganisation within a stable situation are provided
by the manors of Warmington, Cottingham and Kettering. Each of
them had demesnes of medium size, between 200 and 300 acres
being sown in each year. Both Warmington and Cottingham were
two-crop manors in the earliest accounts, sowing little save large
acreages of both wheat and oats, in roughly equal proportions. By
1309–10 Warmington had halved its oats total and grew barley in its
stead; at Cottingham both wheat and oats were halved, with in-
creases in barley and drage and a total decline overall. At Kettering
oats declined by a third, wheat was finally abandoned, rye and drage
were increased. The pattern on the manors which showed major
decline also varied. At Great Easton, going down from 375 to 263
between 1295 and 1310, the decline was in all the crops sown in

roughly equal proportions; at Irthlingborough, decreasing from 156 to 96 over the same period, the decline was most marked in oats. Irthlingborough seems to be the one example on the estate where, within the period studied, we see demesne cultivation in wholesale decline.

On the basis of this analysis the manors in Northamptonshire may be divided into two groups of equal size. The first group comprises the manors nearest the abbey – Warmington, Ashton, Oundle, Biggin Grange and Stanwick. These lay in the Nene valley, and on the western edge of the claylands. Demesne acreage on these manors remained fairly stable, and wheat cultivation was kept at a high level. The second group comprised Kettering, Irthlingborough, Cottingham, Great Easton and Tinwell. Irthlingborough lay on one of the poorest areas of the clays,[1] Kettering on the redlands, and the other three manors on the lighter soils of the uplands. These manors either show major decline, or slight decline accompanied by major reorganisation. On these estates the decline in the amount of oats sown is particularly marked.

In the modern period the agricultural history of these two areas has been completely different. Just before the Second World War the yellow patches in the land utilisation survey, showing abandoned land, were predominantly in the area of the heavy clays.[2] By contrast, the second group of manors then lay on respectable agricultural land. The clays are hard and demanding soils.[3] In periods of high labour costs they are unrewarding, but in times of cheap labour they can be farmed at some slight profit. In the thirteenth century it was tenacious customary obligations which kept demesne cultivation at a high level. Cottingham, Kettering and Irthlingborough lay farther from the abbey to the west of the Nene. Before the agricultural revolution this area seems to have been on the economic margin,[4] and it was here in the late thirteenth century that the movement from demesne cultivations seems to have been most pronounced.

It would be difficult to generalise very far from a situation in three or four manors over a fairly short period of time. There is, however, other evidence to suggest that the abbey was experimenting on these

[1] *Land Utilisation Survey*, ed. L. Dudley Stamp, part 58 (Northamptonshire), by S. H. Beaver (1943), pp. 378–80.
[2] *Land Utilisation Survey* (Northants), pp. 375–6, and part 76 (Hunts) by D. W. Fryer (1941), pp. 442–3.
[3] D. Grigg, *The Agricultural Revolution in South Lincolnshire* (1966), pp. 18–19.
[4] *Land Utilisation Survey* (Northants), pp. 378–81.

manors, and abandoning demesne land because of poor soil and falling yields. The concomitant expansion of sheep farming, which is discussed more fully below, was more marked in the western group, and most marked in the manors where the arable demesne was contracting. It was at Irthlingborough that the abbey leased 'eight acres of the furthest distant and the worst of all the demesne land'.[1] On the opposite bank of the Nene, at Stanwick, one of the freeholders 'enfeoffed various men of a cottage and a virgate of the worst land, which was of least value'.[2] At Kettering several of the customary virgates had parcels of land of between one and eight acres attached to them, several of which are stated to have been demesne land. On the same manor there are references to the leasing of land, tofts and also shops.[3] At Cottingham there was a large item, £6 2s 9d, from the farm of tofts.[4] These entries are certainly allusive, but there is more enterprise here, a manorial administration that seems more self-conscious, than elsewhere in the group.

SHEEP FARMING

The figures for pastoral farming, and for sheep in particular, give a much clearer impression than those for arable farming. That sheep-farming on any scale was a comparatively new development for this estate can be seen when the post-Conquest evidence is examined.

The surveys of 1125 give the first picture of the scale and pattern of stock-rearing. The sheep flocks then recorded were as follows.[5]

Soke of Peterborough		*Northamptonshire*	
Castor	100	Kettering	300
Etton	120	Pytchley	220
Pilsgate	180	Irthlingborough	100
		Stanwick	100
Nottinghamshire		Warmington	129
Collingham	160	(potential of 229)	
Lincolnshire		*Rutland*	
Scotter	16	Tinwell	10
Gosberton	6		

[1] Fitzwilliam A/C Roll 2388, m. 14d.
[2] Black Book, fo. 233r.
[3] Fitzwilliam A/C Roll 233, m. 27r; Fitzwilliam A/C Roll 2389, m. 24d.
[4] Fitzwilliam A/C Roll 2388, m. 16r.
[5] *Chr.P.*, pp. 157–66.

The total number of sheep was 1441, to which could be added the 100 lambs and 60 rams recorded at Etton, which would give a figure of 1601. Well over half the sheep recorded were in the five Northamptonshire manors of Irthlingborough, Stanwick, Warmington, Kettering and Pytchley. 400 sheep grazed on the three manors of Castor, Etton and Pilsgate, in the upland area of the Soke, west of the abbey. The fen area to the north and east of the abbey lay as yet little developed, and had only a moderate number of cattle. Elsewhere, 'the cattle populations were modest, and generally no more than the minimum needed to replenish the plough teams'.[1] Collingham was the only northern manor with a flock of any size. The Lincolnshire manors and the upland manors, which later were to provide the best grazing land on the estate, had no sheep and few cattle at this time.

Between the survey of 1125 and the earliest fragment of account roll the only indication of the scale of sheep farming lies in the vacancy accounts in the Pipe Rolls, with their entries for the profits of wool sold. These are as follows.[2]

1176	£9	12s	4d	
1210	£10	7s	5d	
1211	£12	0s	0d	(including cheese)

In 1211 the wool and cheese were worth only seven per cent of the value of the grain sold, and little more than one per cent of the abbey's total receipts.[3] Figures for the vacancies of 1248 and 1263, giving sheep totals of 1383 and 587 respectively, would seem to suggest that sheep farming was at a fairly low level in the mid-thirteenth century also.[4] The next half-century, on the other hand,

[1] R. Trow-Smith, *A History of British Livestock Husbandry to 1700* (London, 1957), p. 91.
[2] *Pipe Roll 23 Henry II*, p. 104; *Pipe Roll 12 John*, p. 215; *Pipe Roll 13 John*, p. 271.
[3] *Cf.* the figures quoted by Trow-Smith, *British Livestock Husbandry*, p. 170.
[4] Vesp. E.22, fo. 41v. Discussion of the size of sheep flocks is complicated by the question of depreciation during vacancies. Dr Titow has shown that there is clear evidence of this from the Winchester accounts: J. Z. Titow, 'Land and Population on the Bishop of Winchester's Estates. 1209–1350' (Univ. of Cambridge Ph.D. thesis 1962), pp. 44–5, 48–51, and Table IV. All ecclesiastical estates might be subject to the same pressure. Yet in the case of abbatial vacancies in the thirteenth century the prior and convent frequently paid a fine of custody. This happened at Peterborough in 1214 (M. Howell, *Regalian Right in Medieval England* (London, 1962), p. 68 note 1), and seems to have been customary in Edward I's time. A fine of 300 marks was paid in 1274 (*Cal. Patent R.*

saw a major expansion of sheep farming on this estate. On the basis of the 1294–5 figures, which are all that are available, wool sales between 1300 and 1310 would have been rather higher than sales of grain. With expansion came an increasingly centralised administration, which involved a fair degree of specialisation of function among individual manors.

Table 11   *Number of sheep at Michaelmas*

	Western	*Home*	*Northern*	*Total*
1294	2330	not known		
1295	1852	not known		
. . .				
1300	2249	1024	867	4140
1301	2809	1344	1112	5265
. . .				
1307	2975	1824	2104	6903
1308	3615	2172	2208	7995
1309	3040	1537	2090	6667
1310	3160	1102	2232	6494

Since the early fragments of account both relate to the western group, sheep farming here can be studied over a longer period of time than elsewhere. The figures give a very clear picture of expansion. Cottingham had no sheep at all in 1281 and 423 at Michaelmas 1310; Irthlingborough grew from 6 in 1281 to 463 at Michaelmas 1308. Biggin Grange, with 466 sheep at Michaelmas 1294, had a flock of 1096 at Michaelmas 1301, and only slightly less than this in the later 1300s. Cottingham, Great Easton and Kettering, other large manors in the group, show a similar growth. The number of shepherds increased in proportion. Neither Irthlingborough nor Cottingham employed shepherds in 1281, but in 1310 Irthlingborough had one full-time shepherd and one part-time, and Cottingham two full-time shepherds and one part-time. Kettering had four full-time shepherds at Michaelmas 1310.

With this expansion came increased centralisation. In 1281 there was only one inter-manorial transfer of stock, and this was clearly

1272–81, p. 45), and one of 1000 marks in 1299 (Vesp. E.22, fo. 60r). It is assumed for the period of the accounts, therefore, that vacancy depreciation can be ignored. Certainly there is no *prima facie* case for it, since the 1300–1 account (the 2nd year of Godfrey of Crowland) reflects a higher level of sheep-farming than that of 1294–5 (the 20th year of Richard of London).

an exchange.[1] The economic unit was still the manor. In 1295 there was more fluidity, but the transfer of stock was still at a rudimentary stage, and only thirty-nine animals were involved. By 1301 both inter-manorial and inter-group transfers were clearly established, and involved the movement of 834 animals. Among the inter-group transactions, Warmington and Irthlingborough sent ewes to Glinton, while Irthlingborough and Biggin Grange received lambs from Castor and Eye respectively. These transfers made possible a certain specialisation of function, the best example of this being the case of the manors of Kettering and Irthlingborough. In 1295 these manors were self-sufficient. By 1301 all the Irthlingborough ewes in a given year were being sent from there to Kettering for lambing, and its stock replenished from Kettering, in the form either of lambs or of yearlings. This involved not only the movement of sheep but also of shepherds; in 1310 one of the Kettering shepherds spent ten weeks at Oundle and Irthlingborough.[2]

There was expansion too in the home group in the 1300s, but not to so marked an extent, for sheep farming was better established there. In 1301 the bulk of the sheep farming took place on the manors of Eye,[3] Glinton, Walton and Castor; the two former were breeding manors, while the two latter carried flocks of wethers only. Between 1304 and 1306 a lot of capital was devoted to creating a new manor, at Northolm, from the fenland. This manor was entirely pasture land, and it seems to have been both a reflexion of and a stimulus to the centralisation of the group. The reorganisation was extensive. Until the turn of the century the sheep in the Soke of Peterborough had been the responsibility of the individual reeves, as elsewhere on the estate. By 1307 they were under a stock-keeper, who accounted for them separately as the *Bidentes de Nasso*.[4] Three

---

[1] Thirteen yearlings were sent from Kettering to Stanwick, and the same number of ewes received in return.

[2] Fitzwilliam A/C Roll 2389, m. 25d. He is elsewhere described as the shepherd 'custodiente hoggastris': *Ibid*. m. 25r.

[3] The fenland proper had had no sheep in 1125, and it is difficult to say when Eye and Glinton first carried flocks. The surveys of *c*. 1230 show that the colonisation and manorialisation of Eye were sufficiently far advanced for the villeins there to owe the full customary services. Yet at the same time the cowherd's serjeanty tenure (*cf. Chr.P.*, p. 165) was described as follows: 'Hugo vaccarius tenet 1 toftum et 2 acras terre et custodit vaccas, porcos et omnia animalia curie' (Surveys, fo. 185r). If there were sheep among the *animalia curie* they did not rate separate mention. Intensive sheep farming here was probably the creation of a later date.

[4] Fitzwilliam A/C Roll 233, m. 11r; Fitzwilliam A/C Roll 2389, m. 11r–d. The phrase *Bidentes de Nasso* refers to the sheep of the home group only: *cf.* Knowles, *Religious Orders*, I, 42.

manors in the home group had no sheep, but each employed shepherds. In 1310 Boroughbury had two part-time shepherds, Longthorpe one part-time, and Werrington one full-time.[1] Possibly their labour was transferred to other manors; more likely, however, they minded the flocks of the customary tenants. There was specific reference to this at Kettering in 1281, and the practise may have been fairly common.[2]

The Lincolnshire manors also expanded between 1300 and 1310, and by the latter date Collingham, Scotter and Fiskerton each had flocks of between 600 and 800 sheep. In the middle years of this decade Walcot, the most northerly manor, started a flock of its own. The disparate nature of this set of properties, however, seems to have precluded any attempt at transfer of stock or specialisation.

The centralisation which came with this expansion over the whole estate is most marked in relation to the collection and sale of the wool clip. Unfortunately, this very centralisation means that the actual sale of the wool disappears from the account rolls. In 1281 and 1295 the wool was sold from each manor, and the reeve accounted for the proceeds. These entries also give the weight of the fleeces. In 1295

Table 12   *Wool sales 1295*

	Fleeces no.	Weight st lb		Price £ s d			Price per stone s d	
Biggin Grange	303	37		9	17	4	5	4
Cottingham	79	10	7	2	8	1	4	7
Great Easton	242	28	1	6	8	8	4	7
Irthlingborough	105	13	5	3	1	3	4	7
Kettering	187	21		5	5	0	5	0
Oundle	83	7	8	1	14	8	4	7
Stanwick	175	20	7	4	14	0	4	7
Tinwell	136	22		5	0	10	4	7
	1310	160		38	9	10		

[1] Fitzwilliam A/C Roll 2389, m. 2r, m. 8r, m. 5r.
[2] 'In stipendio secundi bercarii custodiente bidentes cotariorum 3s. 2d.' (Add. Ch. 737). There was a very large cottar population on this manor. There is a similar entry from the Crowland manor of Wellingborough in 1321–2: 'in conductione unius garcionis per 4 dies custodientis oves cotariorum dum bercarius fugavit 140 hogettos usque Langetoft, 4d.' (*Wellingborough Manorial Accounts. 1258–1323*, ed. F. M. Page (Northants Rec. Soc., VIII, 1936), p. 125).

the prices paid varied between 4s 7d and 5s 4d a stone, the latter sum being paid for the fleeces of Biggin Grange only. At Scotter the price was 4s 9¾d. The higher figures most probably indicate a heavier fleece, since while the Oundle fleeces weighed 1 lb 4½ oz each, the Scotter fleeces weighed 2 lb 7 oz.[1] There is only one hint as to the destination of the wool: the Kettering account in 1295 recorded that three men of Gilbert of Chesterton came to weigh the wool.[2] This man was one of the greatest wool merchants of the day, and he may perhaps have bought the whole clip.[3] There is, however, no indication of the nature of his contract with the abbey.[4]

The stock-keeper of the *Bidentes de Nasso*, along with the bailiffs of the home and western groups, had general responsibility for the sheep of the whole estate.[5] These three officials supervised the collection of the wool, each manor contributing a share of the expenses involved.[6] This applied equally to the wool of the northern group, which was apparently collected and packed at Fiskerton.[7] The whole clip was sent to Walton, from where it was sold.[8]

The expansion in sheep farming was in contrast to, and, as has been seen, in some measure connected with, a decline in the amount of demesne cultivation. It seems that in most of the anciently settled areas the arable frontier had reached its limit. At Peter-

---

[1] The average weight was slightly over 1¾ lb a fleece. This is rather over the average quoted by Trow-Smith (*British Livestock Husbandry*, pp. 166–8), but rather under that given by R. J. Whitwell ('The English Monasteries and the Wool Trade in the Thirteenth Century', *Vierteljahrschrift für Sozial- und Wirtschaftgeschichte*, II (1904), 15).

[2] Rockingham Compotus, under Kettering.

[3] Eileen Power, *The Wool Trade in English Medieval History* (Oxford, 1941), p. 113. Gilbert also dealt with the nuns of Stamford, paying them £5 for the next year's wool in 1304–5: P.R.O., S.C.6. 1260/1. One of Gilbert's sons was a clerk in the abbey in 1300: Vesp. E.22, fo. 58r.

[4] By contrast, a detailed set of records relate to the more improvident contracts of the neighbouring Cistercian house at Pipewell: Power, *Wool Trade*, pp. 43–4.

[5] The stock-keeper or head-shepherd appears before 1301, since an entry in this account refers to payment of a boy from Michaelmas to Martinmas, 'dum magister bercarius fuit cum Radulpho de Thorneye a tractandis bidentibus ad omnia maneria domini' (Fitzwilliam A/C Roll 2388, m. 3r).

[6] Thus the entry for Tinwell in 1310: 'in expensis Radulphi de Thorneye, Ricardi de Croylande et Johannis de la Bigginge existentes apud Waltonam ultra bidentes tondendos et lanam volupandam et saccandam, per 1 talliam 2s. 2d.' (Fitzwilliam A/C Roll 2389, m. 30r).

[7] Fitzwilliam A/C Roll 2388, m. 21r.

[8] 'In prebendis equorum Ricardi de Croylande et Radulphi de Thorneye circa bidentes tondendos et lanas saccandas et ponderandas, cum prebendis equorum mercatorum 1½ quarteria' (Fitzwilliam A/C Roll 233, m. 7r).

borough, as on several estates, there was probably a partial reaction in favour of pastoral farming.[1]

LABOUR SUPPLY

The composition of the labour force in the age of high farming can be scrutinised in some detail, for the accounts give information on the use made of customary works as well as details of stipendiary and wage labour. By the late thirteenth century stipendiary labourers (*famuli*) provided the bulk of the labour on this estate, as elsewhere.[2] And yet within the estate, from manor to manor and especially from group to group, the variations were considerable. The figures give a further indication of the differing economy of each group of manors.

Each manor, with two exceptions, had the number of labourers that might have been expected. The exceptions were Kettering and Irthlingborough, neither of which in the early fourteenth century employed any full-time ploughmen. Kettering sowed a demesne of slightly under 300 acres in 1301, and Irthlingborough sowed 160 acres. The special character of each of these manors can be seen when the details of their labour force are contrasted with those for neighbouring manors of a comparable size. In 1301 Kettering sowed 283 acres and Warmington sowed 287 acres. Their respective labour forces at this date were as shown opposite.[3] Warmington had an extra carter, Kettering an extra shepherd, but all told the figures are remarkably similar. The exception lies in the absence at Kettering of the very core of the stipendiary servants, the ploughmen. There were six at Warmington, and none at Kettering.

Where the extra labour came from is not immediately apparent in the accounts. Clearly, however, Kettering was a manor well provided with customary services. It had the equivalent of forty full

---

[1] F. M. Page, 'Bidentes Hoylandie', *Economic History* (Supplement to the *Economic Journal*), I (1920), 603–13; Smith, *Canterbury*, pp. 146–56; Raftis, *Ramsey*, pp. 144–6; *Historia et Cartularium Monasterii Gloucestrie*, ed. W. H. Hart, I (Rolls Ser., 33, 1863), p. 39, cited by R. Lennard, 'Agrarian History: Some Vistas and Pitfalls', *Agric.H.R.*, XII (1964), 86–7; Barbara Harvey, 'The Population Trend in England between 1300 and 1348', *T.R.H.S.*, 5th ser., XVI (1966), 40–1. Dr Titow's figures for Winchester, from where alone there is statistical evidence for an earlier period, show the peak level of sheep farming between 1209 and 1350 to have been the 1220s (J. Z. Titow, thesis as cited, pp. 48–52).

[2] The classic study is provided by M. M. Postan, *The Famulus: The Estate Labourer in the Twelfth and Thirteenth Centuries* (Economic History Review Supplement, no. 2, 1954).

[3] Fitzwilliam A/C Roll 2388, m. 10r–11d, m. 15d.

Warmington	s	d	Kettering	s	d
1 Hayward	6	8	1 Hayward	6	8
6 Ploughmen	4	6			
1 Carter	4	6			
1 Carter (pt)	4	1	1 Carter (pt)	3	11
1 Carter (pt)	4	0	1 Carter (pt)	3	6
1 Shepherd	4	6	3 Shepherds	4	6
1 Shepherd (pt)	4	1			
1 Cowherd	4	6	1 Cowherd	4	6
1 Dairywoman	4	6	1 Dairywoman	4	4
1 Miller	4	6	1 Miller	4	2
1 Swineherd	2	3	1 Swineherd	1	0

(pt) = part time

tenancies and three cottages, which provided 6500 works over a full year, far and away the biggest total in the group. The statement of works (*opera*) performed shows that these included a certain amount of ploughing; in 1310 there were 110 works used in ploughing before the crops were sown, and 144 in ploughing the fallow.[1] Yet it is doubtful whether this represented a year's ploughing of a demesne of nearly 300 acres. This work was not done by wage-labourers either, for the only paid occasional work here was that common to the whole estate, the threshing and winnowing done as task-work. The problem can only be satisfactorily solved by presuming that the *opera* section of the account did not include the villein's customary ploughing obligations.[2]

The absence of stipendiary ploughmen at Irthlingborough, on the other hand, is probably explained by a more recent development. Here again it will be useful to compare its labour force with that of another manor of comparable size, in this case the neighbouring manor of Stanwick. The full-time labourers on these manors in 1281 and 1301 were as follows.[3]

[1] Fitzwilliam A/C Roll 2389, m. 26r.
[2] These same two manors, Warmington and Kettering, were compared by Lennard on the basis of the 1125 surveys, and he concluded that, 'the tillage of the demesne must have depended less upon the services of the peasants at Warmington than it did at Kettering' (*Rural England*, p. 379). The early fourteenth-century history of Kettering is little more than a gloss on the twelfth-century survey.
[3] B.M. Add. Ch. 737; Fitzwilliam A/C Roll 2388, m. 14d, m. 13d.

Irthlingborough			Stanwick		
1281	s	d	*1281*	s	d
2 Ploughmen	3	6	1 Hayward	3	6
2 Ploughmen (pt)	3	2	4 Ploughmen	3	6
1 Carter (pt)	2	6	1 Carter	3	6
			1 Shepherd	3	6
1301			*1301*		
1 Hayward	5	0	1 Hayward	allowances	
			4 Ploughmen	4	6
1 Shepherd	4	5	1 Carter	4	6
1 Shepherd (pt)	3	6	1 Dairywoman	3	6

Here there have been ploughmen and they have been dispensed with; and the explanation lies in the figures for the cultivation of the demesne. At Stanwick the amount sown varied between 145 and 165 acres. In 1281 Irthlingborough sowed 180 acres; in 1301 it sowed 159; by 1308 this figure had fallen to below 100. Yet the falling off in demesne cultivation is already marked by the disappearance of the stipendiary ploughmen by 1301. Ploughing obligations seem to have been shifted entirely onto the customary tenants.[1] In 1281 virgates were farmed here for 14s 0d, and in 1295 for 12s 4d. This was little more than half the normal rate of commutation for the estate, and clearly this was related to the extra duties performed.[2] The extent of commutation on each manor was a reflexion of the needs of the demesne; as the extent of demesne cultivation changed, so villein obligations changed in response to it.

On five of the manors in the western group there were sufficient customary works performed to merit a separate section in the account. At Tinwell in 1301 just under a third of the works owed were performed, and at Kettering about forty per cent. At Warmington and at Stanwick the winter and autumn works were accounted

---

[1] In 1281 virgates that were at farm at Irthlingborough owed the following services: 'Preterea debent arare ter in anno cum quot habuerint iunctis in carrucis. Debent eciam pratum falcare et fenum levare, et bladum meterent prius. Et debent cariare bladum per 1 diem cum sociis' (Add. Ch. 737). The equivalent section in 1310 read: 'Preterea debent *totam terram domini arare*, seminare et herciare et sarclare et totum pratum falcare, et quando necesse fuerit domi cariare, et totum bladum metere et domi cariare' (Fitzwilliam A/C Roll 2389, m. 23d – my italics).

[2] At Ashton, where there were no ploughing obligations attached, the rate of commutation for a virgate was 16s 8d (*Ibid.* m. 19d). At Oundle, where there were no obligations at all, the standard rate of commutation was 24s, while customary tenants with a second holding and freeholders were paying 29s and 32s (*Ibid.* m. 20r). The existence of a merchant community at Oundle probably explains a higher level of demand for land.

for separately; only sixteen per cent of the autumn works were sold, whereas the winter figure was sixty per cent.[1] At Great Easton in 1308 none of the autumn works were sold, and sixty per cent of the winter. Taking the western group as a whole, it is apparent that not all the manors owed services, and where they were performed they were kept up almost entirely for the seasonal assistance provided at harvest time. The reaping and binding of grain is always the largest entry in the *opera* accounts, representing in every case at least half of the total work performed. There are frequent entries for the mowing of hay, and the carrying and spreading of manure. There was a bit of weeding, and a bit of hedging and ditching. Apart from these the part played by customary works was negligible.[2] The part played by wage-labour was small also. Threshing and winnowing the grain was done by piece-work, with some assistance from the *famuli* and from customary works. Wage-labourers also did most of what reaping and binding could not be done by customary works.[3]

The grange at Biggin naturally provides an exception to this pattern, and must be considered separately. It is of interest since it is a rare example of a Benedictine grange for which account roll material has survived.[4] In 1310 there were three chief officials, a reeve, a forester and a hayward. The other full-time workmen comprised three carters, twelve ploughmen, four shepherds, one cowherd, one swineherd, and one dairywoman. Three more men were employed part-time, making a total of twenty-eight in all. What these men did not do can be seen from the account rolls. Reaping was done by piece-work, at a rate of $7\frac{1}{2}$d an acre; hay-making was done at the same rate; and the grain was threshed and winnowed by task-workers. There was a wages bill of nearly £50, made up as follows.[5]

---

[1] Fitzwilliam A/C Roll 2388, m. 17d, m. 16r, m. 11r, m. 14r.

[2] As at Crowland (Postan, *Famulus*, p. 4), the villeins quite frequently performed ploughing services when the stipendiary ploughmen were engaged in other work. Thus: 'in eunte ad carrucas dum famuli cariant bladum de Ryssedene (Rushden) ad Stanwigge 3 opera. In eunte ad carrucas dum famuli seminaverunt 2 opera . . . In eunte ad carrucas dum famuli iverunt ad carectas 21 opera' (Rockingham Compotus, under Stanwick).

[3] Occasionally all three forms of labour might be used in the same operation. At Warmington in 1310, 220 quarters of grain were threshed by task-workers, 10 quarters by the *famuli* and 14 quarters by villein works: Fitzwilliam A/C Roll 2389, m. 18d.

[4] *Cf.* Postan, *Famulus*, p. 2.

[5] These figures are worked out to conform with those in Postan, *Famulus*, pp. 27, 41–6.

	£	s	d
Stipends of *famuli*	6	3	9
Food supplied to *famuli*	23	2	3
Wage-labour	20	3	6

In addition to this the villeins of Oundle had certain customary obligations on the grange. They owed one day's carrying hay, and one day's carrying grain; they performed these services between 1300 and 1310 and received payment for them, even though their customary services on their own manor were commuted.[1] This service will have made a minor impact in 1310, but it is interesting since it may well reflect a time when labour from the abbey's nearby manors played more of a part in the running of Biggin Grange than they did in the early fourteenth century.[2]

There was another Peterborough grange, nearer to the abbey, at Belsize in Castor. The customary tenancies of Fletton in Huntingdonshire each sent two men to do a day's work at Belsize, at the abbey's expense.[3] Fletton was five miles away from Belsize; the obligation thus lay on the nearest property of the obedientiary who held the grange, the cellarer, even though several of the abbot's properties lay closer. If there was flexibility within the abbot's part, there was a hard line between abbot and convent. Since none of the cellarer's records survive, there is no information on how this second grange was staffed.

Nearer to the abbey far more of the customary works owed were performed. The amount of work required must have been worked out very exactly, for on five manors a number of virgates were farmed. At Boroughbury in 1309–10, 11 virgates out of 36 were farmed, and at Castor 9 virgates out of 28. When the virgates farmed are removed, it appears that in 1301 under five per cent of the works owed by the villeins of the home group were sold, and this figure would be a lot lower were it not for the fifteen per cent sold at Glinton. Within the manors of this group there is the one extreme

Eye	100 works allowed	
	9 sold	out of 2676

---

[1] Fitzwilliam A/C Roll 2388, m. 12r; *Ibid*. no. 233, m. 23d; *Ibid*. no. 2389, m. 21d.

[2] In 1281, 34 *opera* were sent from Kettering to Biggin Grange. The distance between these manors was a good ten miles.

[3] *Rotuli Hundredorum*, II, 639b.

and on the other

> *Castor* 2342 works allowed
>   186 sold   out of 4784

Fifty-two per cent of the works owed were not performed at Castor, and five per cent at Eye.[1] Eye, which does not appear in *Domesday*, was a hamlet of Peterborough, and was gradually built up as a separate manor in the twelfth and thirteenth centuries. It had a small core of customary holdings, surrounded by a large fringe of small holdings. The latter were of recent origin, and therefore owed little in the way of customary service. A consequence of this was that the villeins at Eye bore the heaviest burden on the whole estate. Just under twenty-five per cent of the works owed are recorded as sent to the abbey (*missis in abbaciam*). The greater number of these works must have been spent on agricultural operations, as is proved by one of the items in a slightly later statement of the duties of the beadle of Boroughbury.[2]

He must receive the works from the manors, and supervise to see that they are well done, in cutting wood under the oversight of the bailiff or his clerk, and making and carrying faggots, and carrying peat; and he should organise the carting of all the carts in Nassaburgh, for the carrying of grain and fuel and other necessities to the abbey, and should keep a check both with the reeve of each manor and with the hearth-keeper.

This was a reserve fund of villein labour, from which the supply of grain and fuel to the abbey, and all the carting works associated with this, were organised within the group on a centralised basis. The unit of organisation was the group. While the *famuli* were ubiquitous here as elsewhere, by far the greater number of customary works owed within this group were performed. This does not represent, of course, anything like a dependence on villein services, but it does represent a substantial use of them as compared with certain other ecclesiastical estates.[3] And that these services were performed goes part of the way to explain the concern of the Peterborough administration with the integrity of the villein tenement.

The northern group shows up very little worthy of remark. None of its manors had any customary holdings at farm in 1301. The

---

[1] Fitzwilliam A/C Roll 2388, m. 3d, m. 6r.
[2] *C.N.* 558.
[3] The Kentish estates of Christ Church, Canterbury, were entirely dependent on wage labour at this date: Smith, *Canterbury*, p. 125.

actual obligations were light compared with those elsewhere on the estate, yet a large number of the works owed were performed. In 1308, fifty-five per cent were performed, twenty-eight were sold, and the rest allowed for various reasons. Demesne cultivation on this group seems to have been slightly increasing at this time.

ENTRY FINES

The last topic to be considered is the level of entry fines, and the circumstances which influenced them.[1] Here the fragmented nature of the accounts is less of a drawback than elsewhere, and there is additional evidence from a number of court rolls. Full particulars of fines are usually given, and something of the substance of the individuals concerned can usually be gathered from these and other records. Information about individuals is presented along with the statistics, for to study entry fines without examining the persons who paid them can be a misleading exercise. This material is examined in detail in Appendix C.

Detailed analysis suggests two points which are of relevance in the context of this chapter. In the first place, fines at the level of the years 1300 to 1310 were almost certainly a good deal higher than they had been between 1280 and 1290. Fragments of an account for four Northamptonshire manors in 1280–1, and one for the manor of Boroughbury in 1290, have as their standard fines amounts of 5s and 10s. The size of the tenancy is not stated, but full holdings predominate in the later sample, and it is probable that these also were full holdings. The second point is that while the burden on the peasantry clearly increased, these fines are not of the size that some studies would suggest.[2] There are around a hundred fines for a virgate or the equivalent here. The highest fine was £5, which was paid on three occasions. This was not a standard fine, it was exceptional, and the reasons for the exceptions have been examined. Another thirteen fines were for five marks or more. This was not exceptional, but it was definitely high. There was perhaps some limit to what a man would pay for access to the means of subsistence; certainly on this estate there was a limit to what he was required to pay. Some of the high fines, and perhaps not a few, were

---

[1] The only full discussion of entry fines for any estate will be found in Dr Titow's work on the Bishopric of Winchester (J. Z. Titow, thesis as cited, pp. 110–27).

[2] See M. M. Postan, 'Investment in Medieval Agriculture', *Journal of Economic History*, XXVII (1967), 587.

paid by men for extra holdings. These men were speculators, and the abbey was taking a high initial premium from them.

If the account roll material makes any single impression it is of considerable intellectual effort and some enterprise, which even so was insufficient to keep arable farming going at the old level. The time of maximum seigneurial profit was not a time of uniform agricultural expansion; and these two phenomena are possibly related. It is perhaps significant that the first complete set of accounts from the central Northamptonshire manors survives from 1294–5, the year which saw the first campaign against villein transactions in free land in that area. The Peterborough apogee of high farming was an administrative achievement on an insecure agricultural base.

9   *Conclusion*

The land market on this estate has been studied, so far as is possible, through family history. The monastic community was itself a family, and it is not entirely fanciful to look at the abbey's history as that of a family. The devolution of property during the twelfth century follows the pattern of lay estates. Seen in this perspective the obedientiaries become the abbot's younger sons, and there is the early and mid-twelfth century fragmentation characteristic of families of baronial rank. There are considerable similarities between the build-up of obedientiary estates and that of knightly estates over the same period.

In such a perspective, the differences between large and small landowners start to shade away, and it is difficult to see the monasteries as predators on the land market.[1] There remains, however, a more basic problem in the very beginning of a land market, which began with baronial property in the early twelfth century, and spread downwards in the social scale over the next hundred years. The charters for knightly properties become abundant in the last quarter of the twelfth century. Before that there is what Duby calls 'an astonishing stability among knightly families'.[2] In the thirteenth century the situation seems, by comparison, to be almost anarchic. The family's attitude to its property seems to have undergone an abrupt change.

In examining this problem, it is important to study a full range of sources covering as many levels of society as possible. At Peterborough, unusually, it is at the lower levels of the land market that the sources are most abundant. Here 'the manor seems to have kept with a wonderful conservatism what we may call its external shape'.[3] But this was perhaps the common tenacity of thirteenth-century feudal records, which will tend to conceal any form of social change? It can be argued that stability was the result solely of seignorial

---

[1] See the argument in my article, 'Large and Small Landowners in Thirteenth-Century England', *Past and Present*, no. 47 (1970), pp. 45–50.

[2] 'Une étonnante permanence des familles chevaleresques'; G. Duby, 'Une enquête à poursuivre: La noblesse dans la France médiévale', *Revue Historique*, CCXXVI (1961), 22.

[3] Maitland, *Collected Papers*, II, 370.

pressure, where all the natural tendencies were towards fragmentation. Sub-division of holdings reveals the existence of a land market, while stability does not 'signify its absence'; 'we must therefore have it both ways'.[1] This is certainly a tenable position, and it could be the correct one. At the same time it is possible to construct a slightly different argument. This points to the stability of the virgated pattern, and to the active land market revealed in the peasant charters, as two quite separate things. Indeed it could be, as has been suggested, that the market in free land assisted rather than impeded this conservation. And it could be that this conservatism reflected peasant attitudes.

Similar observations can be made on the other freehold charters, those which record dealings between freeholders. These are more difficult to interpret, because there is no background of surveys and account rolls against which they may be set. But where there is a full series of charters, showing the previous history of a number of properties granted to the abbey, it is striking how often the grants transfer an individual's acquisitions and not his original holding, which is never seen and can only be guessed at. The land which Ralph the Mason gave to his wife was described as 'my own acquisition and free purchase'.[2] Agnes Pudding gave eight acres of land made up of four parcels; all of them can be traced back, and one of them goes back, two stages earlier, to the Tot fee.[3] The background to Richard of Dene's later and more substantial grant can be traced in a similar way.[4] To draw the line between poverty and piety is often difficult and always invidious. But in either case it is striking that these alienations are in some way controlled.

With knightly families, many of whom were freeholders in all but name, we find the same thing. The smaller knight is distinguished from the freeholder in that his property will tend to be more widely flung. The farthest flung and the smallest of his holdings are the natural portions of younger brothers and, if they are lucky, of sisters also. It is the same property which, in times of stress, he will first lease and then alienate. In the Conqueror's reign and thereafter, the major landowners took great care over which property was subinfeudated.[5] Later the knights, who had in some way suffered from

---

[1] Postan, *C.N.*, p. xli.   [2] Fitzwilliam Charter, no. 43.
[3] Franceys, pp. 58–9.   [4] See Appendix D, note 7.
[5] A calculation well symbolised by the fate of the poor canons of Llanthony who, long in advance of any castle, were the first bulwark of the Weobley honour against a Welsh invasion: Wightman, *The Lacy Family. 1066–1194*, pp. 183–4.

this selection, made similar calculations. They decided what was their core property and what was, to some degree, dispensable. It is this latter which they used to meet the various pressures on them over the succeeding generations. A study of reaction to these pressures, over a long period, is not always possible. Where it is, as in some cases on the Peterborough estates, it suggests that there was a slow process of whittling away, and this provides a necessary background to the various transactions which show these tenancies finally being bought out.

At each of these levels (which do not show different social groups but are rather the products of legal definitions which determine the types of record which survive) the attitude to property seems the same. Its descent was governed by strict rules. Some of these rules were common to each level of society, for the basic concerns of families were the same. One rule which seems particularly general is that concerning 'acquired' land. The patrimony, and land in any way acquired, were kept apart: the latter was freely alienable, the former subject to primogeniture. A knight giving a manor to his younger son, in the second generation of the twelfth century, took care to point out that this was land he had acquired (*de acato meo*).[1] The distinction was basic to Glanville's account of the rules governing the descent of knightly property,[2] and clearly these rules were established custom both in England and in north-west France at the same period.[3] They are certainly custom in Bracton's time, and do not need to be defined.[4] One result of this rule was that where an elder son held 'acquired' land from his father and then inherited the family holding he forfeited the acquisition, 'for the homage drives out the acquisition'.[5]

When we can form a picture of peasant society, from the court rolls of the later thirteenth century and thereafter, we find the same rules governing peasant custom. Basic to peasant inheritance customs, at least in open-field England, was the principle that 'an established holding of land ought to descend intact in the blood of the men who had held it of old . . . Assart land or land "acquired" in

[1] *Sir Christopher Hatton's Book of Seals*, no. 301.
[2] *Glanville*, VII, I (ed. G. D. G. Hall, Nelson's Medieval Texts (1965), pp. 70–1); *cf.* Milsom, int. to *History of English Law*, I, xxxii.
[3] S. Painter, 'The Family and the Feudal System in Twelfth-Century England', *Feudalism and Liberty*, pp. 212–13; G. Duby, 'Au XIIᵉ siècle: les "Jeunes" dans la société aristocratique', *Annales, E.S.C.*, XIX (1964), 841, 842 note 2.
[4] *Bracton* (ed. Woodbine), II, 191, 194.
[5] *Ibid.* II, 192.

any other way could, in many villages, be left freely by will, but an established holding descended according to these rules.'[1] And certainly with many of the peasant holdings that have been considered, it would seem that here as in Bracton 'the homage drives out the acquisition'.[2] The rule is the same in each case, and it is performing the same function. It was a concept designed to give some guarantee of stability while satisfying the family's legitimate demands. It is perhaps no accident that at many levels 'alienation' is a thirteenth-century word.[3]

It is possible that the thirteenth-century land market was not as anarchic as might appear at first sight; that it was the work of people who felt, no less than any monastic corporation, that their land was a sacred trust from their ancestors, although unlike the monasteries they found it an increasing struggle to hand it on.[4] To some extent the break between the twelfth and thirteenth centuries is one of record. Because of the records, work on the twelfth century concentrates upon families, and that of the thirteenth upon holdings. It is true that the twelfth-century knightly families were 'established on the same patrimonies and in the same position of economic superiority as had been their ancestors'.[5] But the patrimony was not everything, and the argument relates more to families than to their holdings. There is some flexibility in the use of the latter during the twelfth century, and some fragmentation. It could be that a closer look at twelfth-century holdings, and a closer look at thirteenth-century families, might tone the distinction down. It might then appear that the twelfth century was less stable than we are led to believe, and the thirteenth century slightly more.

[1] Homans, *English Villagers*, p. 195.
[2] An example of the Alred family, above p. 112–14.
[3] Homans, *English Villagers*, Ch. xiv – 'Alienation'; Sutherland, *Quo Warranto Proceedings*, Ch. vi – 'The Alienability of Franchises'; E. H. Kantorowicz, 'Inalienability: A Note on Canonical Practice and the English Coronation Oath in the Thirteenth Century', *Speculum*, xxix (1954), 488–502.
[4] This attitude is everywhere in the writings of eleventh and twelfth century ecclesiastics (see, for example, R. W. Southern, *St Anselm and his Biographer* (1963), pp. 127ff), while the eleventh and twelfth-century landlord is almost dumb. But was the lay attitude very different from the religious? And was the thirteenth-century attitude very different from this?
[5] 'Etablis sur les mêmes patrimoines et dans la même supériorité économique que leurs ancêtres'; Duby, 'La noblesse', p. 22.

The Disafforestation of the Soke

The first four of these documents show the steps that were taken to disafforest the double hundred of Nassaburgh in 1215. The abbey, the knights and the freeholders appear here as a single community, and the substance of these extracts demonstrates that this community was very far from being an accounting fiction. There were numerous disafforestations in John's reign, but this would appear to be the only detailed archive to have survived. The final document is a list of asserts in Nassaburgh from around 1209; it provides the only comprehensive list of those clearing land in the period which led up to the disafforestation. The figures in these documents have been modernised.

1. *Four knights and a clerk surveyed the woodland, and this document is the result of their survey. It lists the names of the woods and their extent, together with the names of the owners. Eighty-four pieces of woodland are listed here, amounting to slightly under 1600 acres.*

Hec est descriptione boscorum de Nasso Burgi que facta fuit in disaforestacione ipsius Nassi in qua discriptione continetur quot sunt ibi bosci et que sunt eorum nomina et cuius vel quorum sunt et quantum et quot acras quisque boscus continebat tempore disaforestacionis. Haldhauue boscus Ricardi de Bernack continet 40 acras de quibus 30 acre sunt de bosco cooperto et 10 de rifleto. Friday boscus Willelmi de Burthle continet 5 acras et 1 rodam. Burulelund continet 5 acras et 1 rodam. Suttonefrith continet 22 acras. Uuerwode de Suttone continet 29 acras et ½ rodam. Dalhawe Hugonis de Bernak continet 1 acram. Ibidem habet 1 rodam de assarto novo. Mannewode de Uptona continet 8 acras et 3 rodas. Boscus Johannis Fauuel continet 30 acras de quibus 20 sunt de bosco cooperto et 10 de rifleto. Boscus Roberti filii Galfridi de Suthtorp continet 10 acras de quibus 15 sunt de rifleto (*sic*). Litilhawe boscus Roberti de Torp continet 27½ acras de quibus 7½ acre fuerunt de rifleto. Halhawe Galfridi de Uptona continet 5 acras et ½ rodam. Boywode domine Asceline de Watervile et domine Matildis de Dive continet 8½ acras. Seggethewit Galfridi de Uptona continet 2 acras. Uptunefrith dominarum de Uptona continet 7½ acras. Sokkes Galfridi de Uptona continet 3 acras. Northwode dominarum de Uptona continet 16 acras et 1 rodam. Alfledhawe dominarum de Uptona continet 7½ acras. Swinehawe Galfridi de Uptona continet 6 acras. Swinehawe dominarum de Uptona continet 8 acras et 3 rodas. Morhauue Galfridi de Uptona continet 2½ acras. Uptonehawe dominarum de Uptona continet 11 acras et 3 rodas. Hueswode Galfridi de lamare continet 5 acras et 1 rodam de rifleto. Randscort Roberti filii Willelmi de Eylisuurie continet 1½ acram de rifleto. Rhis Pagani de Helpistona continet 8 acras et 3 rodas. Haw eiusdem Pagani et Thurlageswode continet 33½ acras et 1 rodam. Esthawe Radulfi de Mortemer continet 3 acras. Symonwode Galfridi de Northburch continet 27½ acras. Tindhawe Briani de lamare continet 32 acras dimidia roda minus. Nortburswode eiusdem Briani continet 12 acras et 1 rodam. Acherardeswde continet ½ acram. Westwode Walteri de Prestone continet 3 acras et 3 rodas. Suthlund Rogeri de Wodecroft continet 7 acras et ½ rodam unde Walterus de Prestone habet ½ acram. Estlund dicti Rogeri continet 1 acram et 3 rodas. Ibidem idem Rogerus 1 acram et 1 rodam, et Ricardus de Wodecroft 3 rodas, et Martinus de Makeseye ½ acram, et alibi 2 acras. Ereuuardesuuode et Peresuuode Radulfi de Mortemer continent 5 acras. Heath et Netheruuode Radulfi de Mortimer continet 17½ acras. Brendis Ricardi de Watervile continet de bosco cooperto 30 acras et de rifleto 7½ acras. Irengeshauue eiusdem Ricardi 12½ acras. Litlelund eiusdem Ricardi continet 8 acras et 1½ rodam. Methelund eiusdem Ricardi continet 5 acras et 1 rodam. Mukeuuode et Smaleuuode cum Mariscallisuuode eiusdem Ricardi continent 65 acras de quibus 2 acre sunt de rifleto. Einig Radulfi Munioye continet 5 acras de refleto. Einig domini abbatis continet 5 acras de rifleto. Rohauue et Thinferdesland et Wlfhauue abbatis continent 78 acras et 3 rodas unde una mediatas est boscus coopertus et alia rifleto. Frith Toroldi de Castre continet 25 acras. Boscus Radulfi filii Silvestri et boscus Paris et boscus Reginaldi de Astona continent 25 acras. Eylisuuorthe mor abbatis continet 22 acras et 3 rodas. Boscus Willelmi filii Gilberti continet 7 acras et 1 rodam. Abbotishauue, Estrys et Iungeuuode continent 120 acras. Aleuuode abbatis continet 8 acras et de rifleto 1 rodam. Ibidem de rifleto abbatis 11 acre. Ibidem domine de Uptona habent 11 acras de rifleto. Ibidem Willelmus de Euersmue 4 acras et 1 rodam de rifleto. Alfeldesuuode Rogeri de Torpel continet 11½ acras de rifleto. Brenduuode Galfridi de Norburch continet 1 acram de rifleto. Westuuode dominarum de Uptona continet 15 acras et 1½ rodam. Hauuisuuode abbatis continet 18 acras. Astinesuuode boscus Astin continet 3 acras. Boscus Willelmi Abuuetun continet 28 acras. Boscus Radulfi Cordel continet 6½ acras. Boscus persone de Castre continet 16 acras. Ashauue Willelmi de Euremue continet 9 acras. Boscus Illing continet 16 acras. Baketeshauue abbatis continet 8 acras. Ashauue abbatis continet 5 acras. Tikkeuuode Willelmi de Euermue continet 4 acras. Sistremor Roberti de Meltune continet 25 acras. Gilberteshegges Benedicti de Meletone continet 2 acras et 1 rodam de rifleto. Ibidem Ricardi de Watervile tenet 4 acras de rifleto. Louuenhauue, Rouleshauue Roberti de Meletone continent 61 acras et ½ rodam. Willelmus filius Ricardi 1 acram bosci. Ibidem ex alia parte 1 acram et 1 rodam. Robeletesuuode Roberti de Meletone continet 7½ acras. Eisting eiusdem Roberti continet 50 acras et 3 rodas. Tokevile continet 1 acram. Boscus Reginaldi de Meletone et Benedicti continet 3 acras. Lece et Agnes 1 acram de rifleto. Gruneshauue abbatis continet 52 acras. Boscus Willelmi de Gimiles continet 12½ acras. Westhauue boscus Willelmi et Thome de Torp continet 17 acras. Sereslauue et Steruuittig bosci Willelmi et Thome de Torp continent 36 acras. Westuuode abbatis continet 179 acras et 1 rodam de quibus 50 sunt de rifleto. Lund Casuueye Roberti filii Galfridi continet 10½ acras. Northuuode eiusdem Roberti continet 15 acras. Tantinguuode Galfridi de Tot continet 9 acras. Ibidem domina Gundreda 2½ acras de rifleto et veteri assarto 5 acras. Estuuode abbatis continet 94 acras et de rifleto 24 acras.

Text. Swa. fos. 120v–121v.

2. *This document states how the survey was carried out, and how as a result of it the fine was apportioned between the various tenants. The fines here total £361 3s 1½d, leaving a balance of £452 3s 6½d, and presumably also responsibility for the collection, to be met by the abbey. The figures, some of which are given in pounds and others in marks, have been standardised.*

Notum sit omnibus hoc scriptum visuris vel audituris quod nos scilicet Paganus de Helpistona, Henricus Engayne, Hugo de Bernac, Walterus de Ufford, Rogerus Bacun clericus, iurati ad peticionem et instanciam domini Roberti abbatis de Burgo, Rogeri de Torpel, Briani de lamare et Ricardi de Watervile et aliorum militum et francolanorum de Nasso Burgi, boscos et rifleta de Nasso Burgi secundum quod communiter provisum fuit fideliter mensuravimus et secundum iuramentum nostrum appretiavimus. Et ut expresse sciatur quid unusquisque predictorum militum et francolanorum pro boscis et rifletis suis ad deforestacionem Nasci debeat, in hoc scripto sub hac forma expressimus. Willelmus de Burgele £5. Ricardus de Bernak £14 6s. 8d. Robertus filius Galfridi £34 4s. 4d. Johannes Fauuel £7 13s. 4d. Hugo de Bernak 6s. 8d. Domine de Uptona, scilicet Ascelina et Matilda, £46 3s. 0½d. Galfridus de Uptona £3 17s. 6d. Gilbertus de Uptona 17s. 9d. Rogerus de Torpel £10 15s. 9d. Galfridus de Lalme £2 4s. 5d. Paganus de Helpistona £14 3s. 4d. Radulfus de Mortmer £10 15s. 0d. Brianus de lamare £19 12s. 2½d. Rogerus de Wdecroft £2 15s. 10d. Ricardus de Watervile £50 19s. 4½d. Robertus de Meletone £64 13s. 3½d. Galfridus de Northburc £9 3s. 4d. Walterus de Prestone £1 2s. 3½d. Thoroldus de Castro et sui £7 6s. 8d. Willelmus filius Gileberti £1. Robertus filius Willelmi 3s. Willelmus Abuueton £3. Radulfus Cordel £1. Persona de Castro £5. Galfridus Illing £2. Willelmus de Euermu £5. Willelmus filius Ricardi de Meletone £1 6s. 8d. Tokevile 6s. 8d. Benedictus et Reginaldus de Meletone £1 11s. 8d. Willelmus et Thomas de Thorp. £17 13s. 4d. Willelmus de Gimiges £4 3s. 4d. Galfridus del Tot £2. Domina Gundree 5s. Ricardus de Wdecrofte 1s. 6d. Domine Agnes et Lece de Castre 2s. Martinus de Makesheye 5s. Achelardus 4s. Et ut hec prenominata singulorum debita secundum appretiacionem boscorum et rifletorum Nassi per nos factam ad futurorum memoriam fide indubitata perveniat presens scriptum sigillorum nostrorum munimine roboravimus.

Text. Swa. fo. 243r-v.

3. *An undertaking to pay the fine in annual instalments of 720, 300 and 200 marks.*

Universis Christi fidelibus ad quorum audienciam presens scriptum pervenerit Ricardus dei gracia abbas de Burgo et eiusdem loci conventus et milites et francolani qui terras vel tenementa in Nasso Burgi habeant eternam in domino salutem. Noverit universitas vestra quod solvemus domino regi Johanni pro difforestanda tota terra in Nasso Burgi que est inter aquam de Nen et aquam de Weland sicut aque conveniunt in villa de Croyland et de Walmisford sicut magnum chiminum extendit se usque ad stupendestan extra villam de Stanford et de stupendestan per rectam lineam usque ad Weland sub curia monialium de Stanford, ita quod abbacia illa sit infra metas predictas, a proximo Pascha post relaxacionem generalis interdicti Anglie in tres annos subsequentes plene completos 1220 marcas esterlingorum. Ita quidem quod primo anno solvemus 720 marcas, et secundo anno 300 marcas et tercio anno 200 marcas. Et in huius rei testimonium ego Ricardus abbas de Burgo et conventus et milites et francolani de Nasso huic scripto sigilla nostra apposiumus.

Text. Swa. fo. 243r.

4. *The abbot and convent on the one hand and the knights and freeholders on the other come to an agreement concerning assarting in their respective woodland. The chief problem here concerned rights of common. This comprehensive agreement comes a generation before the Statute of Merton, and anticipates several of its provisions. It is notable also in being sealed by six knights, as representatives of the local community.*

Sciant omnes tam presentes quam futuri quod hec est convencio facta inter Robertum abbatem de Burgo et eiusdem loci conventum et milites et francolanos de Nasso Burgi, in pasca proximo post deforestacionem Nassi Burgi, scilicet anno quo relexatum fuit interdictum generale in Anglia. (Ita) quod liceat prefatis abbati et monachis de Burgo infra Nassum Burgi . . . boscos suos proprios videlicet Cotwode, Estwode, Westwode, Parcwode et Casterwode et omnes alios boscos suos quos nunc habent vel habere poterunt in posterum in eodem Nasso, et omnia rifleta sua et omnia alneta sua in Peycherchefrith, Eggerdesle et Talnholt et alibi infra Nassum predictum assartare et excolere et riflatis et haiis includere . . . et de omnibus predictis libere disponere pro voluntate sua sine impedimento vel contradiccione alicuius militum vel francolanorum predictorum aut heredum suorum imperpetuum. Ita tamen quod predicti milites et francolani habeant in predictis mariscis liberum ingressum ad animalia sua pascenda prout consueverunt habere temporibus retroactis. Et similiter liceat militibus et francolanis predictis infra sepedictum Nassum Burgi boscos suos et rifleta sua propria assartare et excolere et de eis libere disponere pro voluntate sua sine impedimento vel contradiccione prefatorum abbatis et monachorum de Burgo vel alicuius alterius. Et si forte inter aliquos ipsorum super pretaxatis aliquando oriatur contencio illa in visneto per arbitrium legalium et proborum hominum de Nasso Burgi assensu patrium electorum terminetur. Et ne aliquis processu temporis contra hanc convencionem eam infringendo vel aliquid discordie suscitando . . . sit prefati abbas et monachi in partibus cyrographi penes predictos milites vel francolanos residentibus sigilla sua apposuerunt et in parte cyrographi penes predictos abbatem et conventum residente sigilla pro omnibus militibus et francolanis de Nasso apposuerunt sex milites subscripti, videlicet Rogerus de Torpel, Brianus de lamare, Robertus filius Galfridi, Radulfus de Mortemer, Ricardus de Bernake, et Paganus de Helpestona. Huius igitur auctoritate cyrographi non licebit alicui predictorum boscum vel rifletum suum vendere vel invadiare vel aliquo modo tradere alicui viro potenti vel religioso ad nocumentum iamdictorum abbatis et monachorum vel aliquorum vicinorum suorum.

Text. Swa. fo. 121r (gloss). This is written in a very small hand opposite the survey of woodland. The text is illegible at a number of points, and no attempt has been made to supply the gaps.

5. *This list is part of the records surviving from the Northamptonshire forest eyre of 1209. It is headed 'the old assarts of Nassaburgh' ('veteri essarta de Nasso Burgi') and presumably dates either to 1209 or to the period immediately before. It gives the name of the tenant, the size of the assart, and the crop sown. The first entry reads, 'domina Azelina de Walterville et Radulpho de Dive habent apud Upton 3 acras inbladiatas avene, de veteri essarto'; and all the other entries are in precisely the same form. The names of the tenants are as they appear in the text, but the other material has been calendared, and numbers added for convenience of reference.*

1 Domina Azelina de Walterville et Radulpho de Dive. At Upton. 3 acres of oats.
2 Paganus de Helpestona. At Helpston. 1 acre of oats.
3 Ricardus de Wdecroft. At Woodcroft. 2 acres of oats.
4 Rogerus de Wdecroft. At Woodcroft. ½ acre of wheat.
5 Walterus de Preston. At Woodcroft. 1½ acres of wheat.
6 Domina Gundreia uxor Gileberti de Bernak. At Cathwaite. 2½ acres of wheat.
7 Salomon frater abbatis Burgi. At Cathwaite. 4 acres of wheat.
8 Willelmus Punzun. At Cathwaite. 2 acres of wheat.

9 Robertus Peverel. At Cathwaite. 3 acres of wheat.

10 Henricus clericus. At Cathwaite. 1 acre of wheat.

11 Ricardus Harold. At Cathwaite. $2\frac{1}{2}$ acres of wheat.

12 Ricardus Punzun. At Cathwaite. $2\frac{1}{2}$ acres of wheat.

13 Ricardus Folesanke. At Cathwaite. 1 acre of wheat.

14 Gaufridus filius Gaufridi. At Cathwaite 'in duobus locis'. $3\frac{1}{2}$ acres of wheat; $\frac{1}{2}$ acre of oats.

15 Willelmus filius Ricardi de Wirintona. At Cathwaite. 1 acre and 1 rood of oats.

16 Gaufridus filius Alizie de Pastona. At Cathwaite. 3 roods of oats.

17 Willelmus Douri. At Cathwaite. $\frac{1}{2}$ acre of oats, 'de feodo Roberti Peverel'.

18 Herbertus Peverel. At Cathwaite. 3 acres of wheat; $\frac{1}{2}$ acre of oats.

19 Ricardus Punzun. At Cathwaite. 1 acre of wheat.

20 Ricardus Harold. At Cathwaite. 1 acre of wheat.

21 Robertus Peverel. At Cathwaite, 'in duobus locis'. $1\frac{1}{2}$ acres of oats.

22 Willelmus Punzun. At Cathwaite. $\frac{1}{2}$ acre, 'dimidia frumenti et dimidia avene'.

23 Johannes de Walton. At Cathwaite. $2\frac{1}{2}$ acres, 'quas Willelmus de Wengam inbladavit frumenti'.

24 Willelmus Punzun. At Cathwaite. 1 rood of oats.

25 Ricardus Harold. At Cathwaite. $\frac{1}{2}$ acre of wheat; $\frac{1}{2}$ acre of oats.

26 Willelmus Puttoc. At Cathwaite. $\frac{1}{2}$ acre of wheat; $\frac{1}{2}$ acre of oats.

27 Segestarius de Burgo. At Cathwaite. 7 acres of wheat, 'de feodo Simone Lengleis'.

28 Salomon frater abbatis. At Cathwaite. 3 acres of oats.

29 Hugo de Bernake. 'Sub Cathuet'. 2 acres of oats.

30 Willelmus Pudding. At Dogsthorpe. $3\frac{1}{2}$ roods, 'dimidia frumenti et dimidia avene, de feodo Roberti de Tot'.

31 Matilla de Shotendon. At Dogsthorpe. 1 acre of wheat; 2 acres of oats, 'de eodem feodo'.

32 Almonarius de Burgo. At Dogsthorpe. 2 acres of wheat.

33 Willelmus filius Roberti. At Dogsthorpe. 5 acres of oats.

34 Hugo Fluri. At Dogsthorpe. $2\frac{1}{2}$ acres of oats.

35 Willelmus filius Azelini. At Dogsthorpe. 5 acres of oats.

36 Beringerius de Estfeld. At Dogsthorpe. 4 acres of oats; $\frac{1}{2}$ acre of wheat.

37 Segretarius de Burgo. At Dogsthorpe. 2 acres of wheat.

38 Abbas de Burgo. At Walton. 4 acres of oats.

39 Willelmus filius Ricardi. At Walton. $1\frac{1}{2}$ acres of oats.

40 Salemon frater abbatis. At Walton. 1 acre of oats.
41 Almonarius de Burgo. At Walton. 1 acre of oats.
42 Abbas de Burgo. At Walton. 3 acres of wheat.
43 'Abbas habet ibidem apud Heuenhawe'. 2 acres of oats.
44 Warinus de Fecham et Rogerus frater suus. At Walton. 2 acres of wheat.
45 Willelmus Puttoc. At Walton. 1 acre of wheat.
46 Emma vidua de Wirintona. At Walton. 1 rood of wheat.
47 Willelmus filius Thoroldi. At Walton. 1 rood of wheat.
48 Willelmus Blakeman. At Walton. 1 acre of wheat.
49 Thomas cum barba. At Walton. 1 acre of wheat.
50 Achilles de Burgo. At Walton. $\frac{1}{2}$ acre of wheat.
51 Willelmus Blakeman. At Walton. $\frac{1}{2}$ acre of wheat.
52 Johannes filius Herberti. At Walton. $2\frac{1}{2}$ acres, 'dimidia frumenti et dimidia avene'.
53 Hugo filius Hugonis de Burgo. At Walton. 1 rood of wheat.
54 Matilla de Sotendon. At Peterborough. 1 acre of wheat; 1 acre of oats.
55 Christiana uxor Petri de Burgo. At Peterborough. 1 rood of wheat.
56 Willelmus filius Beneit. At Peterborough. 1 rood of wheat.
57 Hugo Witlomb. At Peterborough. 1 rood of wheat.
58 Robertus nepos Ade. At Peterborough. 1 acre of wheat; $\frac{1}{2}$ acre of oats.
59 Willelmus Prest. At Peterborough. 1 rood of wheat.
60 Hugo filius Ricardi. At Peterborough. $\frac{1}{2}$ acre of wheat; $\frac{1}{2}$ acre of oats.
61 Gaufridus Roser. At Peterborough. $\frac{1}{2}$ acre of oats.
62 Robertus nepos Davidis. At Peterborough. $\frac{1}{2}$ acre of oats.
63 Matilla uxor Ricardi de Shotendon. At Peterborough. 1 rood of oats.
64 Henricus in Angelo. At Peterborough. 1 rood of oats.
65 Matilla de Shotendon. At Peterborough. $\frac{1}{2}$ acre of oats.
66 Robertus nepos Ade. At Peterborough. 1 acre of wheat; $\frac{1}{2}$ acre of oats.
67 Matilla de Schotendon. At Peterborough. 1 acre of oats.
68 Thomas filius Azelini. At Longthorpe. 1 acre of oats.
69 Willelmus filius Trasteni. At Longthorpe. 3 acres of oats.
70 Catelina de Castre. At Longthorpe. 1 acre of oats.
71 Abbas de Burgo. At Longthorpe, 'apud Westwode'. 21 acres of oats.
72 Betricia uxor Willelmi pastoris de Torp. At Longthorpe. 1 acre of oats.
73 Warin de Pecham. At Longthorpe. $1\frac{1}{2}$ acres of oats.
74 Uxor Willelmi de Higenheie. At Longthorpe. 1 acre of oats.

75 Gaufridus Roser. At Longthorpe. 2 acres of oats.
76 Villata de Torp. At Longthorpe. ½ acre of oats.
77 Rogerus filius Widonis. At Longthorpe. ½ acre of oats.
78 Robertus de Meletone. At Milton. 1 rood of oats.

Text. P.R.O., E. 32/62, membrane 3.

Crops Sown on Northamptonshire Estates

Area under seed in the western group 1309–10

	Wheat	Rye	Barley	Drage	Oats	Peas	Total
Biggin Grange	179½	—	45	27	150½	38	440
Oundle	65	—	22	13	48½	13½	162
Irthlingborough	17	14	22	20½	5	17	95½
Kettering	—	100	—	54	87	23	264
Warmington	118½	—	82	—	48½	16	265
Stanwick	53	—	26	52	—	13½	144½
Cottingham	65	—	42	33½	64½	19	224
Great Easton	97	—	30	35	79	22	263
Tinwell	49½	12	24	7½	26½	3½	123
Ashton	53	—	31	12	46	12	154
Total	697½	126	324	254½	555½	177½	2135

Biggin Grange

	Wheat	Rye	Barley	Drage	Oats	Peas	Total
1294–5[a]		—		32½	192	42	c. 500
1300–1	222	—	33	24½	169	34	482½
1307–8	170½	—	48½	40	170½	39	468½
1309–10	179½	—	45	27	150½	38	440

Oundle

	Wheat	Rye	Barley	Drage	Oats	Peas	Total
1294–5	97½	—	26½	32½	80	—	236½
1300–1	64½	—	26	16	74	—	180½
1307–8	85	—	44	30	62½	12	233½
1309–10	65	—	22	13	48½	13½	162

Irthlingborough

	Wheat	Rye	Barley	Drage	Oats	Peas	Total
1280–1	30	21	17	51½	47½	12	179
1294–5	32	25	15	45	28½	11	156½
1300–1	30½	25½	17	40	26	20	159
1307–8	17½	11	16½	24½	12	14½	96
1309–10	17	14	22	20½	5	17	95½

[a] The membrane is damaged, and the figures for wheat and barley are not legible.

	Wheat	Rye	Barley	Drage	Oats	Peas	Total
Kettering							
1280–1	24	92	28	6	122	—	272
1294–5	4½	86½	18	11	131	9	260
1300–1	—	112	—	30	141	—	283
1307–8	—	122	—	22	116½	15	275½
1309–10	—	100	—	54	87	23	264
Warmington							
1294–5	96	—	27	17	105½	20	265½
1300–1	114	—	100	—	58	15	287
1307–8	128	—	64	—	64½	24	280½
1309–10	118½	—	82	—	48½	16	265
Stanwick							
1280–1	66	—	20	64	—	—	150
1294–5	57	—	21	68½	—	11	157½
1300–1	53½	1	24½	70	—	14½	163½
1307–8	56	—	24	66½	—	13½	160
1309–10	53	—	26	52	—	13½	144½
Cottingham							
1280–1	131	—	8½	8½	113	1½	262½
1294–5	100	—	37½	83	52	?	c. 275
1300–1	membrane missing						
1307–8	78	—	30½	53	70½	23	255
1309–10	65	—	42	33½	64½	19	224
Great Easton							
1294–5	132½	—	51	55	92½	44	375
1300–1	membrane missing						
1307–8	110½	—	38	37½	68½	21½	276
1309–10	97	—	30	35	79	22	263
Tinwell							
1294–5	46½		14			13	
1300–1	48½	5	13	30½	17½	—	114½
1307–8	37	11½	22	5½	59	3	138
1309–10	49½	12	24	7½	26½	3½	123
Ashton							
1294–5	69½	—	21½	28½	50½	16	186
1300–1	68	—	26	13	59	9½	175½
1307–8	51½	—	26½	14½	54	11½	158
1309–10	53	—	31	12	46	12	154

Appendix C

Entry Fines

The surviving account rolls, and a number of court rolls, contain full details of entry fines. The number of years covered is not large, but a clear impression emerges of the level of fine charged for full and half tenancies in the late thirteenth and early fourteenth centuries. The material for each region is presented in this appendix, the general conclusions of which have been presented above, pp. 166–7.

The home group

This provides a sample of six years between 1300 and 1338.[1] In these years fifty-four tenancies changed hands, forty-nine of them full virgates and five half virgates. They may be categorised as follows:

A 9 Fines paid by widows for their husband's holding.[2]
B 15 Fines paid by a son or daughter for the parents' holding.
C 30 Fines paid by apparent strangers, men not 'of the blood' of the previous tenant.

The number of strangers is high. It is possibly significant that in three of the manors of this group (Boroughbury, Castor, and Glinton) a number of the customary tenancies were farmed. In the three rolls between 1300 and 1310, twenty-two strangers entered, and of these eleven were in Boroughbury and six in Castor. It might be that the rules of descent were less tenacious on those tenancies which were removed from obligations towards the demesne.

Among these fifty-four fines only six were for amounts of over two pounds. Four of these fines were of five marks (66s 8d) and two of three and a half marks (46s 8d). It will be observed that these high fines do not occur specifically in any one column; two of the larger fines relate to transactions within a family, and the other four do not. Four out of the nine widows' fines were for a pound or more. Of the fifteen examples of a son or daughter inheriting, six are for a pound and only five for above this amount. Of the thirty for strangers only eight are for more than a pound, and only four for more than two pounds. There is no apparent tendency

---

[1] 1300–1, 1307–8 and 1309–10 (Fitzwilliam A/C Rolls 2388, 233, 2389); 1320–1 (Peterborough D and C Muniments, Court Rolls, Box Ia); 1335–6 and 1337–8 (Fitzwilliam Court Rolls 138 and 140).
[2] At Ramsey a widow did not fine for her husband's holding (Raftis, *Tenure and Mobility*, p. 36). On the other hand, she did pay heriot, while there is no record of heriot at Peterborough.

Table 13   *Entry fines in the home group*

A   Fines paid by a widow for her husband's holding.
B   Fines paid by a son or daughter for the holding of one of the parents.
C   Fines paid by those not apparently related to the previous tenant.
Fines in the left-hand column under each heading are for full tenancies; those in the right-hand column for half tenancies.

A		B		C	
13s 4d*a		6s 8d		10s	
11s		6s 8d		nilg	
10s		13s 4d*a		10s	
13s 4d		66s 8dd		10s	
66s 8db		40s		nil	
20s (13s 4d‡)		16s		13s 4d	
10s		20s*e			13s 4d
	20s	20s*†		30s	
	33s 4dc	20s		26s 8d	
		20s		13s 4d	
		20s		nil	
			66s 8df	6s 8d	
		33s 4d		13s 4d	
				nil	
		20s		20s	
		50s		20s	
				13s 4d	
				46s 8d	
				66s 8dh	
				40s	
				10s‡	
				10s	
				40s‡	
				46s 8d	
				16s 0¼d	
					66s 8di
				13s 4d‡	
					nilk
				30s‡	
				20s	

* Indicates a tenancy with land additional to the customary holding; the amount is usually stated in a separate note.
† Indicates that a corrody was granted to the previous tenant.
‡ Indicates fines paid for the marriage of a widow. Widows marrying within a year of their husband's death appear in column *A*, and those marrying after this in column *C*.

for a certain type of succession to carry a standard fine. The nearest approach to this would be the son's 20s, but even here less than half the fines in category *B* are for this amount. The higher fines seem more to be related to the status of the parties than to the nature of the land or the type of transaction.

The western group

The sample in this group is four of the years between 1294 and 1310.[1] In these years fifty tenancies changed hands, forty of them full virgates and the rest half virgates. They divide up as follows, the number of half tenancies being given in brackets:

A 15 (5) Widows. Seven out of the ten widows holding full tenancies married again in the year that they took up their husband's holding, i.e. within a year of his death.
B 14 (2) Sons and daughters of the previous tenant.
C 21 (3) An apparent change of family; six of these fines were paid for the marriage of a widow.

The highest entry for a standard holding in this group is again five marks: this occurs twice, at Oundle in 1308 and at Warmington in 1310. There are four examples of higher fines, but each of these has some special feature. Two of them, for six and a half marks each, occur at Kettering in 1310. Robert Henriot took over his mother's holding, which was stated to comprise a messuage, a virgate, seven acres of demesne and some meadowland; and he also got permission to bake his own bread. The same amount is accounted for by a widow's fine for a messuage, virgate

---

[1] 1294–5 (Add. Ch. 737); 1300–1, 1307–8 and 1309–10 (Fitzwilliam A/C Rolls 2388, 233, 2389).

---

a The widow of Ascelin the reeve (1300–1) and Walter the son of Ascelin (1303–4), for a virgate and 3 acres *de molend*.
b Alice the widow of Robert of Thorpe. A high fine; possibly she was a member of the family of Robert of Thorpe.
c The widow of Richard the carter, for a cottage and 7½ acres. Eye: 1337–8.
d Robert son of Richard Alred.
e Richard Hunne, son of a former reeve of Boroughbury, for a virgate and 3 acres at farm. 1341.
f Walter Hunne, for a messuage and 16 acres which his father had held; possibly a demesne lease. Werrington: 1307–8.
g A virgate taken at farm by Richard of Crowland, bailiff of this group of manors. Boroughbury: 1300–1.
h Simon son of Simon in le Wro, for a messuage and a virgate. Glinton: 1307–8.
i John of Helpston, for a messuage and half-virgate which Alice Carter surrendered to his use, to hold for 13s 4d a year. Walton: 1320–1. Possibly this was a member of the family which had sold the small Helpston fee a generation earlier (*Pytchley*, pp. 148–9).
k Lease for nine years, on condition that specified improvements were made to the property. Glinton: 1337–8.

Table 14   *Entry fines in the western group*

A		B		C	
33s 4d		20s^e		15s^k	
13s 4d (26s 8d‡)		20s†		13s 2d*^l	
20s (33s 4d‡)		20s		26s 8d*†	
20s			6s 8d		40s
6s 8d (13s 4d‡)		30s		40s	
	24s*^a	26s 8d		50s	
30s (20s‡)		30s			20s
	20s	86 8d*^f		100s‡^m	
13s 4d		66s 8d*^g		80s^o	
20s (30s)‡*^b			40s*^h		30s‡
	20s*^c	20s		40s‡	
26s 8d (60s)‡*^d		30s		30s	
40s (40s‡)		30s†^i		30s	
	26s 8d	40s		40s‡^p	
	13s 4d			30s	
				30s	
				40s‡^h	
				30s^q	
				13s 4d‡	
				20s‡	
				66s 8d^r	

* Represents a tenancy with land additional to the customary holding.
† Indicates that a corrody was granted to the previous tenant.
‡ Indicates a fine paid for the marriage of a widow.

a Messuage and a half-virgate and 3 acres *de mollond*. Cottingham: 1300–1.
b William of Cransly, for a messuage, cottage, virgate and 8 acres of land. Kettering: 1307–8. Cransly was an adjacent parish.
c Cottage, 10 acres and an acre of demesne. Kettering: 1309–10.
d Richard son of Robert of Burton, for a messuage, virgate and two pieces of meadow. Kettering: 1309–10. He was possibly from Burton Latimer, another neighbouring parish.
e Messuage and a virgate, held at will. Great Easton: 1294–5.
f Robert Henriot, for a messuage, virgate, 7 acres of demesne, meadowland unspecified, and that he might bake his own bread. Kettering: 1309–10.
g Thomas son of William of Peakirk, for a messuage and a virgate when his father dies. Oundle: 1307–8.
h Father surrenders a half-virgate on marrying a woman who holds a full tenancy, and his son takes over the half-virgate. Tinwell: 1300–1.
i Son to hold a messuage and a virgate on his father's death. Warmington: 1309–10.
k A woman pays 15s for a 'stranger's' holding, which she surrenders to the use of a man who pays 20s entry fine and grants her a corrody. Cottingham: 1300–1.
l Messuage, half-virgate and 6 acres in *le Stibbings*. Cottingham: 1300–1.
m Henry Sanag, for the marriage of a widow holding a messuage and a half-virgate. Irthlingborough: 1307–8.

and meadowland (26s 8d), and a £3 fine paid for her marriage, but strictly this was two fines and not one. The other two examples come from Irthlingborough in 1308. Henry Sanag paid £5 for the marriage of a widow who held a half virgate. He was not to be liable to serve as reeve; this was a concession, for which he would pay. He was also to keep the tenancy in good repair; an order to this effect is unusual, and perhaps suggests that he came from another village. The other fine here was of £4, paid for an unspecified tenancy, which a man claimed to hold of the abbey. The figures of over five marks are therefore exceptional, and the circumstances are usually explained in the record. The average fines for a full tenancy came some way below the five-mark level. The lowest were from widows taking up their husband's holding. The fine here could be as low as 6s 8d, was often a mark or a pound, and very seldom more. A man marrying a widow who held a full tenancy would pay slightly more, commonly two marks or two pounds. A son entering his father's holding, either during the father's lifetime or on his death, usually paid something of the same sort; all but two out of twelve fines here were between £1 and £2. For half-virgates in this group there were two fines of 20s, one of 26s 8d, one of 30s and one of 40s. Forty shillings for a half-virgate was on the same level as five marks for a virgate, definitely on the high side. Anything above this was exceptional.

The northern group
This table relates to three of the years 1300 and 1310.[1] There are forty-one entries:

A   12   Widows.
B   12   Sons and daughters of the previous tenant.
C   17   An apparent change of family; eight of these fines were paid for the marriage of a widow.

To compare the amounts paid here with the figures for the other groups is difficult, since the social structure of the area was very different, and the unit of tenure not the same. This, however, is not an insuperable problem. 'The great body of the individual holdings recorded in the texts . . . vary between half a bovate and two bovates. They are planned, this is, on the same general scale as the villein tenancies of the south.'[2] This comment on a body of twelfth-century Danelaw charters applies also to

[1] 1300–1, 1307–8 and 1309–10 (Fitzwilliam A/C Rolls 2388, 233, 2389).
[2] F. M. Stenton, *Documents Illustrative of the Social and Economic History of the Danelaw* (1920), pp. xix–xx.

o Henry son of Simon, a relief 'for the land which he claims to hold of the abbot in Irthlingborough'. 1307–8.
p Peter Mounsterel of Barton. Kettering: 1307–8. Barton was an adjacent parish.
q Surrendered because of poverty. Warmington: 1294–5.
r John son of Richard Hayward and his wife, for a messuage and a virgate for their lifetimes. Warmington: 1307–8.

Table 15 *Entry fines in the northern group*

A		B		C	
26s 8d	T+3	5s	T+½	2s‡	T+1
10s	T+1	40s	M+3	13s 4d‡	T+1
3s	T+½	20s	T+½	20s	M+virgate
20s	M+1	40s	M+1½	2s	?+2
13s 4d	T+1	66s 8d	?+2	26s 8d‡	M+1
16s	T+1	60s	T+2	40s	M+1
20s	M+2	40s	T+1	40s‡	M+1
26s 8d	M+1½	80s	M+2	60s	?+2
30s	T+1	16s	T+1	100s	T+1
40s	T+1	20s	M+3	60s‡	M+2
50s	M+2	16s 6d	T+1	66s 8d	M+2
50s	M+2	13s 4d	M+2	40s‡	T+1
				20s	M+1
				13s 4d‡	T+2
				26s 8d	M+1
				6s 8d	½
				100s‡	T+1

‡ Indicates that the fine was paid for the marriage of a widow.

T = Toft ⎱ The number given following these represents the
M = Messuage ⎰ number of bovates.

the customary tenancies seen on these Peterborough manors in the early fourteenth century. The scale was roughly the same; perhaps, with a twenty-acre bovate,[1] the man with a toft and two bovates was slightly better off than a man holding a messuage and a virgate elsewhere on the estate. This would seem to be reflected in the level of fines for two bovates, which is slightly higher also. It is more difficult to generalise with this group, however, because the sample is small, and the differences between manor and manor are considerable. The fines were highest at Fiskerton, which was the biggest manor in the group. The highest fine was £5, paid in 1308 by Alexander the forester for a toft and a bovate that had been surrendered to his use. From the size of the fine it must be very likely that this was an additional tenancy for him, and had been purchased. The same man paid five marks two years later, for a messuage and two bovates. From the coincidence of these two entries we can identify Alexander as an important tenant, and in two other entries we find that he had a ferry at Barlings at farm and a toll of peat-cutting. There is another five mark fine, also for two bovates, in 1301, and a £4 fine for the same amount of land in 1310; both of these were paid by sons for their father's holding.

[1] *Ibid.* pp. xxviii–xxx.

The lowest fine for two bovates was £3; the fines for single bovates were 30s or £2. Scotter, on the other hand, took no fine of over £2. At Thurlby the fines were in general as low, but there was a £5 fine paid in 1310 by one Robert Drinckedregges for the marriage of a widow holding a toft and a bovate. The man probably came from another village.

Survey of Paston Manor

An anatomy of a thirteenth-century manor. This is a survey of the sacrist's manor of Paston, which was built up in the second half of the thirteenth century from a number of freeholds. The names both of the holding and of the original tenant are given, and many of the original charters can be traced in the sacrist's register. The survey is clearly a stage removed from the formation of the manor, and so must date from some time in the fourteenth century.

Memorandum quod totum mansum ubi est nunc manerium de Pastona cum gardino et crofto in quo est herbagium et mediatas crofti que adiacet dicto manerio que est nunc terra arabilis continent: Item 20 acre terre que iacent in quadam quarentena que vocatur le Schortbacwong. Item quarentena que vocatur le Nab continens 10 acre terre.[1] Item 3 acre terre iacentes ex opposito Soliscroft fuerunt Ascelini Yunder, que quidem Ascelinus ecclesiam Burgi et eiusdem sacristiam de dictis feoffavit, et ad totam vitam suam habuit victo suo necessaria in sacristia.[2] Item quarentena sub Estwode continens 50 acre terre, quondam Roberti Tot qui aliquando fuit unus de dominis in Pastona. Et est memorandum quod pro 40 acris terre ibidem sacrista solvet celerario conventus per manus elemosinarii 40s., quia ille 40 acre terre pertinent ad manerium de Belasise. Item 20 acre terre iacentes in le Longbacwong, que fuerunt dicti Roberti Tot et Ade bercarii; residuum crofti terre arabilis quod iacet manerio quod non fuit dicti Ascelini Yunder fuit dicti Roberti Tot.[3] Item quarentena que vocatur Gravelecroft continens 8 acre terre que fuit aliquando Roberti Scully de Pastona. Item quarentena continens 8 acre quod vocatur Gernouniswong, quondam Roberti Gernoun de Burgo.[4] Item cotagium cum 2 acris terre in crofto iacente iuxta Simonem Aubrey

---

[1] *C.N.* 524 is a grant by Alice of Scotter, the widow of a former steward, of 9½ acres in *le Nab*, in return for the life tenancy of a similar amount of land in *Rumpele* (*C.N.* 523). Date: 1250–63.

[2] Ascelinus Tunder occurs twice in the early thirteenth century (Swa. fos. 221r, 229r). In a later charter the son of Henry the clerk of Paston made over 3 selions of land, 'quas Ascelinus Tunder quondam de sacrista de Burgo tenuit' (Franceys, p. 61; 1246–50). But the documents recording Ascelin's grant to the sacristy do not survive.

[3] The dealings of the Tot family with the abbey are considered above, pp. 44–5. These parcels of land are most likely part of their demesne, leased to the abbey in 1222 (Franceys, pp. 40–1), and probably never reclaimed.

[4] This land was granted by Richard son of William of Werrington to Margaret his daughter, on her marriage to Robert Gernun (Franceys, pp. 98–9; *c.* 1250–65). This was leased for nine years in 1275 and shortly thereafter granted to the abbey (*Ibid.* pp. 88–9, 98).

ex parte occidentali quondam Ade le Schephirde predicti.[1] Item 3 acre terre iacentes in le Middilwong que fuerunt Willelmi de Revisby de Pastona.[2] Item quarentena que vocatur Hailiswong continens 9 acre quondam Thome Festedeu. Item quarentena que vocatur Neviliswong continens 10 acre; preterea 3 acre, quarum una acra et dimidia fuerunt Agnetis Undirwode, et una acra et dimidia fuerunt Thome Undirwode, quas habuerunt Johannes de Secford per escambium.[3] Item quarentena que vocatur Schukkiswong continens 8 acre. Item quarentena in le Holmes continens 8 acre. Et una acra et dimidia quas tenet Johannes le Taylour de Pastona pro 18d. per annum que fuerunt Ricardi Den qui dictas terras contulit monasterio Burgi et sacristie eiusdem. Et habet quolibet anno de sacristia 6s. ad participacionem.

Due acre et dimidia prati in Grenhirst fuerunt quondam Reginaldi capellani qui habuit moram suam in sacristia Burgi.[4] Item una acra prati ibidem fuit aliquando Roberti de Bucston.[5] Item due acre ibidem fuerunt Ricardi de Schotingdon. Item una triroda ibidem et una triroda apud Totisgore fuerunt Thome Scully. Illa parcella prati que vocatur le Bak fuit extracta de marisco, et nunquam solvit decimam, et est indecimabilis.

Text. Franceys, pp. 426–7.

[1] Adam's grandson occurs in 1299 (*Ibid.* pp. 83–4).
[2] A William of Revesby clerk occurs in 1269 (*Ibid.* p. 82).
[3] The key to this and the remaining entries is a charter of Richard of Dene, by which he granted the abbey 29 acres and 1 rood in Peterborough and Paston (*Ibid.* p. 26; *c.* 1270). This land had been acquired in a large number of transactions over the previous twenty years (*Ibid.* pp. 50–5, 108–10). Two of the parcels of land can be firmly identified. (1) The 8 acres in Schukkiswong is the largest of the grants of William of Neville, 'in cultura que vocatur Chukkeswong' (*Ibid.* pp. 52–3). (2) The 8 acres in le Holmes is the main part of the charter of Richard of Scotendon, 7½ acres 'in le Holmes' (*Ibid.* pp. 54–5). The 10 acres in Nevilswong probably comprised a number of William of Neville's other alienations (*Ibid.* pp. 48–54).
[4] Reginald the chaplain of Botulf bridge leased this land for nineteen years from Richard of Scotendon on 1 May 1269, giving him 28s for it. On 29 June 1270 he bought the property for 6 marks (*Ibid.* pp. 81–2).
[5] Robert of Buckston sold John Aubrey an acre of meadow in Grenehirst (*Ibid.* p. 90).

Bibliography

MANUSCRIPT SOURCES

PETERBOROUGH RECORDS:

LONDON   *British Museum*
Egerton 2733.
Additional MS. 25288.
Additional MS. 39758.
Additional charter. 737.
Cotton MS.
    Cleopatra. C. i, ii.
    Faustina. B. iii.
    Nero. C. vii.
    Vespasian. E. xxi, xxii.
Society of Antiquaries.
MS. 38.
MS. 60.

PETER-
BOROUGH   *Dean and Chapter Library.*
MS. 1.
MS. 5.
MS. 6.
MS. 7.
MS. 39.
Dean and Chapter Muniments.
Court Rolls.
Account Rolls.

KETTERING   *The Duke of Buccleuch.*
Register of George Franceys, Sacrist.
Series of Charters.

ROCKINGHAM
CASTLE   *Sir Michael Culme-Seymour.*
Account roll for 1294-5.

OTHER RECORDS:

BRITISH MUSEUM	Additional MS. 37022 (Pipewell).
	Additional MS. 54228 (lay cartulary, Hotot).
	Stowe MS. 937 (Pipewell).
	Cotton MS. Caligula A. xii (Pipewell).
	Cotton MS. Tiberius E. v (St James, Northampton).
	Sloane MS. 986 (lay cartulary, Braybrooke).
	Sloane Rolls. xxxi. 3–7 (lay records, Basset).

PUBLIC RECORD OFFICE	Forest Proceedings (E. 32), 37–8, 62, 248–9.
	Feet of Fines (CP. 25(1)), 93, 170–6.
	Ministers Accounts (S.C.6), 1260/1.

LAMBETH PALACE LIBRARY	Records of the Court of Arches, MS. Ff. 291 (Fineshade).

NORTHAMP-TONSHIRE RECORD OFFICE	Fitzwilliam collection.
	Account Rolls.
	Court Rolls.
	Charters.
	Box 1062 (lay cartulary, Griffin).
	W. T. Mellows' transcripts.

CAMBRIDGE UNIVERSITY LIBRARY	Additional MSS. 3020/1 (Thorney).

PRINTED SOURCES

Abbreviatio Placitorum, ed. W. Illingworth (Rec. Com., 1811).

Anglo-Saxon Chronicle, trans. G. N. Garmonsway (Everyman edn., 1953).

Book of Fees (3 vols, London, 1920–31).

Book of William Morton, ed. W. T. Mellows, P. I. King and C. N. L. Brooke (Northants Rec. Soc., XVI, 1954).

Bracton. De Legibus et Consuetudinibus Angliae, ed. G. E. Woodbine (4 vols., Yale, 1922); same ed., *Bracton. On the Laws and Customs of England*, trans. S. E. Thorne (2 vols., Harvard, 1968).

Calendar of Charter Rolls, I–IV (1903–12).

Calendar of Close Rolls, 1227–1349 (31 vols., 1892–1913).

Calendar of Inquisitions Post Mortem, I–VI (1904–10).

Calendar of Miscellaneous Inquisitions, I–II (1916).

Calendar of Patent Rolls, 1216–1348 (22 vols., 1891–1913).

Calendar of the Plea Rolls of the Exchequer of the Jews, I–II (ed. J. M. Rigg, 1905, 1910), III (ed. H. Jenkinson, 1929).

Carte Antiquae Rolls 1–10, ed. L. Landon (Pipe Roll Soc., new ser., XVII, 1939).

Carte Nativorum. A Peterborough Abbey Cartulary of the Fourteenth Century, ed. C. N. L. Brooke and M. M. Postan (Northants Rec. Soc., XX, 1960).

Cartulary of St. Werburgh, Chester, ed. J. Tait (Chetham Soc., LXXIX, 1920).

Cartulary of Missenden Abbey, ed. J. G. Jenkins, pt. III (Historical Manuscripts Commission, JP. I, 1962).

Cartularium Monasterii de Rameseia, ed. W. H. Hart and P. A. Lyons, (3 vols., Rolls Series, 79, 1884–93).

Cartularium Abbathiae de Rievalle, ed. J. C. Atkinson (Surtees Soc., LXXXIII, 1889).

Cartulary of Snelshall Priory, ed. J. G. Jenkins (Bucks Rec. Soc., IX, 1952).

Cartulary of Tutbury Priory, ed. A. Saltman (Historical Manuscripts Commission, JP. 2, 1962).

Cartulary of the Cistercian Abbey of Old Wardon, Bedfordshire, ed. G. H. Fowler (Beds Hist. Rec. Soc., XIII, 1930).

Catalogue of Ancient Deeds in the Public Record Office (6 vols., 1890–1915).

Chronicle of Hugh Candidus, ed. W. T. Mellows (1949).

Chronicle of Jocelin of Brakelond, ed. H. E. Butler (Nelson's Medieval Texts, 1949).

Chronicon Abbathiae Ramesiensis, ed. W. D. Macray (Rolls Series, 83. 1886).

Chronicon Monasterii de Abingdon, ed. J. Stevenson (2 vols., Rolls Series, 2, 1858).

Chronicon Petroburgense, ed. T. Stapleton (Camden Soc., XLVII, 1849).

Compotus of the Manor of Kettering for A.D. 1292, ed. C. Wise (1899).

Court Roll of Chalgrave Manor, 1278–1313, ed. M. K. Dale (Beds Hist. Rec. Soc., 28, 1950).

Curia Regis Rolls, I–XV (1922–72).

Documents illustrating the Rule of Walter de Wenlok, Abbot of Westminster. 1283–1307, ed. B. Harvey (Camden Soc., 4th ser., II, 1965).

Domesday Book, I–II (Rec. Com., 1783), IV (Rec. Com., 1816).

Durham Episcopal Charters 1071–1152, ed. H. S. Offler (Surtees Soc., CLXXIX, 1968).

Eadmer's History of Recent Events in England, trans G. Bosanquet (London 1964).

Earliest Northamptonshire Assise Rolls 1202 and 1203, ed. D. M. Stenton (Northants Rec. Soc., V, 1930).

Early Yorkshire Charters, I–III, ed. W. Farrer (1914–1916), IV–XII, ed. C. T. Clay (Yorks Arch. Soc., rec. ser., extra ser., I–X, 1935–65).

Estate Book of Henry de Bray, ed. D. Willis (Camden Soc., 3rd ser., XXVII, 1916).

Facsimiles of Early Charters from Northamptonshire Collections, ed. F. M. Stenton (Northants Rec. Soc., IV, 1930).

Facsimiles of English Royal Writs to A.D. 1100, ed. T. A. M. Bishop and P. Chaplais (Oxford, 1957).

Feet of Fines 10 Richard I (Pipe Roll Soc., XXIV, 1900).

Feudal Aids, 6 vols. (1899–1920).

Feudal Documents from the Abbey of Bury St Edmunds, ed. D. C. Douglas (London, 1932).

Fitznells Cartulary, ed. C. A. F. Meekings and P. Shearman (Surrey Rec. Soc., XXVI, 1968).

Gesta Regis Henrici Secundi Benedicti Abbatis, ed. W. Stubbs (2 vols., Rolls Series, 49, 1867).

Henry of Pytchley's Book of Fees, ed. W. T. Mellows (Northants Rec. Soc., II, 1927).

Historia et Cartularium Monasterii Gloucestrie, ed. W. H. Hart (3 vols., Rolls Series, 33, 1863–7).

Historiae Anglicanae Scriptores Varii, ed. J. Sparke (London, 1723).

Liber Eliensis, ed. E. O. Blake (Camden Soc., 3rd ser., XCII, 1962).

The Lincolnshire Domesday and the Lindsey Survey, ed. C. W. Foster and T. Longley; int. F. M. Stenton (Lincs Rec. Soc., XIX, 1924).

Literae Cantuarienses, ed. J. B. Sheppard (3 vols., Rolls Series, 85, 1887–9).

Matthaei Parisiensis Chronica Majora, ed. H. R. Luard (7 vols., Rolls Series, 57, 1872–83).

A Medieval Miscellany for D. M. Stenton, ed. P. M. Barnes and C. F. Slade (Pipe Roll Soc., N.S., 36, 1962).

Memoranda Roll 10 John, ed. R. Allen Brown (Pipe Roll Soc., N.S., 31, 1957).

Monasticon Anglicanum, W. Dugdale (London, edn. of J. Caley, H. Ellis and B. Bandinel, 1846).

Oseney Cartulary, ed. H. E. Salter, I (Oxford Hist. Soc., LXXIX, 1929).

Papsturkunden in England, ed. W. Holtzmann, I–II (Berlin, 1935–6).

Peterborough Chronicle 1070–1154, ed. C. Clark (2nd edn., Oxford, 1970).

Peterborough Local Administration, I, ed. W. T. Mellows (Northants Rec. Soc., IX, 1939).

Pinchbeck Register, ed. Lord Francis Hervey (2 vols., Brighton, 1925).

Pipe Roll 31 Henry I, ed. J. Hunter (Rec. Com., 1833).

Pipe Rolls 2–4 Henry II, ed. J. Hunter (Rec. Com., 1844).

Pipe Rolls, 5 Henry II to 17 John (Pipe Roll Soc., 1884–1964).

Pleas before the King or his Justices, ed. D. M. Stenton, I–IV (Selden Soc., LXVII–III, LXXXIII–IV, 1953–67).

Records of the Templars in England in the Twelfth Century, ed. B. A. Lees (London, 1935).

Records of the Trial of Walter Langeton, ed. A. Beardwood (Camden Soc., 4th ser., 6, 1969).

Red Book of the Exchequer, ed. H. Hall (3 vols., Rolls series, 99, 1896).

Regesta Regum Anglo-Normannorum, I (ed. H. W. C. Davis, 1913), II
(ed. C. Johnson and H. A. Cronne, 1956), III (ed. H. A. Cronne and
R. H. C. Davis, 1968).

The Registrum Antiquissimum of the Cathedral Church of Lincoln, ed.
C. W. Foster and K. Major (9 vols., Lincs Rec. Soc., 1931–68).

Registrum Epistolarum Johannis Peckham Archiepiscopi Cantuariensis, ed.
C. T. Martin (3 vols., Rolls Series, 77, 1882–5).

Registrum Roberti Winchelsey, ed. R. Graham, I (Canterbury and York
Soc., LI, 1952).

Rolls and Register of Bishop Oliver Sutton 1280–1299, ed. R. M. T. Hill,
(6 vols., Lincs Rec. Soc., 1948–69).

Rotuli de Dominabus, ed. J. H. Round (Pipe Roll Soc., 35, 1913).

Rotuli litterarum clausarum in turri Londinensi asservati, ed. T. D. Hardy
(2 vols., Rec. Com., 1833–4).

Rotuli Selecti, ed. J. Hunter (Rec. Com., 1834).

Rotuli Curie Regis, ed. F. Palgrave (Rec. Com., 1835).

Rotuli Hugonis de Welles, episcopi Lincolniensis: A.D. 1209–1235, ed.
W. P. W. Phillimore, (3 vols., Lincs Rec. Soc., 1912–14).

Rotuli Hundredorum, ed. W. Illingworth and J. Caley, (2 vols., Rec.
Com., 1812–18).

Select Cases in the Court of King's Bench under Edward I, ed. G. O.
Sayles, I (Selden Soc., LV, 1936).

Select Pleas of the Forest, ed. G. J. Turner (Selden Soc., XIII, 1901).

Sir Christopher Hatton's Book of Seals, ed. L. C. Loyd and D. M.
Stenton (Oxford, 1950).

Starrs and Jewish Charters, preserved in the British Museum, ed. I.
Abrahams, H. P. Stokes and H. Loewe (3 vols., Cambridge, 1930–2).

Taxatio Ecclesiastica Angliae et Walliae (Rec. Com., 1802).

Visitations of Religious Houses in the Diocese of Lincoln, ed. A. H.
Thompson, III (Lincs Rec. Soc., XXI, 1929).

Wellingborough Manorial Accounts 1258–1323, ed. F. M. Page
(Northants Rec. Soc., VIII, 1936).

SECONDARY WORKS CITED

Allison, K. J., etc. *The Deserted Villages of Northamptonshire* (University of Leicester,
Department of English Local History, Occasional Papers, no. 18, 1966).

Altschul, M. *A Baronial Family in Medieval England: the Clares, 1217–1314*
(Baltimore, 1965).

Baker, A. R. H. 'Some Fields and Farms in Medieval Kent', *Archaeologia Cantiana*,
LXXX (1965), 152–74.

'Open Fields and Partible Inheritance on a Kent Manor', *Econ.H.R.*, 2nd ser.,
XVII (1964), 1–23.

Barrow, G. W. S. *Robert Bruce* (London, 1965).

Bazeley, M. 'The Extent of the English Forest in the Thirteenth Century',
Transactions of the Royal Historical Society, 4th ser., IV (1921), 140–72.

Beardwood, A. 'The Trial of Walter Langton', *Trans. of the American Philosophical
Soc.*, new ser., 54, pt. 3 (1964).

Bennett, H. S. *Life on the English Manor. A Study of Peasant Conditions 1150–1400*
(Cambridge, 1937).

Berliere, U. 'Innocent III et la réorganisation des monastères bénédictins', *Revue Bénédictine*, XXXII (1920), 22–42, 145–59.

Beveridge, W. 'The Yield and Price of Corn in the Middle Ages', in *Essays in Economic History*, ed. E. M. Carus-Wilson, I (London, 1954), 13–25.

Bonenfant, P. and Despy, G. 'La noblesse en Brabant aux XIIᵉ et XIIIᵉ siècles', *Le Moyen Age*, 4th ser., 13 (1958), 27–66.

Boutruche, R. *La crise d'une société: seigneurs et paysans du Bordelais pendant la guerre de cent ans* (Paris, 1947).

Bridges, J. *The History and Antiquities of Northamptonshire* (London, 1791).

Cam, H. M. *Liberties and Communities in Medieval England* (Cambridge, 1944).

Cheney, C. R. *Episcopal Visitation of Monasteries in the Thirteenth Century* (Manchester, 1931).

Chew, H. M. *English Ecclesiastical Tenants-in-Chief and Knight Service* (Oxford, 1932).

Colvin, H. M. 'A list of the archbishop of Canterbury's tenants by knight-service in the reign of Henry II', *Medieval Kentish Society* (Kent Records, XVIII, 1964), 1–40.

Complete Peerage, by G.E.C. (revised edn., ed. V. Gibbs, H. A. Doubleday & G. H. White, London, 1910–59).

Constable, G. *Monastic Tithes from their Origins to the Twelfth Century* (Cambridge, 1964).

Corbett, W. J. 'The Development of the Duchy of Normandy and the Norman Conquest of England', *Cambridge Medieval History*, V (Cambridge, 1926), 481–520.

Coulton, G. G. *Five Centuries of Religion*, II (Cambridge, 1927).

Cronne, H. A. *The Reign of Stephen* (London, 1970).

Darby, H. C. *The Draining of the Fens* (Cambridge, 1940).
  The Medieval Fenland (Cambridge, 1940).

Darby, H. C. and Terrett, I. B. *The Domesday Geography of Midland England* (2nd edn. Cambridge, 1971).

Davis, R. H. C. *King Stephen* (London, 1967).
  'What happened in Stephen's Reign', *History*, XLIX (1964), 1–12.
  'An unknown Coventry charter', *E.H.R.*, LXXXVI (1971), 533–45.

Denholm-Young, N. *Seignorial Administration in England* (Oxford, 1937).
  Collected Papers (Cardiff, 1969).
  History and Heraldry. 1254 to 1310 (Oxford, 1965).

Dodwell, B. 'Holdings and Inheritance in Medieval East Anglia', *Econ.H.R.*, 2nd ser., XX (1967), 53–66.

Donkin, R. A. 'Settlement and Depopulation on Cistercian Estates', *Bulletin of the Institute of Historical Research*, XXXIII (1960), 141–65.
  'The English Cistercians and Assarting, *c.* 1128–*c.* 1350', *Analecta Sacri Ordinis Cisterciensis*, XX (1964), 49–75.
  'The Cistercian Grange in England in the Twelfth and Thirteenth Centuries', *Studia Monastica*, 6 (1964), 95–144.

Douglas, D. C. 'Some Early Surveys from the Abbey of Abingdon', *E.H.R.*, XLIV (1929), 618–25.
  Review of *Hugh Candidus*, in *E.H.R.*, LXIV (1949), 538.
  The Norman Achievement (London, 1969).

Du Boulay, F. R. H. *The Lordship of Canterbury* (London, 1966).

Duby, G. *Rural Economy and Country Life in the Medieval West*, trans. C. Postan (London, 1968).

'Une enquête à poursuivre: La noblesse dans la France médiévale', *Revue Historique*, CCXXVI (1961), 1–22.

'Au XIIe siècle: les "Jeunes" dans la société aristocratique', *Annales, E.S.C.*, XIX (1964), 835–46.

'The Diffusion of Cultural Patterns in Feudal Society', *Past and Present*, no. 39 (1968), 3–10.

Dugdale, W. *The History of Imbanking and Draining of Divers Fens and Marshes* (2nd edn., 1772).

Emden, A. B. *A Biographical Register of the University of Oxford to A.D. 1500*, 3 vols. (Oxford, 1957–9).

Emery, R. W. *The Jews of Perpignan in the Thirteenth Century* (New York, 1959).

Farrer, W. *Honors and Knights' Fees*, 3 vols. (London and Manchester, 1923–5).

Finch, M. E. *The Wealth of Five Northamptonshire Families* (Northants Rec. Soc., XIX, 1956).

Fisher, D. J. V. 'The Anti-Monastic Reaction in the Reign of Edward the Martyr', *Cambridge Historical Journal*, X (1952), 254–70.

Foss, E. *The Judges of England*, III (1851).

Genestal, R. 'Le Parage Normand', *Bibliothèque d'Histoire du Droit Normand* (2e sér. études, I. fasc. 2, Caen, 1911).

Génicot, L. *L'économie rurale Namuroise au Bas Moyen Age. II. Les hommes – La noblesse* (Louvain, 1960).

Gibbons, A. *Early Lincoln Wills* (Lincoln, 1888).

Green, C. 'Excavations on a Medieval Site at Water Newton, in the county of Huntingdon', *Proceedings of the Cambridge Antiquarian Society*, LVI–LVII (1964), 68–87.

Grigg, D. *The Agricultural Revolution in South Lincolnshire* (Cambridge, 1966).

Gunton, S. *The History of the Church of Peterburgh* (1686).

Hall, H. and Nicholas, F. J. 'Manorial accounts of the Priory of Canterbury, 1260–1420', *Bulletin of the Institute of Historical Research*, VIII (1931), 136–55.

Hallam, H. E. *Settlement and Society. A Study of the Early Agrarian History of South Lincolnshire* (Cambridge, 1965).

Harmer, F. *Anglo-Saxon Writs* (Manchester, 1952).

Hart, C. R. *The Early Charters of Eastern England* (Leicester, 1966).

Harvey, B. 'The Population Trend in England between 1300 and 1348', *Transactions of the Royal Historical Society*, 5th ser., XVI (1966), 23–42.

Harvey, P. D. A. *A Medieval Oxfordshire Village. Cuxham 1240 to 1400* (Oxford, 1965).

Hill, J. W. F. *Medieval Lincoln* (Cambridge, 1948).

Hilton, R. H. 'Gloucester Abbey Leases of the late Thirteenth Century', *University of Birmingham Historical Journal*, IV (1953–4), 1–17.

'Rent and Capital Formation in Feudal Society', *Second International Conference of Economic History. Aix-en-Provence. 1962* (Paris, 1965), 33–68.

'Freedom and Villeinage in England', *Past and Present*, no. 31 (1965), 3–19.

Review of *C.N.*, in *E.H.R.*, LXXVII (1962), 323–6.

Hollister, C. W. *The Military Organization of Norman England* (Oxford, 1965).

'The Knights of Peterborough and the Anglo-Norman Fyrd', *E.H.R.*, LXXVII (1962), 417–36.

Holt, J. C. *The Northerners* (Oxford, 1961).

Magna Carta (Cambridge, 1965).

Homans, G. C. *English Villagers of the Thirteenth Century* (Cambridge, Mass., 1941).

Hoskins, W. G. *Essays in Leicestershire History* (Liverpool, 1950).

    The Midland Peasant. The Economic and Social History of a Leicestershire Village (London, 1957).

Howell, M. *Regalian Right in Medieval England* (London, 1962).

Hyams, P. R. 'Legal Aspects of Villeinage between Glanvill and Bracton' (Univ. of Oxford, D.Phil thesis, 1968).

    'The Origins of a Peasant Land Market in England', *Econ.H.R.*, 2nd ser., XXIII (1970), 18–31.

Jacob, E. F. *Studies in the Period of Baronial Reform and Rebellion. 1258–67* (Oxford, 1925).

John, E. *Orbis Britanniae* (Leicester, 1966).

Kantorowicz, E. H. 'Inalienability: A Note on Canonical Practice and the English Coronation Oath in the Thirteenth Century', *Speculum*, XXIX (1954), 488–502.

King, E. J. 'The Peterborough "Descriptio Militum" (Henry I)', *E.H.R.*, LXXXIV (1969), 84–101.

    'Large and Small Landowners in Thirteenth Century England', *Past and Present*, no. 47 (1970), 26–50.

    'Two Charters of Liberty', *Northamptonshire Past and Present*, V, pt. 1 (1972–3).

Knowles, M. D. *The Monastic Order in England* (2nd edn. Cambridge, 1963).

    The Religious Orders in England, 3 vols. (Cambridge, 1948–59).

Kosminsky, E. A. *Studies in the Agrarian History of England in the Thirteenth Century* (Oxford, 1956).

The Land of Britain. The Report of the Land Utilisation Survey of Britain, ed. L. Dudley Stamp, pts. 58–9 by S. H. Beaver (Northamptonshire and the Soke of Peterborough, 1943), pt. 75 by D. W. Fryer (Huntingdonshire, 1941).

Leland, J. *The Itinerary of John Leland the Antiquary* (2nd edn., 1744).

Lennard, R. *Rural England. 1086–1135* (Oxford, 1959).

    'Agrarian History: Some Vistas and Pitfalls' *Agricultural History Review*, XII (1964), 83–98.

    Review of Duby (1953), in *E.H.R.*, LXX (1955), 99–102.

Levett, A. E. *Studies in Manorial History* (Oxford, 1938).

Loyd, L. C. *The Origins of some Anglo-Norman Families* (ed. C. T. Clay and D. C. Douglas, Harleian Soc., 103, 1951).

Maitland, F. W. and Pollock, Sir F. *The History of English Law*, 2 vols. (2nd edn., Cambridge, 1898).

Maitland, F. W. *Collected Papers*, 3 vols. (Cambridge, 1911).

Matthew, D. J. A. *The Norman Monasteries and their English Possessions* (Oxford, 1962).

A. Mawer (ed.), *Chief Elements used in English Place-Names* (English Place-Name Society, I (2), 1924).

McFarlane, K. B. 'Had Edward I a "policy" towards the Earls ?', *History*, L (1965), 145–59.

Mellows, W. T. *The Local Government of Peterborough* (Peterborough, 1919–23).

Miller, E. *The Abbey and Bishopric of Ely* (Cambridge, 1951).

    'The Background of Magna Carta', *Past and Present*, no. 23 (1962), 72–83.

    'England in the Twelfth and Thirteenth Centuries: An Economic Contrast ?', *Econ.H.R.*, 2nd ser., XXIV (1971), 1–14.

Milsom, S. F. C. Int. to Pollock and Maitland, *History of English Law*, 2nd edn. (Cambridge, 1968 reprint), I, xxiii–xci.

Morris, W. A. 'The Office of Sheriff in the Early Norman Period', *E.H.R.*, XXXIII (1918), 145-75.

Morton, J. *The Natural History of Northamptonshire* (1712).

Page, F. M. *The Estates of Crowland Abbey* (Cambridge, 1934).

'Bidentes Hoylandie', *Economic History* (a supplement to the *Economic Journal*), I (1920), 603-13.

Painter, S. *Studies in the History of the English Feudal Barony* (Baltimore, 1943). *Feudalism and Liberty* (Baltimore, 1961).

Pearce, S. V. 'A Medieval Windmill, Honey Hill, Dogsthorpe', *Proceedings of the Cambridge Antiquarian Society*, LIX (1966), 95-103.

Peck, F. *Academia tertia Anglicana; or, the Antiquarian Annals of Stanford* (1727).

Pevsner, N. *The Buildings of England. Bedfordshire and the County of Huntingdon and Peterborough* (Harmondsworth, 1968).

The Place-Names of Northamptonshire, J. E. B. Gover, A. Mawer and F. M. Stenton (Place-Name Society, x, Cambridge 1933).

Platt, C. *The Monastic Grange in Medieval England* (London, 1969).

Plucknett, T. F. T. *The Legislation of Edward I* (Oxford, 1949). *The Medieval Bailiff* (Creighton Lecture for 1953, London, 1954).

Postan, M. M. 'Medieval Agrarian Society in its Prime. England', *Cambridge Economic History*, I (2nd edn., Cambridge, 1966), 548-632.

The Famulus. The Estate Labourer in the Twelfth and Thirteenth Centuries (Economic History Review, Supplement no. 2, Cambridge, 1954).

'Village Livestock in the Thirteenth Century', *Econ.H.R.*, 2nd ser., XV (1962), 219-49.

'Function and Dialectic in Economic History', *Econ.H.R.*, 2nd ser., XIV (1962), 397-407.

'Credit in Medieval Trade', *Econ.H.R.*, I (1928), 234-61.

'The Chronology of Labour Services', reprinted slightly revised in *Essays in Agrarian History*, ed. W. E. Minchinton, I (1968), 75-91.

'Investment in Medieval Agriculture', *Journal of Economic History*, XXVII (1967), 576-87.

Power, E. *The Wool Trade in English Medieval History* (Oxford, 1941).

Powicke, F. M. *King Henry the Third and the Lord Edward* (Oxford, 1947). *The Thirteenth Century* (Oxford, 1953).

'Observations on the English Freeholder in the Thirteenth Century', *Wirtschaft und Kultur: Festschrift... Alfons Dopsch* (Leipzig, 1938).

Review of Homans (1941), in *E.H.R.*, LVII (1942), 496-502.

Prestwich, J. O. 'Anglo-Norman Feudalism and the Problem of Continuity', *Past and Present*, no. 26 (1963), 39-57.

Review of Hollister (1965), in *E.H.R.*, LXXXI (1966), 103-110.

Putnam, B. *The Place in Legal History of Sir William Shareshull, Chief Justice of the King's Bench, 1350-61* (Cambridge, 1950).

Raftis, J. A. *The Estate of Ramsey Abbey* (Toronto, 1957). *Tenure and Mobility. Studies in the Social History of the Medieval English Village* (Toronto, 1964).

Richardson, H. G. *The English Jewry under Angevin Kings* (London, 1960).

Richardson, H. G. and Sayles, G. O. *The Governance of Medieval England* (Edinburgh, 1963).

'The King's Ministers in Parliament, 1272-1377, pt. 1', *E.H.R.*, XLVI (1931), 529-50.

Robertson, A. J. *Anglo-Saxon Charters* (2nd edn., Cambridge, 1956).

Rogers, J. E. Thorold. *A History of Agriculture and Prices*, I (1866).
Round, J. H. *Feudal England* (1895).
    The Commune of London (1899).
Rouse, E. C. and Baker, A. 'The Wall Paintings at Longthorpe Tower, near
    Peterborough, Northants', *Archaeologia*, XCVI (1955), 1–57.
Sanders, I. J. *English Baronies. A Study of their Origin and Descent. 1086–1327*
    (Oxford, 1960).
    Feudal Military Service in England (London, 1956).
Sawyer, P. H. *Anglo-Saxon Charters. An annotated list and bibliography* (London, 1968).
Slade, C. F. *The Leicestershire Survey* (Leicester, 1956).
Smith, R. A. L. *Canterbury Cathedral Priory* (Cambridge, 1943).
    Collected Papers, ed. M. D. Knowles (London, 1947).
Southern, R. W. *St Anselm and his Biographer* (Cambridge, 1963).
    Medieval Humanism and Other Studies (Oxford, 1970).
    Western Society and the Church in the Middle Ages (Harmondsworth, 1970).
Stenton, F. M. *Types of Manorial Structure in the Northern Danelaw* (Oxford, 1910).
    Int. to *Documents Illustrative of the Social and Economic History of the Danelaw*
    (London, 1920).
    Int. to *Transcripts of Charters relating to Gilbertine Houses* (Lincs Rec. Soc., XVIII,
    1922).
    The First Century of English Feudalism (2nd edn., Oxford, 1961).
    Preparatory to Anglo-Saxon England, ed. D. M. Stenton (Oxford, 1970).
Stones, E. L. G. 'Sir Geoffrey le Scrope (*c*. 1285–1340), Chief Justice of the King's
    Bench', *E.H.R.*, LXIX (1954), 1–17.
Sutherland, D. W. *Quo Warranto Proceedings in the Reign of Edward I* (Oxford, 1963).
Tait, J. 'Knight-Service in Cheshire', *E.H.R.*, LVII (1942), 437–59.
Tawney, R. H. *Business and Politics under James I* (Cambridge, 1958).
Thorne, S. E. 'English Feudalism and Estates in Land', *Cambridge Law Journal* (1959),
    193–209.
Titow, J. Z. 'Land and Population on the Bishop of Winchester's Estates 1209–1350'
    (Univ. of Cambridge, Ph.D. thesis, 1962).
    'Some Differences between Manors and their Effects on the Condition of the Peasant
    in the Thirteenth Century', *Agricultural Hist. Rev.*, X (1962), 1–13.
Tout, T. F. *Chapters in the Administrative History of Medieval England*, 6 vols.
    (Manchester, 1920–33).
Treharne, R. F. 'The Battle of Northampton', *Northamptonshire Past and Present*, II,
    no. 2 (1955), 73–90.
Trow-Smith, R. *A History of British Livestock Husbandry to 1700* (London, 1957).
Vinogradoff, P. *Villainage in England* (1892).
    English Society in the Eleventh Century (Oxford, 1908).
    Collected Papers, 2 vols. (Oxford, 1928).
Waites, B. 'The Monastic Grange as a Factor in the Settlement of North-East
    Yorkshire', *Yorkshire Archaeological Journal*, XL (1962), 627–56.
Whitelock, D. *Anglo-Saxon Wills* (Cambridge, 1930).
    'The Dealings of the Kings of England with Northumbria in the Tenth and
    Eleventh Centuries', in *The Anglo-Saxons*, ed. P. Clemoes (London, 1959).
Whitwell, R. J. 'The English Monasteries and the Wool Trade in the Thirteenth
    Century', *Vierteljahrschrift für Sozial- und Wirtschaftgeschichte*, II, I (1904), 1–34.
Wightman, W. E. *The Lacy Family in England and Normandy 1066–1194* (Oxford, 1966).
Williams, G. A. *Medieval London. From Commune to Capital* (London, 1963).
Wood-Legh, K. L. *Perpetual Chantries in Britain* (Cambridge, 1965).

Index

Aaron the Jew, 44–5
Abbot family, 116, 117n
Abingdon (Berks), Benedictine abbey, 6
Abovetown, Robert, 107; William, 173
account rolls, as sources, 4
Achurch, John de (abbey steward), 135
Addington, 29n; Richard of, 29n
aids, see tallage
Ailsworth, 56–7, 65, 109; assarts in, 72, 77
Ailsworth, Hugh the sokeman of, 56;
  Leofric of, 56; Ralph son of Robert of,
  57; Robert of, 56; Robert son of
  William of, 173–4; William of, 56;
  William son of Gilbert of, 173–4;
  William son of William of, 57
Aldwincle, 33, 91, 140n, 141–2, 144
Aleby, Alice of, 49
Almoner (surname), Adam, 60, 65–6;
  Thomas son of William, 59–60
Alred family, 112–14, 117n, 124, 184n
Alwalton (Hunts), 92–3, 98, 141–4
Amewell, William of (abbey bailiff), 65,
  68n
Anglicus family, 58, 78
Anlafestun, 7
Ansford, 24
arable farming, 150–4
Armston, hospital, 107n
Ashby de la Laund (Lincs), 145n
Ashton, 8, 151, 153, 162n, 180–1
Ashton family, 63, 67, 173
assarting, see colonisation
Aswig, 8
d'Aubigny, William, 31
Aubrey family, 138n, 189–90
Avenel fee (table 2, no. 31), 25–6; Avenel,
  24; William, 65

Bacon, Roger (clerk), 174
bailiffs, 127–8, 136–9
Bainton, 90
Barlings (Lincs), 187
Barnack fee, 137; Geoffrey of, 33;
  Gilbert of, 32, 36, Gundreia wife of,
  174, 176; Hugh of, 172, 174, 177;
  Richard of, 172, 174, 176
Barton, 186n
Basset family, 36, 46n; Ralph, 21;
  Richard, 20, 31
Bassingbourne fee (table 2, no. 10), 24,
  29n; tenants of, see Waterville, Hugh of
  (Bassingbourne)

Bekingham, Elias of, 133–4
Belsize, abbey grange, 62, 67–9, 76–8,
  189; labour supply, 164
Benefield, 8; rector of, 82
Berkhamstead, Ralph of, 65–6
Berwick, John of, 133–4
Bethwaite, 77–8
Biggin, abbey grange, 81–2, 131–2, 145,
  147–8, 151, 153, 156–9, 163–4, 180;
  vineyard, 82
Biggin, John of (abbey stock-keeper), 159n
Binnington (Yorks), 10
Blakeman family, 65, 108, 122, 178
Blevet, William, 41
Boroughbury, see Peterborough, manor of
Borret, 10n
Boston (Lincs), fair, 128, 136
Botulfbridge (Hunts), Reginald the chap-
  lain of, 68, 190
Bourn (Cambs) barony, 39
Bourne (Lincs) barony, 21–2
Bradley (Leics), Augustinian priory, 83n
Bray, Henry de, 46, 121n
Braybrooke, Robert of, 41
Bretnon family, 109
Bringhurst fee (table 2, no. 25), 25; John
  of, 113; Theobald of, 25
Brito, Robert, 56
Britwell, Richard of, 119
Buckston, Robert of, 190
building, 119–22, 138
Burghley fee (table 2, no. 16), 24; Geoffrey
  of, 24; William of, 24, 32, 172, 174
Burmund, 29n
Burri, Godric, 56
Burton Latimer, Richard son of Robert
  of, 185n
Bury St Edmunds (Suffolk), Benedictine
  abbey, 32; abbot Samson, 126
Butler, Robert, 62–3

Camoys, John de, 39; Ralph de, 39
Canterbury, archbishopric of, 14–15;
  council, 135
Canterbury Cathedral Priory, 150n, 165n
Carlton, 49
Carter, Alice, 184n; Richard, 184n
castles, see Rockingham
castle-guard, commutation of, 26
Castor, 5, 18, 56, 62–5, 67, 76–7, 80, 123,
  130, 132, 138n, 141–2, 144, 147, 151,
  154–5, 157, 164–5, 182; assarts in, 72;

Index